570R
51

William Wallace

Man and Myth

GRAEME MORTON

SUTTON PUBLISHING

First published in the United Kingdom in 2001 by
Sutton Publishing Limited · Phoenix Mill
Thrupp · Stroud · Gloucestershire · GL5 2BU

Reprinted in 2001

British Library Cataloguing in Publication Data
A catalogue record for this book is available from the British
Library.

ISBN 0-7509-2379-2

Typeset in 11/14.5 pt Sabon.
Typesetting and origination by
Sutton Publishing Limited.
Printed and bound in England by
J.H. Haynes & Co. Ltd, Sparkford.

To
Sam for the 'bluckling'

To
Evie for the drawing

To
*Ange for the quartering
(and threats of disembowelling)*

The frontispiece of *The Scottish Chiefs
and the Heroism of Sir William
Wallace*, by Jane Porter. (*National
Library of Scotland*)

Contents

List of Illustrations

Acknowledgements

To provide even this cursory analysis of 700 years of examples of the Wallace myth has resulted in a number of debts. The framing of my approach to this study is dependent on the writings and my conversations with Bob Morris and David McCrone. Offers (with my grateful acceptance) of yet more examples of Wallaciana have come from Steve Boardman, Linos Eriksonas, Adam Fox, Kino Iwazumi, Michael Lynch, Angela Morris and Trevor Griffiths. Each has broadened my understanding of periods and themes not usually my own; I wish I could have rewarded them better. Elspeth King provided a more than useful link to the archives on the National Wallace Monument and has led the way in the commemoration of the 700th anniversary of the Battle of Stirling Bridge. The archivists of the Council Archives in Edinburgh and Stirling, and the librarians at the Special Collections department of Edinburgh University Library, the Mitchell Library in Glasgow, the National Library of Scotland and the public libraries of Aberdeen, Ayr, Edinburgh, Perth and Stirling have all been remarkably helpful. It has been much appreciated. I would also like to thank Jane Crompton and Clare Jackson at Sutton Publishing for their patience. I apologise for missing so many deadlines.

A number of the ideas expressed here have been developed in discussion over the last few years with students who have taken the British National Identity option or have signed-up for the Scotland: Society and Politics MSc programme at Edinburgh University. Again, I wish I could have done better justice to their many original ideas and challenging criticisms. Some of the material in the chapters here has previously been published in 'The Most Efficacious Patriot: the heritage of William Wallace in nineteenth-century Scotland', *The Scottish Historical Review*, Vol. LXXVII, 2: No. 204 (1998). I hope what I have now produced is not too familiar to some.

Finally, I must thank my family who have endured distance and neglect, especially as this work neared the final stages. It is to them that I dedicate this book.

ONE

National Myth

A cry rose from the Highlanders as from the tomb: 'Wal-lace! Wal-lace! Wal-lace!' Louder, louder . . . 'Wal-lace! WAL-LACE!'

'You have bled with Wallace!' He slid his broadsword from its scabbard. 'Now bleed with me!' – Robert Bruce at Bannockburn.

In the year of our Lord 1314, patriots of Scotland, starving and outnumbered, charged the fields of Bannockburn. They fought like warrior poets. They fought like Scotsmen. And won their freedom.[1]

Do you feel proud? Do you wish you were Scottish? Did a smile come upon your lips when you read these three extracts? What is the done thing? What is sincere? How *should* one react to the emotions of nationalism? It's ephemeral, as woolly as Highland cattle. It's as powerful an ideology as any the world has thought of. Nationalism has a grip over us, whether we think it or not, whether we want it or not. It is made out of straw, it is made out of bricks, it is made out of myth. National myth is the core of our culture. It tells us who we are. It tells us where we are from.

Studies abound on what is the nation.[2] The search goes on to discover its essence, its organic being, its face as much as its heart. Not so many years ago politicians and academics were content to locate that nation in the political structures which came about at the end of the First and Second World Wars. The United Nations embodied these newly enshrined rights to national self-determination after 1945. However, this was the essence not of the nation, but of the nation-state, conjoined twins of classical simplicity. State and nation go together, it seems so natural. Scotland had already tried to make its claim, petitioning the American President Woodrow Wilson in 1918 to gain recognition in the international arena.[3] The claim was not sanctioned, size was important, Scotland was too small to sustain a state and, in any case, it had one, in London, at Westminster. The conjoined twin was fixed in a model of Siamese elegance: Scotland, being awkward, was ignored. The Revd James Barr made clear this grievance at an address commemorating Wallace at the patriot's most likely birthplace, Elderslie, in 1921:

> The Government taught [Ireland] during the war to advocate self-determination for all nations great and small, the shaping of their own destinies, the choice of their own constitutions. They had granted it to many a people in Europe, cut them adrift from the Commonwealth in which they were embedded, and given them full independence. They had even organised plebiscites to know the mind of the people. Can we do less for the people at our own doors? Can we claim less for ourselves?[4]

Scotland was sent homewards to think again who it was, although the people of Scotland did not have to ponder very long, if at all. The (non-)reply from Wilson was merely replicated at the end of 1945, the United Nations was a United (Nation-)States. In any event, it did not really matter. No shuddering halt was experienced in the national train of thought: Wallace was not forgotten. National identity had long been nurtured in areas quite separate from the formal political process, national or international, and kept up its independence and its coherence, irrespective of so many challenges. In the constitutional and administrative arrangements established in the Union between England and Scotland in 1707, in the cultural accommodation these two nations reached from the second half of the eighteenth century and the non-interference of Westminster during the age of *laissez-faire*, Scotland had no need and no time to focus its national identity on the state or the demand for a state. The argument has been presented elsewhere,[5] but its conclusions impact on how we study the Wallace myth in Scotland.

Scottish national identity has – from the eighteenth century most clearly – been located in its civil society. Normally one finds civil society in opposition or in distinction to the state, although the definition of the concept has changed over time and still today can mean different things to different people. It can range from the family to governmental institutions and quangos.[6] Most accept that it is a set of structures between these two boundaries, comprising the associations and institutions which are part of society's response primarily to rapid (urban) change.[7] A number of particular circumstances make this especially important to Scotland. Scotland's governance – as distinct from its government (Westminster) – was enacted locally through its civil society. By its 'governance' is meant the ability to intervene in the problems of housing, destitution, crime, immorality and other aspects of social welfare. In the ideology of good government and in the practicalities of good management, the state was deliberately kept (and kept itself) distant from this role. The sociologist Tom Nairn analysed the rift between the Westminster state and Scottish civil society in order to explain how mistaken we are to regard Great Britain and now the United Kingdom as a coherent nation-state.[8] Better to call it a state-nation or, in James Mitchell's analysis, a union not a unitary state, because of the agreements, bargains and compromises which hold its component nations together.[9] The gap is where Scottish national identity has flourished because it was where the governance of the nation was to be found.[10] This governance was enacted through political managers, municipal councils and the institutions and organisations of civil society.

Reconceptualising a nation's governance, when it is in union with three other nations, is a difficult prospect – not to be followed up in these pages. Instead, it can be found through the notes to this chapter and these citations help explain two phenomena relevant to the study of William Wallace as a national myth in Scotland. The first is the constant interplay – and co-existence – of Scottish and British national identities since 1707; the second is the explanation for why a strong identification with the Scottish nation – despite monarchical and parliamentary union – so rarely was manifest in the demand for an independent Scottish parliament. Both themes will dominate and structure the rhetoric of commemoration in the story of Wallace, to be joined by more recent and more complex identities. By reflecting on reactions to the three extracts at the beginning of the chapter, from which the screenplay to *Braveheart* was born, is to emphasise how inclusive national identity is, encompassing innumerable viewpoints. It is national *identity*, not *nationalism*, and rarely ever has it been captured entirely by political parties. There have been a number of political organisations since the 1850s which have mobilised some version of national identity. Sometimes their focus was on parliament – certainly since the Scottish Home Rule Association in the 1880s – and the call for a federal or a devolved structure has been stronger than the call for an independent parliament in the century which followed.[11] These have been organisations to join, where membership is akin to a declaration of intent, a fan club and in the chapters ahead their fanatical interpretation of the Wallace story will be unearthed.

However, national identity has been more expansive than that. In time, fanaticism may account for those of you who felt rather proud to be Scottish when reading the three extracts. What about if you wished you *were* Scottish, to claim the spirit – the geist – of freedom, which the memory of Wallace and Bruce actualise so powerfully. Do not worry, you are not alone. There is evidence of black slave workers in the Southern states of America who revelled in the vivacity of 'Scots Wha Hae Wi Wallace Bled', universalising its theme of emancipation as their own personal cry,[12] while the 'white settlers', following the well-worn trail in search of a rural idyll, but looking for a sense of community that Scotland seems best to enjoy, are defined by their purchase of the Scottish lifestyle.[13] Buying the Shetland croft is a major commitment, the holiday-home in Perthshire or Berwickshire or Sutherland is more a composite shift: keeping a foot in both core and peripheral cultures. The view from the community overseas – the expatriate one – enhances cultural identification from a range of peoples. Here the egalitarian tradition and that of freedom are bandied as the essence of a homeland still loved, but remaining distant.

If, after reading those extracts, it was a smile that came across your lips, then do not think your know-it-all, seen-it-all-before satisfaction, or sarcasm, makes you immune from the pull of nationality. From a study of tourist nick-nackery we know that irony is no shield from heritage consumption and acceptance of the shortbread-tin image.[14] One and one's guests might laugh at the antics of the two sentry guards outside Edinburgh Castle, but you have still chosen to stop there when touring the city.

What about those for whom the quotes meant nothing, who had never heard of Wallace or Bruce, or ever thought that 'freedom' was an issue? You may not be cognisant of the main markers of your identity, but you remain governed by them. It's a banal nationalism, hidden from consciousness and it permeates everyday actions.[15] The appearance of flags above prominent buildings and at football matches, the singing of songs – anthems, folk ballads, playground chants – surround us with reminders of who we are. It is no state ceremonial, it is no royal command performance, but it is a nationalism of the everyday, one that has great significance in Scotland, where a British identity may be promoted by the state, but the Scottish element of this dual identity is found free-floating in civil society.[16] To be sure, you cannot escape reminders of your nationality, just like you cannot escape your gender or your class without difficulty and conscious effort. One can change nationality by changing citizenship (becoming American or Australian, for example) and one can deny one's ethnic origins by offering a more open and inclusive (not exclusive or xenophobic) version of nationalism.[17] There are many choices and opportunities that can be taken or ignored. Nevertheless, they are manifestations of the breadth and flexibility and, ultimately, the indelibility of national identity.

So it is the case that the story of William Wallace is fuelled by evidence from all of these categories: the nationalist movements, organisations in civil society, expatriate groups, disenfranchised peoples, as well as poems and songs from those who lack any formal organising principle. The Wallace myth is part of up-front political nationalism, of both civic and ethnic complexion, and it is part of the nation's banal nationalism. It is a truly universal story.

For the remainder of this chapter the task is to explain the wider background of the Wallace story in Scotland's history. Why do we need the Wallace myth at all?

FITTING WALLACE INTO THE NATIONAL MYTH

What is it about nations that makes them fall back on heroes from the past? Folk heroes help us make sense of the past and add to our understanding of the future. In a survey of the greatest Scots in history conducted by *Who's Who* in Scotland, Wallace polled 169 votes to take second place from Bruce (third with 161 votes), both well behind Robert Burns' runaway victory with 268 votes, but safely ahead of Walter Scott down in seventh place with sixty-three votes.[18] Heroes are remarkable for their persistence in the national consciousness. There is a child in every adult, and an insatiable desire for valour and romance, for swashbuckling adventure. We want glory as much as we want continuity over time but it is difficult not to sound trite when offering words on the importance of myth and historical stories. There is much truth in Roy Foster's assertion that '(t)he idea of nationality as narrative is becoming a cliché . . .'.[19] Nevertheless, it retains enduring importance. Most influentially, Benedict Anderson's 'imagined community' unfolds through the transition from the contents of vernacular literature to common understanding: 'a hypnotic confirmation of the solidity of a single community'.[20] It magnifies the 'one, yet many' of national life.[21] The push given by new technology from the eighteenth century created first a provincial press and then a national press which enabled, in Gellner's words, 'sustained, frequent and precise communication between strangers'.[22] The national story comes from this change: and it is not singular, but plural. A range of stories is manifest. They remind us that the processes of globalisation and modernity go together and have gone together for longer than many theorists, who stress the novelty of these social and economic processes, care to admit.[23]

These operations are not just about the internet and trans-national organisations, their roots go back to whenever regional identities were subsumed by national identities and when links were made across national boundaries. The letter from Wallace and Murray to the mayors of Lübeck and Hamburg, to kick-start Scotland's trading relationship with central Europe in October 1297, offers a good example of the early phase of the globalisation process. Of course, these processes have intensified in recent decades and, as Hall has argued, the result today is that our identity has become a 'movable feast'. It is something that is very temporary and 'any one of a range of identities would be used, although only usually for a short period before a new identity becomes fashionable'.[24] The national community from the days of Wallace onwards is a plural, comprising many different identities. The transition from personal identity to national identity may be common and the two badges may be broadly compatible at the journey's end, but many versions of Scottishness can be included along the way.

In a study on the meaning of Englishness, by way of contrast, it was found in the literature and other writings on England, that national identity is multi-dimensional. With no discrete texts – but, instead, debates linked to specific historical circumstances – the nation's identity is constructed on shifting sands. The same is true for Scotland, if not more so, the result of the British state's failure to capture Scotland's civil society (the home of its national identity). This narration, then, is about values, beliefs and attitudes – it is a state of mind.[25] It may be an over-used concept in nationalism studies, but narration remains fundamental, especially in the stateless nations. Accordingly, Stephen Cornell has attempted to delineate the processes involved in constructing the narrative. He has done so by postulating three interrelated steps. The first is the selection of the story or the events which comprise the story; then the emplotment of the story where the events are linked to each other in a logical way and then, finally, the all important interpretation of the narrative, where its significance is stressed to the reader/listener/viewer.[26]

As the story of Wallace unfolds, it should transpire that Scots have never been that good at revising their history. Emplotment is remarkably static in the popular imagination. The cult of revisionist history which is so lively – and one might say, cut-throat – in (Northern) Ireland, is much more genteel upon returning to the ferry-port at Cairnryan.[27] Still, this is not to deny that debates abound: the 'political bias' of the medieval chronicles, the 'distortions of Unionism', 'cultural inferiorism' or the pro-independence bias of nationalist historians.[28] These are themes we will return to and are strong narratives, but revisionism has not always been welcomed. Prebble and Tranter still dominate the shelves in the airport bookshops, although Devine and Lynch are making headway in the train stations.[29] The fault of being on the periphery – of accepting oneself as being parochial – has created, Craig argues, a sense of self-hatred. Held down and holding ourselves down, 'by the colour of our vowels'[30] or the colour of our tartan and the discourse of kailyardism, a literature long associated with Scotland's failure to face urban industrial reality and political maturity.[31] Craig sums up this pull on Scottish discourse in the following terms:

> The richness of the core cultures into which peripheral writers have attempted to integrate themselves in order to benefit from their accumulated wealth [of a literary tradition] is a richness maintained precisely by dominant cultures' ability to insist that those from the periphery contribute their individual talents to the maintenance of its traditions. . . . what we see are the workings of a system of cultural exchange designed to enhance the core and impoverish the periphery and thereby to maintain the power relations between them.[32]

This inferiorist discourse has been challenged with irony, through the television comedy *Rab C. Nesbitt* ('See if I met Van Gogh in the lavvy o' the Two Ways? I would dae a U-turn in case he chibbed me wi' his palette knife . . .') and the writings of James Kelman and Irvine Welsh.[33] But the lack of self-confidence has sustained the rather frail suggestion in nationalist discourse that the more Scottish history the better, getting published or broadcast what we can and being grateful for it. The over-excitement which greeted the decision of Hollywood to film *Braveheart* is offered as just such an example[34] – a 'we are not worthy' strand of cultural weakness. Current historiographical debates have centred more on the historians of the past, especially those writing in the eighteenth and nineteenth centuries, than today.[35] Scots, it seems, are scared of their history: fearing their history is not important enough or fearing that it will be 'found out', because of their failure to embrace political independence after 1707. The danger is that we go to the other extreme and think the true Scotland is somehow out there, to be found, that if we explode the myth then we get to the facts. Alas it is not possible, nor is it desirable. The myth is as much the truth as the truth itself, at least as far as identity formation is concerned. It is not just that the myths dominate – are hegemonic – but there is no essential culture to find because there is no such culture. McCrone has likened the search for the authentic Scottish culture as a hunt for Lewis Carroll's snark, which does not exist.[36] Who is the true Scot after all: you or me? Why? The Historiographer Royal for Scotland, T.C. Smout, framed this question in a contemporary example. His conception circles around a number of identities, each born out of a range of cultures:

> How can a person in the Outer Hebrides, speaking Gaelic, crofting, a member of the Free Church, have a common identity with a person in Glasgow, speaking a Lowland dialect, working as a software engineer, a follower of no religion save Rangers football club?[37]

We all come to our national identity through the plural – our identities – and forge key elements of different cultures (our religion, our gender, our TV preferences) when we interact with it. Clearly, we, ourselves as individuals, engage in the reproduction of myth-making, fractured by our own experiences, but its collective importance is to the nation and to national identity. It is of particular relevance to a peripheral nation such as Scotland, where myth-history has been the admission ticket to recognition by core cultures.[38] If, by contrast, we have a true history, are we able to join

9

the big boys as equals – is our history now prudent? The shame is that the ticket is a forgery, a black-market reproduction. No good for face-saving, but sufficiently powerful for nation-building. Where would Scotland's tourism be, if it were not a peripheral nation, allowing its visitors to enjoy 'the peripheral principle'.[39] Who comes for the weather? Revelling in being peripheral is a Scottish art, it is one reason why the dual identities of Scottishness and Britishness are so powerful, allowing their claimants to flip between the two. The pull of myth-history sustains this duality and is the route in to theories of nationalism from either ends of the debate. Both the modernists and the pre-modernists, to use the simplest divides in a complex range of positions, legitimate the use of myth in their explanations of what is nationalism and where did it come from. Gellner's analysis of nationalism, which is a product of modernism and industrialisation, lays much on the fabrication of the past, forming the ideology with which nationalism brings the nation into being.[40] As McCrone stresses, it is not Benedict Anderson's 'imagined community' here, it is fabrication, invention – and hence Gellner finds a ready niche for myth-history.[41] Even in the political theories which place the rise of the nation-state as the primary form of governance, there remains room for the myth-hero to make this political project work.

So, too, is myth a key element in the primordialist position (a controversial term nowadays[42]), or the more common position adopted by the pre-modernist, or 'anti-modernist'. Here national identities are formed in and out of much older group and ethnic identities. Llobora goes as far to say that Gellner and the modernists are wrong to stress the modern fabrication of nations, stating in reply that all such identity-creations have medieval roots.[43] This would be a valid criticism of the bald invented 'tradition literature', where emphasis is placed on the modernity of events, ceremonies and traditions which were presented with explicit (but bogus) ancient and historical overtones.[44] The more nuanced retort from Gellner is not to dismiss the importance of older loyalties to structuring modern (in particular) state nationalism, but rather to say it is inessential to their creation. Some nation-states are forged closely from past loyalties, some are not – and that is his point.[45]

10

Nevertheless, examples abound from around the world of the use of myth-history to maintain continuity with these pre-modern attachments. The Spanish obsession with the past, which developed in the nineteenth century around Basque, Catalan and Galician identities and which came to a head in 1898, developed out of a concept of 'nation' first developed in the sixteenth century.[46] A Serbian sense of being 'special', elect peoples, based on history, mythology and Serb purity has sustained a more ethnic form of nationalism.[47] These debates mirror those of the chosen people of Israel, based on the Old Testament and archaeological discoveries.[48]

Closer to home, England has long claimed to be an elect nation, singled out by God as an instrument of Divine Providence, as in Bede's *Ecclesiastical History of the English People* (written in 731), to be Jerusalem, an ancient people and a people in communication with God.[49]

> Many of Bede's characters and situations are 'mere English' at its best: his own character and sober wisdom, devoted yet not uncritical, austere yet widely acquainted with human need and interests, have many times seemed to be reincarnate in the best figures of our history.[50]

The influential scholar and educationalist Ernest Barker distilled Englishness from the intellectual continuity of the Greek city state and the Glorious Revolution of 1688, allied to a remarkable optimism in the character of the English people (or Englishman?) based on the squire or gentleman and the long-held acceptance by the state of social and religious pluralism.[51] The past is, indeed, a foreign country, to be visited selectively, such are the connections which can be made with the present.[52] Where would Scotland be if it were not for the Wars of Independence and the two medieval leaders William Wallace and Robert Bruce? Scotland, without doubt, is 'dream rich' – with a ready supply of myth-making icons.[53] For the pre-modernists, there is a recognition of nationalism's modernity, but a continued stress on shared myths of origin, community and history.[54] Or, in the words of Smith, 'the historical embeddedness of

11

the nation in much older ethnic frameworks'.[55] To repeat the well-known aphorism of Thomas Mann: 'Very deep, very deep is the well of the past. Should we not call it bottomless?' Smith argues that such depth has allowed nationalists to 'return, rediscover and reappropriate traditional customs, symbols and ceremonies' and no better examples can be found than the appropriation of heroes and sagas:

> Muhammad and Moses have ceased to be prophets and servants of God, and have become national leaders *par excellence*; mythological bards like Oisin (Ossian) and Vainamoinen have become exemplars of ancient Irish and Finnish national wisdom; the heroes of *Ramayana* have become prototypes of Indian national resistance.[56]

Smith maintains it is not the use of these heroes which is of greatest import, but 'the fervour of the believing masses'. It shows the power of the ethnic past and the heroic myth.[57] It is more than mere common sense to argue that myth is important to national identity. It is not just that we can never remember our history and have to rely on a common knowledge of '. . . all the parts you can remember, including 103 Good Things, 5 Bad Kings and 2 Genuine Dates'.[58] The former Royal Yacht *Britannia* is advertised as a heritage attraction with the sub-heading 'History You'll Remember'.[59] The political commentator Neal Ascherson has stated that the public perception of Scottish history remains 'chaotic'. This was no insult to historians, he claimed, but to signify that time is used not to enforce perspective, but to enhance dislocation, creating '. . . a scrapbook of highly coloured, often bloody tableaux whose sequence or relation to one another is obscure'.[60] Getting history wrong is important to identity formation as much as the bits of history we get right. Peripheral nations, especially, attempt to reclaim their own narratives from the core and this exaggerates the process of selection and compartmentalisation of the past. Holistic history contains too many narratives from the enemy: it is not suited to nationalist history.

The nation, then, has to have its stories, its own songs. A good example of this is the debate over the national anthem. Interestingly, both Scotland ('Flower of Scotland') and Wales ('Land of my Fathers') have developed their own semi-official national anthems to rival 'God Save the Queen'. A national anthem has been a double-edged sword for union and colonial states. Here, now, is 'The Voice of South Africa', which was written in 1918 by an Afrikaner poet as an alternative to 'God Save the King'. It was an attempt to channel Afrikaner consciousness against foreign imposition:

> In our body and our spirit,
> in our inmost heart held fast,
> In the promise of our future
> and the glory of the past;
> In our will, our work, our striving,
> from cradle to the grave –
> There's no land that shares our loving,
> and no bond than can enslave.
> Thou has borne us and we know thee.
> May our deeds to all proclaim
> Our enduring love and service
> to thy honour and thy name.[61]

The first performance of the National Anthem in Britain was in 1745 at Drury Lane, having first appeared in print the year before. Its somewhat fluid content and simple rhythm allowed a range of versions to gain attention. Some were especially loyal, such as in the example of verses added to ease George III through his illness in 1811:[62]

> Back to his frame and mind,
> Fair health and pow'rs refin'd
> Once again bring;
> To thee with streaming eye
> His trembling people fly
> Oh! hear a nation cry;
> God save the King!

Others had been cruel and threatening, as one parody produced in the 1790s shows:[63]

> To the just Guillotine,
> Who shaves off Heads so clean,
> I tune my String!
> Thy power is so great
> That ev'ry Tool of State
> Dreadeth thy mighty weight,
> Wonderful Thing!

The nineteenth century produced a number of Chartist-inspired rewrites and in 1918, as war was ending, a competition was suggested to find the best verses for the National Anthem to recognise the contribution of the nations of the British Empire. Here is an extract from one of the entrants which incorporated Commonwealth countries:[64]

> Wide o'er the linking seas,
> Polar and tropic breeze
> Our song shall bring.
> Brothers of each Domain,
> Bound but by Freedom's chain,
> Shout, as your Sires, again –
> 'God save the King!'

The Scots, of course, were not averse to a bit of fun here too. Theodore Napier, whose involvement with the Scottish Home Rule Association in the 1880s we will see in later chapters, was Honorary Secretary of the Legitimist Jacobite League of Great Britain. On their behalf he produced *The Royal House of Stuart. A Plea for its Restoration, being an appeal by a loyal Scotsman*, published in 1898, with the aim of supporting HRH Louis of Bavaria (née Mary of Modena) or her legitimate descendants, 'who but for the Act of Settlement, would now be reigning as Queen Mary III of Scotland and IV of England and Ireland'. His plea ended with his own version of 'God Save the Queen':

God save our gracious Queen!
Long live our noble Queen!
God Save the Queen!
Send her victorious,
Happy and glorious
Soon to reign over us!
God save the Queen!

Amen

Songs carry stories, folk songs are for the people, national anthems
are for the people and their parliament. Scottishness in civil society
and Britishness through the state, has sustained informal and formal
nationalism, to use the categories devised by Eriksen.[65] Scottish
national identity has not been captured by its state, so it has been
able to develop many interlocking levels of informal nationality.[66]
That is the structural underpinning of Scottish national identity, its
sociological origins. It has been that stateless nation where, from
electoral polls and other survey work, we know how mistaken it has
been to equate national identity with votes for the Scottish National
Party.[67] National identity is invested in so many areas of Scottish
culture and life and the Wallace story says as much about Scottish
culture as it does about the nation's politics.[68] The narration of the
nation is not artificial or merely virtual, but the ties that bind it are
cultural, spiritual and historical.[69] The story of Wallace does not
make the Scottish nation, but it has carried its culture, it has carried
its identities.

The ease with which the Wallace story fits the core sociological
framework of Scotland's national identity is plain enough. Wallace is
a safe bet for civil society. He was not noble by birth, more
bourgeois than anything else.[70] He was not part of the Scottish
'state', and his knighthood and his Guardianship of Scotland, for a
year after the Battle of Stirling Bridge, was seen as reward for a man
promoted through the ranks by his own efforts, rather than pulled
up by patronage and birth. Religiously a Protestant, with a
Protestant version of Blind Harry's patriotic verse to confirm it in
1570,[71] he was a suitable role model for post-Reformation Scotland

15

and certainly so in the eighteenth and nineteenth centuries.[72] He was no Highlander, although there are Highland claims to his memory and his rustic simplicity, honesty, strength and prowess on the battlefield was easily likened to the noble savage, so portrayed in the late eighteenth-century view of the Scottish Highlands.[73] Nor was he a Jacobite, although this did not stop his deeds of valour appearing in Jacobite songs. However, it did ensure his commemoration would focus Scottish nationhood (freedom) on parliament and governance, not monarchical restoration. It fitted in with longer term religious processes in Scottish nationhood, which Hearn has termed a 'covenanted people'.[74] For religion, but more generally, too, Wallace was the one to back, rather than the equally colourful Charles Edward Stuart four hundred and fifty years later. He better fitted, in Craig's terminology, the richness of the core culture, than did Bonnie Prince Charlie, particularly the Whig constitutional heritage that was to become so important to intellectual debates after the Union.[75] Wallace's technique of guerrilla warfare after the failure of his set piece approach at the Battle of Falkirk, although perhaps not very successful at times,[76] added to the sense of his own personal independence. Being outlawed while remaining the leader of others fitted the sense of obligation and self-service of civil society as it developed in the post-Enlightenment years (without, of course the then abhorrent blood spilling). More acutely, however, it added the romantic appeal of the outlaw, living beyond the law, but sanctioned by the moral economy of the people.[77] Wallace's career began and ended 'as a forest bandit, living free and defiant in "outlaw" wise'.[78] It added structure to which fabrications could be hung. To quote Keen once again:

> he became the hero of a ten years' war against the English, who had three times rescued his country from their yoke; he became the leader of the Scottish forces in immense pitched battles at which either he was not present, or which were not fought at all; and the lives lost in the struggle against him ran into hundreds of thousands. He became a muscular giant whose strength was all but irresistible: he took part in battles upon the

sea and in Gascony, concerning his role in which history remains silent. He became the chosen champion of Philip the Fair of France, and held parley with the Queen of Edward I of England, who was dead before his historical career opened.[79]

Finally, of course, Wallace was a hero who pre-dated the Union of 1707. He was not sullied by early eighteenth-century politics ('bribery'), nor by reaction to the quiet spread of Anglicisation. Not Scotland after Union, but Scotland during the Wars of Independence was his time. Not negotiation with England, but capture and execution by England. His story, for the nationalist, is not compromised, hence his suitability for carrying Scotland's identity and, as it has been suggested, it is the medieval period to which the modern nations of the eighteenth and nineteenth centuries return when they seek to establish their authenticity and authority. It seems as if the story of Wallace can do no wrong. All the boxes have been ticked: the Wallace myth has the strength to carry Scotland's national identity over the centuries. Before we resurrect the myth and show how those other than the nationalists have tried to capture its sentiment, the next task is to uncover what the sources tell us about the man.

TWO

Life in Sources

HOW MUCH DO YOU KNOW ABOUT WALLACE?

(1) When was Wallace born?
(2) Where?
(3) When was the Battle of Stirling Bridge?
(4) Who did Wallace defeat?
(5) When and where was Wallace killed?[1]

The skill with which medieval and early modern historians can resurrect the past from so very limited historical records is something at which those of us more used to the comfort of the resource-rich centuries of the modern period can only marvel. There might be some bad handwriting to deal with on occasion and the pleasure of data overload too, but we do not have the triple challenge of key sources written in contentious Latin, early Scots (with some amazing fonts in the original printed sources) and the tiresome disappearance, destruction and falsification of sources. These are challenges, too, for historians of the modern world, but such problems are nowhere near as acute. The recorded world of William Wallace is not an extensive one, so this account is weighted in favour of the myth, rather than the man.

There are three additional problems which confront us: many of Scotland's national records were taken or destroyed in 1296 at the behest of Edward I, when the Stone of Destiny was also removed to Westminster Abbey. Probably the most complete historical record of Wallace's actions comes from his enemies, not the Scottish side, which itself is not unbiased. Finally, of course, there is the Harry factor. He gives what appears to be an authentic account of the actions of Wallace, in the form of an epic poem compiled in the fifteenth century, claiming legitimacy from a contemporary source. But the claim is false and we are left with no more than a rousing and rather bloodthirsty story.

What is known about Sir William Wallace through the documented evidence is remarkably limited. There are only a handful of items extant which come from the man himself: four writs and charters, a note guaranteeing safe passage for three monks and the trading letter produced in the name of Wallace and Murray while they were stationed in Haddington on 11 October 1297 and sent to the merchants of Lübeck and Hamburg.[2] He was born in either Elderslie in Renfrewshire or Ellerslie in Ayrshire, although no-one can be confident that Mackay's 'discovery' favouring the latter is accurate (with the implication that the Scottish National Party may have spent much of the twentieth century marching up and down the streets of the wrong birthplace).[3] Indeed, Lewis Spence offered the same choice in 1919.[4]

Wallace was born around 1270, the second son of Sir Malcolm Wallace, and not quite the proletarian, in spite of even contemporary accusations over his ignoble birth.[5] His initial prominence is found within the English chronicles which do, for once, back up Harry's verse, telling of Wallace's revenge exacted upon Sir William Heselrig, Sheriff of Lanark, for the death of his wife, or mistress, in 1297.[6] Wallace's victory over a larger English army, under de Warenne, at the Battle of Stirling Bridge in the same year, is widely found, including the grisly fate which befell the English Treasurer Hugh de Cressingham. The accusations here and at the Battle of Falkirk, over the actions of the Scottish nobility, are much harder to pin down. Wallace's knighthood is confirmed in a number of different sources, although again there are doubts. A charter in his name was authorised as 'William Wallace, knight, guardian of the kingdom of Scotland and commander of its armies in the name of the famous prince the Lord John, by God's grace illustrious king of Scotland, by consent of the community of the realm'.[7] His knighthood appears to be self-anointed, but accepted and commonly used by others.[8] His appointment as Guardian in 1297 is more sure, not least because the chronicles record his resignation (or removal) from this position after defeat at Falkirk in 1298.[9] It had some firm foundations, but the earliest sources remain problematic, as Lord Hailes explained:

> I have drawn up this account of the actions in Falkirk from the testimony of the English historians. They have done justice to the courage and steadiness of their enemies, while our historians have represented their own countrymen as occupied in frivolous unmeaning contests, and, from treachery or resentment, abandoning the public cause in the day of trial.[10]

He continues in a footnote:

> There is scarcely one of our writers who has not produced an invective against Comyn or an apology for Wallace, or a lamentation over the deserted Stewart.[11]

It is his major engagements with Edward's forces which appear in most of the contemporary accounts, backed up by the records of the English royal court showing the needful organisation to support the campaign in Scotland. These records include compensation for those who lost horses in the exchanges. It allows some estimates as to the scale of the losses on the battlefield, on the English side at least. After those events little is heard of the patriot, although evidence exists – albeit conflicting – of his visit to France in 1299 or 1300.[12] He returns to Scotland and stays in hiding and the English records report Edward's rejection of the suggestion of peace with Wallace.[13] This hard-line response appears vindicated, as Wallace is betrayed by Sir John Mentieth which led to his capture, trial and execution. All this is reported in the documents which supported Wallace's trial, including the list of crimes which comprised the charges laid against him.[14]

It is evident, and will become clearer in the pages which follow, that what corroboration there is to the biography of Wallace the man comes from two sides, both of which are biased in their function as propaganda.[15] It inevitably casts doubt upon the validity of cross-referral as a means to gaining the balance, offering yet more encouragement for the mythographers to have their way. Not only the chronology and events of Wallace's life, but his motivations and the motivations of those around him, as well as his feelings and personality, are no more than mere surmise. With no personal artefact surviving, no self-reflective diary or letters, in order that we may construct an inkling to his character, the opportunities for fabrication are almost boundless.[16] The chronicles do offer some account of speeches and battle cries at some of the key events, but they are not directly of his time and their authenticity in this respect – despite replication – is very much open to question. Notwithstanding these persistent difficulties, we must work with the sources that survive: that takes us to a number of the earliest extant chronicles of Scottish history which start the debate on the historical Wallace.

John of Fordun's *Chronica Gentis Scotorum* (*c.* 1370) is the first of the early Scottish narratives to mention Wallace, although the actions of those around him, and his betrayal by Menteith, are hinted at in earlier accounts.[17] Fordun's five books[18] are described as the basis of every history prior to the death of James I, 'the indispensable groundwork of our annals' for the twelfth and thirteenth centuries.[19] It is believed that Fordun arranged his chronicle in response to Edward's removal of the early accounts from the Scottish libraries,[20] with the result that he made his compilation primarily from the English chronicles.[21] It is at this point that the origins of the myth begin to form, as the work of Edward Cowan has demonstrated. In Fordun's tale Wallace rose from his 'den' and we are told that he resigned his Guardianship to fight with the plebeians. His defeat at the Battle of Falkirk was due to the perfidiousness of the established aristocracy who resented this upstart. We have the lowly-born Wallace, the man of the people, and are offered sympathy for the treachery he received from the nobles of Scotland. Spice was added to this narrative by Fordun accusing Bruce of hastening the defeat at Falkirk by attacking the Scottish army with his troops.[22] Instructively, Fordun was much less enthusiastic for Bruce than Barbour's renowned epic verse from 1375.[23]

Work by Bannerman on MacDuff of Fife shows the aristocratic betrayal of Wallace to be less than complete, however. MacDuff sent his two sons to fight with Wallace at Falkirk and for this he earned the tag of 'principled patriot'.[24] There is acceptance that Fordun's work is accurate, with his use of contemporary material from the thirteenth century, but that his choice of examples was presented to demonstrate the importance of an independent Scottish nation and Scottish monarchy.[25] This dominant, patriotic narrative was continued in the two chroniclers who wrote in the first half of the fifteenth century: the prior of Lochleven, Andrew of Wyntoun, who completed the *Orygynale Cronykil of Scotland* in the 1420s and the Abbot of Inchcolm Abbey, Walter Bower, whose *Scotichronicon* was a continuation of Fordun and a product of the 1440s.[26] Wyntoun was supported by Sir John Wemyss of Leuchars and Kincaldrum (1372–1428) and Bower's patron was Sir David Stewart of Rosyth (d. 1444).[27]

In Bower's account it is Wallace who taught the Scots to fight, but this was done to free Scots held captive by the English.[28] The English who were defeated in 1297, 'at a bridge on the river Forth beyond Stirling', were described as 'savage'. Victory was offered as a 'celestial gift to the faithful Scots'. Indeed, the Scots were celebrated for the destruction they caused to the English lands as far as (the appropriately named) Stainmore in Northumbria.[29] It was accompanied by Wallace's order that 'all Englishmen (both regular and secular clergy and laymen) [be expelled] from the kingdom of Scotland'.[30] This chronicle offered no criticism of the barbarity of Wallace's actions. Bower produced the most complete early description of Wallace's family background and of his exploits. His outline of Wallace's physical appearance is remarkably similar to the language used by Harry on page 54:

> He was a tall man with the body of a giant, cheerful in appearance with agreeable features, broad-shouldered and big-boned, with belly in proportion and lengthy flanks, pleasing in appearance but with a wild look, broad in the hips, with strong arms and legs, a most spirited fighting-man, with all his limbs very strong and firm.[31]

22

His virtues were extolled as a handsome man which won him the
'grace and favour of the hearts of all loyal Scots', to be generous and
a helper of the poor and of widows, a distinguished speaker, who
abhorred treachery and meted out his own justice upon thieves and
robbers.[32] There are also key moments from his warring career: his
slaying of the English sheriff of Lanark; his success, upon becoming
Guardian, in getting all the magnates in Scotland under his authority
which gave him the confidence to attack the English-controlled
fortified towns and castles.[33] Other events are detailed, but it is in
the description of Wallace's betrayal by the aristocracy in the years
1297–8 that some of the most emotive language is used:

> So while Scotland by the shrewdness of the guardian was
> making a surprising, in fact a successful recovery, since every
> man remained safely on his own property and cultivated the
> land in the usual way and very often triumphed over his
> enemies, the magnates and powerful men of the kingdom,
> intoxicated by a stream of envy, seditiously entered a secret plot
> against the guardian under the guise of expressions of virgin-
> innocence but with their tails tied together.
>
> What stubborn follies of fools! Wallace did not force himself
> into rulership, but by choice of the estates he was raised up to
> be ruler after the previously nominated guardians had been
> removed.[34]

Bower blames their jealousy upon Wallace not being a man of
their rank. However, there is no mention of Bruce's attack on the
Scottish lines, just his and the nobility's abandonment of the field
and a rather chastened Bruce being spurned into rejecting the
English side on the accusation of 'womanish cowardice' made by
Wallace.[35] Thereafter, as the historian Alan Young points out, Bower
was keen to present Bruce as the key patriot-king.[36] It was a path
first trod by Fordun and enhanced by Wyntoun; they turned
Alexander III into a model king in their respective patriotic glosses.[37]
Wyntoun does offer some detail on the early history of Wallace and
of his fights in Lanark and the Battle of Stirling Bridge.[38] The defeat

at Falkirk in 1298 is described around the actions of the Comyns, not Bruce:[39]

> The Cwmynys kyn all halyly
> Fyrst lefft the feld; and, as behoẅyd,
> Syne Willame Walayis hym remoẅyd:
> For he persaẅyd gret malys
> Agayne hym scharpyd mony wys.
> Wythowtyn dowt that ilke day,
> Quhen mony Scottis fled away,
> Quhare eẅyre thai hapnyd to be ouetane,
> All thai ware slayne downe evryilkane,
> The Inglis men had halyly
> Off that jowrnay the ẅyctory.

It is Wallace's first appearance in a chronicle produced in the Scottish vernacular, compiled around 1420, about sixty years before Harry's *Wallace*.[40] John Mair (John Major) littered his *Greater Britain* (1521) with connections between Wallace and the heroes of classical antiquity: 'Like Hannibal or Ulysses he understood to draw up an army in order of battle, while like another Telamonian Ajax he could carry out the fight in open field'. In his *In Quartum Sententiarum* he likened Wallace to Achilles.[41] Mair repeats Bower's interpretation on the eve of the battle at Falkirk that the betrayal of the magnates was the cause of Wallace's defeat, but that, 'it is a feature of nobles generally – to prefer the yoke of a superior to that of an inferior', adding that he believed they wished to weaken the power of both Wallace and King Edward to facilitate their own return to power.[42] There is no mention of the attack on Wallace's troops by Bruce in this history.[43] Mair's proof of the execution of Wallace – placing it at the Tyburn gallows (Smithfield) on 24 August 1305 – is based on a simple reference to 'the English chroniclers'.[44] It was evidence he would not otherwise rely on: despite mention in the chronicles of Wallace visiting France on two occasions, Mair found no such corroboration in the Latin chronicles or in the French accounts, so was inclined to believe that the story was untrue.[45]

The English sources contain an equal measure of rhetoric and one-sided narrative. Alexander Grant has pointed out that the *Lanercost Chronicle* contains much on English 'depredations in Scotland':[46] it was written during the reign of Edward I and it corroborates a few of the main events in the public life of Wallace.[47] We are told that the Glasgow Bishop Robert Wishart conspired with James the Stewart to invoke the uprising against Edward, not by their own deeds, but by 'caus[ing] a certain bloody man, William Wallace, who had formerly been a chief of brigands in Scotland, to revolt against the king and assemble the people in his support'.[48] The Battle of Stirling Bridge is described, focusing on the Scots' tactics of allowing just enough of the English army to cross the bridge before the slaughter began. The atrocities which followed are highlighted: the Treasurer of Scotland, Hugh de Cressingham, was skinned on the orders of Wallace, a broad strip of the skin being used to make either a baldrick for Wallace's sword or horse girths, as other writers have claimed.[49] Wallace and his supporters chased the survivors as far as Berwick, before 'putting to death the few English that they found therein', moved to Northumberland where they 'wast[ed] all the land, committing arson, pillage and murder', did the same in Carlisle before returning to Northumberland 'to lay waste more completely what they had left at first'.[50] The priory of Lanercost is just eight miles from Carlisle,[51] so the consternation of the writers – if that was where it was written – is understandable.[52] Unlike the gloss of Fordun or Wyntoun, Wallace's exploits are not seen as justified, whether inside or outside the law. The 'outlaw tradition' in popular mythology gives legitimacy to those who champion the underdog, protecting the poor or the widowed when faced by unbending and cruel authority.[53] Wallace's morality is the first heroic myth to be undermined in the *Lanercost* account. As well as chasing the English survivors at Stirling Bridge to their death, he was also accused of cruel treachery: he besieged the English in April, bringing 'famine in the castles' and 'when they had promised to the English conditions of life and limb and safe conduct to their own land on surrendering the castles, William Wallace did not keep faith with them'.[54] With this sort of black propaganda, it is no surprise that the English victory at Falkirk was greeted with great acclaim. The chronicle quoted the estimates of Walsingham that 60,000 Scots were defeated and Hemingsburgh that 56,000 was the true figure, despite both, Maxwell tells us, being far in excess of the total of Wallace's resources.[55] The English victories prompted a number of verses:[56]

> Berwick, Dunbar, and Falkirk too
> Show all the traitor Scots can do.
> England exult! thy Prince is peerless
> Where thee he leadeth, follow fearless.

Praise of the King of England

The noble race of Englishmen most worthy is of praise,
By whom the Scottish people have been conquered in all ways.
England exult!

The Frenchmen break their treaties as soon as they are made
Whereby the hope of Scotsmen has been cheated and betrayed
England exult!

O disconcerted people! hide yourselves and close your gates
Lest Edward should espy you and wreak vengeance on your plates
England exult!

Henceforth the place for vanquished Scots is nearest to the tail
   [i]n clash of arms.
O England victorious, all hail!
England exult!

Of William Wallace

> Welsh William being made a noble
> Straightway the Scots become ignoble.
> Treason and slaughter, arson and raid,
> By suff'ring and misery must be repaid.

Following the capture and execution of Wallace, the following lines were penned:

> The vilest doom is fittest for thy crimes
> Justice demands that thou shoudst die three times
> Thou pillager of many a sacred shrine
> Butcher of thousands, threefold death be thine!
> So shall the English from thee gain relief,
> Scotland! be wise, and choose a nobler chief.

Believed to be the best English source for Scottish affairs, the *Chronicle of Lanercost* perpetuated the propaganda against Wallace. Its language has prompted Fiona Watson to label it xenophobic, while acknowledging the fear in the north of England that Edward was underestimating their security against Wallace's threat.[57] Yet the chronicle blames many of Scotland's future ills on Alexander III's wife Yolande, not least his desire to be with her on the stormy night which cost his life.[58] Edward I took up the position of feudal superior in Scotland, ordering the necessary historical proof to be uncovered to back up his claim.[59] It involved more manipulation of the evidence, in a highly complex and confusing way which does little to give security to our historical understanding.[60]

Other corroborating evidence does exist which fleshes out aspects of the military engagement between the two nations. The army assembled by Edward on his return from fighting in France in 1298, and in anger at the defeat at Stirling Bridge, was estimated to be one of the largest of his reign. The work of Michael Prestwich has uncovered the great detail of its organisation which, he concludes, was the basis from which victory could be expected.[61] The valuation rolls show the number of horses invested by the English in the campaign at over 1,350.[62] Reports in England suggested that Edward wished to capture all the Scottish leaders. Interestingly, the English records consulted by Prestwich do indicate Wallace's speech to his troops at Falkirk: 'I have brought you to the ring; now hop if you can', so this is not, perhaps, the invention of later generations.[63] He also shows that the English sources were often sceptical of

Edward's gains after Falkirk because of the Scots' reluctance to engage them in battle. This wasted the time of the great armies assembled at great logistical expense, with siege machinery and prefabricated bridges put into place.[64] Financial help was forthcoming from the archbishop of York, with a lot of the supplies for Edward's army coming from Yorkshire.[65]

Where all the sources are richest is at the death of Wallace. His birthday remains a doubt, but his death was eulogised. His crimes were listed, not discussed, and he was made to wear a laurel crown, indicating English contempt for his rule of the northern kingdom. He was accused, in the documentation at his trial, of issuing writs in the name of King John against the sovereignty of Edward.[66] He was to die by hanging, disembowelling and execution, with his intestines being burned and his body quartered. Each punishment was to reflect one of his crimes, of robbery, murder, treason and sacrilege.[67] Thus his martyrdom at Smithfield made the myth complete.

WHAT TO DO WHEN THE SOURCES ARE FEW:
THE LATER HISTORIOGRAPHY

The eventual failure of the English to conquer Scotland in the early fourteenth century is attributed to continued resistance by the Scots, but this should not be taken too far. Alexander Grant argues that 'With the notable exception of the Douglases, the Murrays, and William Wallace, few Scots can be found steadily and consistently supporting the cause of independence.'[68] Not only was there great inconsistency of support, feuding between Bruce, Comyn and Balliol, but medieval society remained ambivalent in its conception of independence. The focus was on the king, not the kingdom, making it a very subordinate form of freedom, one further subsumed by the authority of the church.[69] Fiona Watson, too, warns against simplistic notions of national identity for this period. She reiterates that national identity was much more about king than it was about kingdom, and she does so to make the point that it is precisely this type of qualification which is lost in the transition from history to myth when used to structure a modern national identity.[70]

The greatest exponent of historical myth has been Blind Harry, whose *Wallace*, an epic verse of 11,861 lines, was turned out in eleven books and is believed to date from around 1474 to 1479.[71] The poem was the start of the historiographical genre which has relied upon a lack of verifiable historical facts about Wallace. Modern research into Wallace was part of the mania for all things bibliographical, which took such inspiration from the historical writings of Walter Scott and his patronage of the Bannatyne Club. Indeed, the leading cataloguer on these and the many kindred historical clubs divides them into 'pre-Waverley', 'Waverley' and 'post-Waverley' societies, in recognition of the novelist's import.[72] Given intellectual support by Thomas Thomson and David Laing, societies such as the Bannatyne Club and the Maitland Club took research into the annals of Scotland to an impressive level of documented scholarship in the nineteenth century. They also did much to inspire interest in Scottish identity, something that, it is claimed, was catastrophically lost with the demise of these societies in the middle of the century.[73] The Maitland Club's *Documents Illustrative of Sir William Wallace, his life and times* was compiled by John Stevenson and presented by Robert Rodger in 1841.[74] It was produced in the firm belief of the heroic quality of the man and his centrality to Scotland's well-being in a time of war:

> Extraordinary circumstances give birth of extraordinary characters. The same exciting causes which produced a Tell in Switzerland, a Cromwell in England, and a Bonapart in France, raised up a Wallace and a Bruce in Scotland.[75]

It contains a wide miscellany of documents in Latin, with no translation offered. But of most importance was a facsimile of the letter from Murray and Wallace to the merchants of Lübeck and Hamburg offering the Scottish ports to trade with Germany, resurrecting the shipment of hinds and wool.[76]

> It has been made known to us by trustworthy merchants of the Kingdom of Scotland that you out of your own goodwill have shown counsel, help and favour in all causes and business

touching us and said merchants, although there have been no previous deserts of ours, wherefore our thanks are so much the more due to you, as well as fitting remuneration, for which we desire you to be so good as to cause proclamation to be made among your merchants that they can have safe access with their merchandise to all the ports of the Kingdom of Scotland, for, thanks be to God, the Kingdom of Scotland has now, by battle, been recovered from the power of the English. Farewell.[77]

They made these overtures as they had control – particularly administrative control – over Scotland and needed recognition for Scotland's economic independence from Edward's jurisdiction.[78] As we have already seen, the Lübeck letter forms one of the few extant artefacts which are directly associated with Wallace. It is a story that sums up so much of the Wallace myth. That this control, or confidence, was short-lived has been lost in the importance later generations have attached to the existence of something Wallace may have touched. There is no proof he ever wrote or saw the letter, although it has clearly been compiled and sent in his name with his and Murray's seal. In the 1990s it re-enters the historical debate like no other source in the Wallace story. Edinburgh at that time was blessed with an extension to the Royal Museum of Scotland in Chambers Street. The museum offered a history of the nation from its geological beginnings to the twentieth century.[79] It opened on St Andrew's Day, 1998. There was an immediate outcry, for there was no mention of Wallace. The Museum of Scotland had nothing to say on the national patriot of Scotland. Why? The answer: there was no artefact to display. There were, of course, early editions of Blind Harry's *Wallace*, but that was text, better placed in a display cabinet in the National Library of Scotland, not a museum. The belief persisted that the Lübeck letter was destroyed during the Second World War, when German bombers destroyed the archives in London.[80] At least this appeared to form the museum's argument, as it was presented in the press. However, a journalist with *Scotland on Sunday*, who made a few phone calls, 'discovered' the letter in an archive in Lübeck. Seemingly, the Scottish historical community had somehow lost track of it. Now it was located, the newspaper had found it, the journalist had her story and she could be a contender for young journalist of the year.[81] The historical community hit back, pointing out that the letter was never lost, despite some published statements to the contrary. The museum would have been directed to it, if only it had asked. *Scotland on Sunday* was accused of refusing to publish letters from a leading Scottish historian which undermined their claims of 'discovery'. Legal proceedings were instigated. The holders of the letter allowed the Scots to borrow it, for an extended period.[82] At last Scotland's new national museum had a display, albeit text, and a portrait.

It is the best example to show how the historiography on Wallace has been a key element in debates over Scottish history. The conjunction of *Braveheart* (1995) and the referendum vote for a Scottish Parliament (1997) made Scots feel important, because they had been recognised to be so. Recognised, that is, by Hollywood and Westminster. Now our history should mature along with our democracy as the consequence of this fusion, was the argument. However, is this any advance on the peripheral culture which, as was shown in the argument of Cairns Craig in the previous chapter, produces a sense of self-hatred, a Scotland restrained 'by the colour of our vowels'?[83] The cry for maturity implies a previous, indeed a current, state of immaturity. Scotland needs the truth, not some myth is the belief. Now Scotland has reached the high-table, the kilt should be dispensed with and the business suit, instead, should be worn. Yet medieval historians will emphasise how relatively minor Wallace's impact was during his short life and even shorter mastery of Scotland's national affairs. They have led the campaign for Murray's role at Stirling Bridge to take precedence over the then more junior Wallace in the history books.[84] It will be a hard job. The legacy of Wallace has obscured too many facts. This should be accepted as the history of the nation, not the search for 'truth' to avoid the self-applied suspicion of being peripheral. All nations of the world are made up from half-remembered stories, of myths and legends and convenient forgetfulness about history that is uncomfortable. The classic statement from Ernest Renan, writing in the 1880s, that the nation is a spiritual entity which embraces shared memories (sacrifices) and is propelled by shared futures, is based on cultural transmission by getting history 'wrong'.[85]

A feature of the Wallace myth is that enough of its history can be established from the chronicles, but the lack of corroborating evidence thereafter seems, surprisingly, to matter a great deal. Opinion-makers in Scotland now want the real history of Scotland to go with the real Scottish nation and parliament. *Scotland on Sunday* dedicated its supplement to paraphrasing the great satire on English history by Sellar and Yeatman *1066 and All That* with *1707 and All That. How well do you know Scotland's history?*[86] The debate on the lack of knowledge of Scottish history among schoolchildren and the adult population of Scotland had surfaced once again.[87] The questions at the beginning of the chapter are an example of this. So, too, are the popular stories of the nation published in conjunction with the newspapers *Scotland on Sunday* and the *Daily Record*.[88] That Scotland's imagined community is based on false history seems to matter. It is important to historians and it is meaningful to the history that is taught, but fighting over the real Christian name of Wallace's father is immaterial to nation-building.[89] The lack of corroboration in the sources has allowed the Wallace myth to gather momentum at various times over the centuries. This is how nations are held together. Still, the fear of being peripheral has made this nation uncomfortable with its myths. That should not be the case but it is. Scotland is again hunting the snark, the true history of Wallace, although, to be fair, this time there are real sightings to go on. The populist historiography is unsettled because it does not have all the answers. Knowing when Wallace was born, or his marital status or the name of his father, will not change his status as Scotland's foremost patriot since the fifteenth century, as the sources give just enough to fire the national imagination by recounting the main events of his life. Not having the answers to the rest is the elixir of myth: it has made Wallace the nationalist icon of the ages. Searching for the true facts of Wallace is a task best left to the historian, yet it is to miss the point of how and why the myth is important. The facts are not the reason why he is remembered as a meaningful historical actor in the first place.

THREE

Blind Harry

Although I cannot say sow crae just as broad as I once could I can read about Wallace, Bruce and Burns with as much enthusiasm as ever and feel proud of having been a son of Caledonia, and I like to tell people when they ask, 'Are you native born?' 'No sir, I am a [S]cotchman,' and I feel as proud as I am sure as ever Romans did when it was their boast to say, 'I am a Roman citizen'.[1]

The myth of Wallace was born from sporadic facts in the early chronicles. Fordun's *Chronica Gentis Scotorum* was followed by Bower and Wyntoun who manufactured a story which lauded the courageous deeds of this ignoble man. Each narrative gave its own slant when fixing Wallace's support or opposition to Bruce, but the parameters of the myth had been put in place. Nor did the myth weaken with the excessive spilling of English blood. Bower paraded Wallace's actions as a 'celestial gift' offering justification from 'up high' to English death and mutilation.[2] The *Lanercost Chronicle* described Wallace as that 'certain bloody man', but such opposition was no brake on the momentum.[3] The validity of the chronicles is based on their position as the great annals of Scottish history which touch Wallace's time, or are claimed as the earliest extant compilers of sources closest to contemporary Wallace.

However, several difficulties arise with the translation of these texts, and none more so than with the motivation to elevate Wallace as the people's champion. As was seen from the arguments of Alexander Grant and Fiona Watson, national identity was focused on king, not kingdom.[4] Emphasising this, Reid's historiographical analysis of the nationalist content of the early chronicles used the monarch, Alexander III, as the indicator for his definition of national identity.[5] Nationality equalled king, not people and not necessarily territory either. This suggests we have a version of Scottish national identity within which Wallace does not fit clearly. He may have been fighting for King John, but the universality of nationhood is one of freedom: of peoples, not kings. As the stories in the following centuries show, it is the people's freedom which comes to shine. The origins of the Wallace myth have not, therefore, been constrained by the chronicles, yet they give credibility to the history of the man, and they have contributed to the myth in their valorisations and biases. Thereafter, it has been Harry, whose epic verse celebrating Wallace's exploits – including many things he never did – has been the genesis of so much Wallaciana and the basis of patriotic inspiration for generations. The philanthropist and industrialist Andrew Carnegie, remembering his days in Scotland in the 1840s, tells of a life of setbacks and challenges, but when faced with such decisions he would ask himself 'what would Wallace have done?'[6] The answer came from his own youth, from Harry's *Wallace*, and the ensuing versions of the story which flooded forth.

WHO WAS BLIND HARRY?

The *Wallace* is written in decasyllabic couplets, the earliest known example in any lengthy, Scottish verse.[7] This structure alone emphasises its literary merit and its place in Scottish history. Its author, Harry, however, is a most mysterious figure. The accounts of the Lord High Treasurer, in 1490, record payments made to 'Blind Hary' for what appears to be the reciting of poetry and song,[8] and John Mair[9] (1470–1550) provides the contemporary evidence that Harry was blind from birth, a suggestion which continues to add a wonderful poetic and romantic flourish to the tales:

> There was one Henry, blind from his birth who, in the time of my childhood, fabricated a whole book about William Wallace, and therein he wrote down in our native rhymes – and this was a kind of composition in which he had much skill – all that passed current among the people of his day.[10]

However, there is no extant manuscript which is traced to Harry's hand and the earliest copy is that transcribed by John Ramsay in 1488, the year after he transcribed Barbour's *Bruce*.[11] Of the attempts to date the *Wallace*, the most convincing work comes from Mathew McDiarmid who concluded that it was produced between 1474 and 1479, by comparing the known whereabouts of individuals for whom the sources are greater.[12] Harry first appeared as the named author of the *Wallace* in the 1645 edition published by Robert Bryson. He becomes Henry, commonly called Blind Harry, in Morrison's 1790 edition and was confirmed as 'Henry the Minstrel' in John Jamieson's 1820 edition.[13] It was in the Victorian period that his chivalric reputation was confirmed with this new designation.[14] Unfortunately, these changes raised more doubts about verifying the authenticity of its writer. It was suggested by J.T.T. Brown in 1900 that the author of the *Wallace* might even have benefited from Barbour's transcriber John Ramsay as a collaborator. The earliest known manuscript of the *Wallace* was for a long time bound with *The Bruce* in the Advocates Library before being separated.[15] However, the accusation against Ramsay has been dismissed by others then and earlier.[16] Sibbald discarded this view a century previously by arguing that Harry must have written this text because it was in a universally understood form which required no tinkering from Ramsay. The reasoning: that Harry was a wandering mendicant and the quality of the text was appropriate for someone of such status.[17] It is a typically assumptive argument of the type too often used as evidence when corroboration is missing in this story. Another, from the nineteenth century, is that 'Blind Harry' was a pseudonym for some unknown author; this was used as an argument to deflect from the poem's anti-Englishness. It comes from a period of British integration between Scotland and England, when unionist-nationalism, not xenophobia, marked this identity, but few have been prepared to project this harmony back to the time of Harry.[18] According to McDiarmid, some of the early twentieth-century historians

wished its author to be some eminent personage from the political and social world of its day who preferred to remain incognito, such a strong expression of anti-English sentiment not then being in accord with government policy or Christian values – though the latter view obviously reflects liberal enlightened Britain better than fifteenth-century Scotland.[19]

With so little to go on, the creator of the *Wallace* has remained largely an unknown figure. Only one name is commonly accepted: Henry or Harry (or Hary in the Scottish usage).[20] His mystique is wrapped in a cloak of classical genius: as the Scottish Homer, where Harry was a man who overcame blindness from birth to make great insights into the Scottish character, which he so dramatically displayed in his only literary work. His reputation became that of a free spirit, an outsider, free from authority. Schofield, writing in 1920, neatly sums up the transition:

> And, now, to give him more dignity, scholars write his name on the title page of editions, and elsewhere, in the form 'Henry the Minstrel', as if the 'blind' were too doubtful, the 'Harry' too familiar, and only 'the Minstrel' worthy to stand as the poet's memorable designation[21]

The image which Schofield satirises is one which came to dominate in the Victorian period through a love of chivalry in the first third of the century, romanticism in the middle decades, and then able to survive the decades of earnest record compilation by Scotland's bibliographical and historical clubs. It is typified as the inspiration for two patriotic historians of the late nineteenth century. John Veitch in his analysis on Scottish poetry in 1887 described Harry as 'truly a wandering minstrel – blind, aged and poor'.[22] It was as if being sighted, young and financially solvent was not to be countered in this patriotic script. John Hill Burton eulogised that 'Harry was a blind wandering minstrel, but he belonged to the days when his craft might be that of a gentleman'.[23] Veitch stated confidently that Harry's only means of subsistence came from 'the voluntary gifts of his patrons',[24] and Burton stated that '. . . while [Harry] addressed the commonality to rouse their patriotic ardour, he was received at great men's tables'.[25] It mirrors easily the tales of the minstrel from Sherwood Forest and the merry men surrounding Robin Hood where much of the myth is based on paraphrasing a few key ballads.[26] Strong themes around the freedom of living in the forest as an outlaw and the hardship of such a life, echo throughout Harry's verse:

> King Edwardis self could nocht get bettir wyn
> Than thai had thar, warnage and vennysonne
> Off bestial in to full gret fusioun
>
> . . .
>
> Now lycht, now sadd; now blisful, now in baill;
> In haist, now hurt; now soroufull, now haill;
> Nowe wieldand weyle; now calde weddyr, now hett;
> Nowe moist, now drowth; now waverand wynd, now wet.[27]

Even less is known about Harry than Wallace, so it is no surprise that retrospective romanticisation was an easy accomplishment. His simpleton image was tied to the ignoble birth of the patriot. Henderson's successful *Scottish Vernacular Literature*, first published in 1898 and reaching a third edition in 1910, used the lowly origins of Harry as an excuse for the historical deficiencies and stylistic gaffes in the poem.[28] The poem is error-strewn because it is the work of an uneducated poet. It was curious logic and acted as a powerful piece of myth-making. It comes straight from the rhetoric of the Scottish and English chronicles in their respective glorification and vilification of the feats of the lowly, noble William Wallace.[29]

Just as Fordun's treatment of Wallace was inspired by his belief in the independence of the Scottish nation, through the independence of the Scottish kingship, so Harry's verse can be seen as a product of its times.[30] Harry's anti-Englishness has been construed as opposition to the pro-Englishness of James III. Macdougall suggests that the *Wallace* was used as propaganda by the Duke of Albany to oppose the treaty between Scotland and England in 1474 and there is evidence that the duke's steward, James Liddale, was used as a source in the epic verse.[31] Indeed, along with Liddale, Harry received the patronage of Sir William Wallace of Craigie.[32] The main editions of the *Wallace* are detailed as follows.[33]

1	Manuscript in Advocates Library	1488
2	'A Fragment', Edinburgh, Chepman & Myllar	?1508
3	The Actis and Deidis – Robert Lekpreuik	1570
4	The Life and Acts – Henry Charteris	1594
5	Robert Charteris	1601
6	Adro Hart	1611
7	Adro Hart	1618
8	Andro Hart	1620
9	Edward Raban for David Melvill	1630
10	James Bryson	1640
11	R. Bryson	1645
12	George Lithgow (Gideon Lithgow)	1648
13	Society of Stationers	1661
14	Gideon Lithgow	1661
15	Robert Sanders	1665
16	Andro Anderson	1666
17	Andrew Anderson	1673/5
18	Published in Glasgow by Robert Sanders	1684
19	Published in Glasgow by Robert Sanders	1685
20	Published in Glasgow by Robert Sanders	1690
21	Published in Glasgow by Robert Sanders	1699
22	Printed in the Year	1701
23	Heirs and Successor of A. Anderson	1709
24	Heirs and Successor of A. Anderson	1711
25	Heirs and Successor of A. Anderson	1713
26	Robert Sanders	1713
27	Published in Belfast by James Blow	1728
28	Alex Carmichael & Alex Miller	1736/7
29	John Robertson & Mrs McLean	1747
30	Published in Glasgow by Archibald McLean	1756
31	Printed in the Year 1715 but suppressed until	1758
32	Three Volumes by R. Morrison Jnr	1790
33	James Ballantyne & Co.	1820
34	Published in Glasgow by Ogle & Co.	1869
35	Scottish Text Society	1889
36	Scottish Text Society	1938
37	Scottish Text Society	1968

Exactly how many reprints were published is debatable.[34] For twenty years a monopoly was granted for its publication by the Privy Council to the Edinburgh printer Thomas Finlayson (1611–31), which held except for Andrew Hart's editions.[35] The publishing history is, indeed, very similar to that of Barbour's epic. McKinlay lists twelve popular edition of the *Bruce* between 1571 and 1914, seven critical editions from 1790 to 1909, three editions of 'Gordon's *Bruce*' in 1615, 1718 and 1753 and seven editions of 'Harvey's *Bruce*' in the eighteenth century, with a further ten editions by 1859.[36]

The early publications by the printers Chepman and Myllar tended to be in the vernacular style because of the market for the reading public, with the work of Dunbar being the most notable.[37] The first printed edition of the *Wallace* exists as fragments from 1508, no new edition is known until 1570. In between there is evidence of the tales of Wallace entering Scottish folklore among the peasantry. The *Complaynt of Scotland*, compiled in 1548 and published the next year, recorded shepherds telling tales of Wallace and Bruce.[38] The vernacular language of the *Complaynt* and of Harry was much more accessible than the Latin chronicles of Fordun, Bower and Lanercost, and it fits the imagined community thesis for the transmission from the interior world of text to the exterior thought-world of a nation's identity, solidifying the single community.[39] The excellent research of George Brunsden, has, however, cast some doubt on the existence of all these different editions of the *Wallace*, but verifies that the majority were valid and extant, with many copies produced, and which stand alongside the undoubted sales success of Hamilton of Gilbertfield's 'translation' in 1722.[40] A key point from Brunsden's researches into the use of Scots in each of the revised transcriptions and editions of the *Wallace* is how stable the use of the language had been, and how remarkably similar Gilbertfield's text was: an abridgement clearly, but less a radical modernisation of the vernacular. Craigie has been one of the more influential authors to declare that Harry was more popular than Barbour throughout the eighteenth century because of the modernising text of Gilbertfield (although adding that Harry's text must have been impressively robust to have survived this treatment).[41] But the view that the text was transformed into something universally understandable has, it appears, been overstated.[42] The preface to the Henry Charteris edition of Harry's *Wallace* from 1594 is far more intelligible today than, say, the chronicles of Bower from the 1440s. Its preface is also important for placing Wallace on a pedestal as the national hero compared with heroes of other nations. It is the language of nationalism:

Lyke as in al natiounis from time to time (gude Reidar) hes flourischit monie Nobill and vailzeand men as amangis the Israelites, Iosue, Gedeon, Iepthe, Samson, David, the Machabeis: amang the Romainis, Brutus, Quintus Fabius, Scipio, Pompeius magnus, Iulies Cæsar: amangis the Carthaginenses, Hannibal: amangis the Greikis, Themistocles, Alcibiades: amangis the Thebanis, Epaminondas: amangis the Macedonians, Alexander the greit: amangis the Persianis, Cyrus, Darius: amangis the Frenchemen, Charles the greit: amangis the Germaines, the Henryis, and the Otthois: amangis the Britonis, Ambrose, Arthur, & swa furth in al Regions. Euin swa in this our Realm, hes florischit mony nobill Princes & notabill men, quha hes not feirit to expone their lyfes, and guidis to all kinde of jeopardies, & hazardis againis their maist cruel! and strang adversaris, for the defence and maintenance of yair liberties & commoun wealth As King Caratak maist vailzeand, althocht infortunate, as wrytis Cornelius Tacitus, King Corbreid, Galdus, ye twa Kennethis, Gregore, Robert Bruce, Grahame, Thomas Randall, & Schir Iames Dowglas. And besides all thir & mony ma, in this Regioun florischit William Wallace (of quhome we ar to entreit) quha justly in vailzeantnes may be co-pit (all circumstances being considderit) to be posteriour to nane of all thir yat hes preceidet.[43]

It is pointed out by Brunsden that the language of the reprints of Harry changed most with Hart's edition of 1618. Thereafter, the idiom alters little from the mid-seventeenth century, with little variation in the style of Scots in the century following that.[44] A difference can be found from the 'Catholic' 1488 manuscript and the Protestant version published by Robert Lekpreuik in 1570, but that was a change of interpretation not of style, designed to catch the mood of patriotic Protestantism.[45] That Hamilton of Gilbertfield was not the great moderniser of the Wallace story, as oft portrayed, suggests that if the consumption of accessible and readable text drove the Wallaciana of the nineteenth century, then it was nothing new in respect of the *Wallace* itself (while noting that this movement's almost exclusive use of English was confined to the pastiche of the story rather than a re-presentation of Harry). The story did not need Hamilton of Gilbertfield for it to be understandable to the majority of the Scottish people. But this did not stop Hamilton impacting upon a number of notable individuals which successfully channelled the story along cultural-political lines. This result was more likely the outcome of its abridgement than its claimed-for revision of the Scots language, negating the need for a glossary, but it spun the myth a little further.[46]

Of greatest significance was the sway Hamilton's text had on Robert Burns, which confirmed its place in the popular consciousness. Two instances are cited by Maurice Lindsay in his *History of Scottish Literature*. The first finds Burns writing to Mrs Dunlop, who claimed descent from Wallace: 'The first books I met with in my early years, which I perused with pleasure, were the lives of Hannibal and Sir William Wallace' (15 November 1786).[47] His oft-quoted lines to Dr John Moore are stronger still: 'the story of Wallace poured a Scottish prejudice in my veins which will boil along there till the floodgates of life shut in eternal rest' (2 August 1787).[48] Indeed, Burns claimed to have taken the last stanza of 'Scots Wha Hae' from the 'common stall' edition of the *Wallace*, 'a couplet worthy of Homer':[49]

> (i) *Scots Wha Hae*
> Lay the proud usurpers low!
> Tyrants fall in every foe!
> Liberty's in every blow!

(ii) *Wallace*
A false usurper sinks in ever foe;
And liberty returns with every blow

Other leaders of Scotland's self-image, literary, intellectual and industrial, can be summoned to support the influence of the tales of Wallace upon their lives. James Hogg, the poet from Ettrick who wore the garb of the peasant shepherd, recalled that:

It was . . . in the eighteenth year of my age, that I first got a perusal of the *Life and Adventures of Sir William Wallace* and the *Gentle Shepherd*; and though immediately fond of them . . . I could not help regretting deeply that they were not in prose.[50]

In his teenage years, Thomas Babington Macaulay revelled in the stories of Wallace he heard from his father, favouring the superiority of 'Scotch blood' and of Scottish missionary work.[51] The industrialist and philanthropist from Dunfermline, Andrew Carnegie, commissioned a bust of Burns for the National Wallace Monument,[52] and he recalled the *Wallace* from his youth for his autobiography:

It was from my uncle I learned all that I know of the early history of Scotland – of Wallace and Bruce and Burns, of Blind Harry's history, of Scott, Ramsey, Tannahill, Hogg, and Fergusson. I can truly say in the words of Burns that there was then and there created in me a vein of Scottish prejudice (or patriotism) which will cease to exist only with my life. Wallace, of course, was our hero. Everything heroic centred in him.[53]

The *Wallace* and *The Bruce* were, along with the plays of Sir David Lindsey, the works which were still popular into the eighteenth century and beyond.[54] It cannot be ascertained which editions so inspired Hogg, Macaulay and Carnegie, but the publishing history of the *Wallace* suggests that once Hamilton's abridgement was published, it dominated the marketplace if not the comprehension of the story, with a new edition every decade in the eighteenth century and ten editions between 1802 and 1857.[55] Then there was a gap when, despite a few notable prose editions, Hamilton's verse was not updated until 1998.[56]

THE APPEAL AND DISTRUST OF HARRY

To the romantics, the greatness of the verse comes from the appeal of its author. Robertson's *Lives of the Scottish Poets* (1821) made this explicit.[57] It added to the debate on the mystique of the text. It is not great poetry, Robertson continues, but if it was produced by someone who was blind, that person should be ranked along with Barbour or Chaucer.[58] Could this verse glorifying the deeds of this great national patriot be the work of someone who was blind? Could it be, perhaps, that the text was a celestial gift to commend what had been God's glory? The debate over Harry's blindness is indicative of the evidence used to support or decry this verse. Whoever wrote the *Wallace* was clearly educated and well travelled – it is not the product of someone who was either lowly born or who led a sheltered and narrow life, handicapped by the lack of sight. The author's education is evident from the use of French and Latin throughout the text.[59] It was claimed in the 1709 edition of the *Wallace* that it had been 'turned from Latin into Scots metre by one called Blind Harry'.[60] In Harry's words: 'Eftir the pruiff geyffin fra the Latin buk/Quilk master Blayr in his tym vndertuk'.[61] There is also the use of much contemporary and near contemporary literature which suggested the poet was both sighted and educated.[62] Chaucer, Barbour and Eglinton being the most notable authors whose work shimmers often into view.[63] In the view of McDiarmid this is evidence that 'it was Hary, not Blind Hary who constructed the poem'.[64] Added to these doubts is the remarkably detailed and vivid use of Scotland's scenery and regional differences in telling of Wallace's progress and deeds during the few short years of his front-line activity and the longer years of his exile, which would not be possible by imagination alone.[65]

It is the romanticisation of Harry which adds so much to the tale. Walter Scott's *Tales of a Grandfather* did much to enhance the myth, as with the creation of Bruce's spider.[66] Robertson likened Harry to Homer and therefore like him blind from birth,[67] while Watson accepted Mair's statement affirming the poet's blindness without question.[68] W.T. Fyfe stated that because Harry was blind he employed others to read for him. Indeed, Fyfe, writing in 1920, was prepared to cite Harry himself as the evidence that the poet used Blair's Latin biography as the source.[69] Henderson and Schofield have blamed inaccuracies in the book on Harry's blindness[70] and Henderson suggests that he could have been blind and still be able to show the feelings of the seasons:

> Some have indeed argued, from what is termed his 'feeling for nature', that he must at one time have possessed the faculty of sight. But this 'feeling' is shown merely in his references to the influences of the seasons, and to the charms of a spring or summer morning – influences and charms to which the blind are specially susceptible; and indeed the very general character of his recorded impressions of nature is almost proof positive that he was born blind.[71]

Neilson used John Mair and William Dunbar to insist that Harry was blind, but argued that the infirmity did not commence until his later years.[72] John Veitch agreed with Patrick Fraser Tytler that Harry could not have been blind from birth, but his evidence is no more than circumstantial, based on the likely activities of a wandering minstrel needing to travel to meet the market for his work: Harry travelled the country 'carrying his rhymes in his memory as his stock-in-trade, reciting them by lowly hearth and in lordly hall, and touching with his own patriotic flame the hearts of all ranks of his countrymen'.[73] James Moir, too, believed Harry could not be blind from birth, and again the reason comes from the content of the text, not historical corroboration.[74] Others looked to define 'blindness', such as W.A. Craigie, who suggested that Harry could have been blind at some time during his life or merely called 'Blind' because he suffered from less than perfect sight.[75] He was unable to offer a definitive answer and concluded that whether Harry was blind or not, or, indeed, whoever it was that compiled the verse (there is no name on the early editions), it should not impinge on its judgement as a piece of literature. In McDiarmid's analysis of these arguments from the turn of the nineteenth century, his conclusion is that Harry wrote the text as an old man (dying three years after receiving payments recorded in the Treasurer's Accounts), who lost his sight late in life.[76] It was a more conservative view, but offered a safer yield in a field of partial evidence. Without knowing the state of Harry's blindness, if at all, nor even who the author really was, speculation had overtaken analysis.

Sobriety should also be called for once the accusations of Harry's plagiarism are listed. For a blind and lowly-born man, he had a terrible tendency to borrow the work of others. J.T.T. Brown has produced one of the most thorough studies of the origins of Harry's text. Instructively, he offers a contrast of Harry with Wyntoun which goes beyond the justification that the sources were common, where the texts mirror each other in the speeches made at key events:[77]

Wyntoun, Book VIII, Ch. 13

Twelf hundryne nynty yhere and seuyn
Fra Cryst wes borne, the kyng of hewyn
Willame Walyays in Clyddisdale,

Swa thay made thame on a day
Hym for to set in hard assay;
Of his lang swerd in that entent
Fyrst thai made hym argwment
Intil Lanark Inglismen,
Quhare a multitud war gaddyrd then
Ane a tyt made at hys sword.

W: 'Hald stylle thi hand & spek thi worde'
I: Wyth thi sword thow mais gret bost'

45

W: 'Tharefore thi dame made lytil cost'

I: 'Quhat caus has throw to were the grene?'
W: 'No cause bot for to make the tene.'

I: 'Thow suld nocht bere sa fare a knyf,'

W: 'Swa sayd the preyst that swywyd thi wyf;'
'Sa lang he cald that woman fayr'
'Quhill that his barne wes made thi ayre'

I: 'Methink thow drywyw me to scorne'

W: 'Thi dame wes swywd or thow wes borne'
Fra that kest thai na ma wordis;
Bot swne wes tyte owt mony swordys

Harry's *Wallace*, Book VI, l. 107

Twelff hundreth zer, tharto nynte and sewyn
Fra Cryst wes born the rychtwis king off hewyn,
Wilzham Wallace in to gud liking gais,
To Lanrik come
Ane argwnde thaim, as thai went throuch the tovn
The starkest man that Hesylrig than knew,
And als he had of lychly wordis ynew.
He saluist thaim as it war bot in scorn,
'Dewgar, gud day, bone Senzhour & gud morn'
Quhom scornys thow? quod Wallace quha lerd the?

W: 'Hald still thi hand', quad he, '& spek thi word'.
I: 'With thi lang suerd thow makis me kill bost'
W: ''Tharoff', quod he, 'thi deme maid litell cost'.
I: 'Quhat caus has throw to were that gudelye greyne?'
W: 'My maist caus is bot for to mak the teyne'
I: 'Quat suld a Scot do with so fayr a knyff?'
W: 'Sa said the prest that last janglyt thi wyff;

'That woman lang has tellit him so fair,
'Quhill that his child worthit to be thine ayr'

I: 'Methink', quod he, 'thow drywys me to scorn'
W: 'Thi deme has beyne japyt or thow was born.'
The power than assemblyt thaim about;
Twa hundreth men that stalwarth war & Stout.

George Neilson, on the side of Barbour in this weighty literary contest, has shown Harry's debt to *The Bruce*, with events ascribed to Wallace which were after the patriot's death and in fact concerned King Robert.[78] He cites the example of a French knight who praised the prowess and integrity of Bruce transmuted into an example of praise for Wallace and the successful use of a key stratagem to win the only historical Battle of Lowdonhill which is attributed to Bruce, but which Harry takes for the triumph of Wallace.[79] In the *Calendar of Documents* Joseph Bain castigated the integrity of Harry,[80] citing his plagiarism from Barbour:

> Bruce has been fortunate in his historian. While the real fame of his precursor Wallace has been obscured by the legendary exploits chronicled by the Blind Minstrel, Barbour's great work is a worthy tribute to his hero, and in all essential points stands the test of historical criticism.[81]

Its failure as a piece of history has truly returned to the fore. It started in earnest when Harry was placed in comparison with the chronicles by Hailes in the 1770s. Moir in the 1880s stated that a third class masters student in scientific research would point out that it is not possible to completely dismiss Harry's account, yet it is the historian who has the greatest difficulty with his slipshod use of chronology.[82] The comparisons with Barbour were without doubt a central feature of the literary analysis and helped to sustain an interest in the poem. *The Bruce* was close to being a chronicle, the *Wallace* was an imagined epic. John Barbour (?1316–96) was a contemporary of Chaucer, with the first reference to each other in 1357. Barbour was then likely to be in his forties, which indicates that his boyhood years overlapped with Bruce's reign and evidence suggests that he knew some of Bruce's contemporaries when he came to compile the verse.[83] Andrew of Wyntoun confirms that John Barbour was the author of *The Bruce* and we gain a number of pieces of detail from the poem, in contrast to the misleading work of Harry.[84] Few other than John Jamieson regarded Harry as the greater poet over Barbour and most – but not all – found some literary merit in its rude fire.[85] Perhaps Agnes Mure Mackenzie is closest when she regarded the *Wallace* as the forerunner of the Waverlies: 'for Harry was neither historian or romancer'.[86]

STORIES BORN OUT OF BELIEF

Belief in the honesty of Harry and the truth of *Wallace* is typical of much of the nineteenth-century Wallaciana in that it was patriotism, not historical corroboration, which replenished popular knowledge. Intellectuals eventually could distil their acceptance of Harry as a piece of literature: not as stylistic as Barbour, but intrinsically important nevertheless. It was the historical context that was more problematic. The most vociferous critic of Harry's verse from the eighteenth century, whose text was still current into the 1820s and beyond, Lord Hailes, based his criticism on those who used Harry as an historical account: 'It would be lost labour to search for the age, name and condition of an author who either knew not history, or who meant to falsify it'.[87] Its modern equivalent was when Cowan criticised Mackay's futile use of Harry as an historical source, declaring such effort more than wasteful.[88] Mackay himself had criticised John Mair for falling 'into the trap of rejecting out of hand stories which he could not corroborate from independent sources'.[89] But where is the real folly? A *Wee Guide to William Wallace*, by Duncan Jones in 1997, was aware of the myths which surround Wallace, and that Harry should be treated as a historical novelist. However, this concise account, 'based as far as possible on firm evidence', lacks discussion of the chronicles until the very end, with no other sources cited nor secondary reading offered to attest to its firmness in fact.[90] In a similar vein, Alan McNie's compilation of *Clan Wallace* (1986) offered a condensed text of James Taylor's *Pictorial History of Scotland* (1859), with no source criticism made.[91] And this is the case with Carruth's *Heroic Wallace and Bruce* (1986),[92] which is in stark contrast to Elspeth King's similarly pictorial production which does keep the sources firmly in view.[93] Only Gray and Fisher, who have written the longer popular accounts in the late twentieth century, have made a serious attempt to engage with the mythmaking, with the latter's short bibliographical essay worthy of note.[94]

This chapter has overflowed with assumption and non-corroborated evidence. Harry as history has been disproved, but just as the nineteenth-century enthusiasts and critics refused to face up to reality, so its fabrication is allowed to persist today. *Braveheart*, of course, has been the prime example of this trend. It is not maliciousness which sustains this need to believe in Harry and his creation, nor is it stupidity. It is patriotism which says that you cannot prove *everything* in Harry's story is wrong, so the historian's dismissal is unwarranted. Finally, it is the patriotism which frames the next phase in the creation of the Wallace story, the chapbooks, short histories, poems and ballads which mushroomed in the nineteenth century. As the reprints of Harry waned, this new phase took little cognisance of the criticism of Hailes or historians of their own time. It was stated by John Finlay in 1804 that it was patriotic fervour which had kept Harry's *Wallace* at the forefront of patriotic myth-making.[95] Yet in the judgement of Tytler, although the marvels of Harry must be questioned, and often condemned by calm judgement, still the verse should be '. . . trod by the patriotic pilgrim rather [than] investigated by the careful antiquary', this being the reason why the story has endured.[96] Brunton, for example, wanted England to know that it was only the English sources which record the story of Cressingham being skinned by Wallace, so how can this slur be trusted?[97] However we absorb these debates, it must be remembered that getting history wrong is an essential of national identity.[98] Here we find the patriots weaving the evidence into an appropriate pattern. Harry has achieved this in a way unmatched by even the most patriotic of the medieval chroniclers. As the publishing industry expanded from the middle of the eighteenth century, so the story of Wallace was rewritten and reproduced in many different forms. Harry's verse was not enough: Wallace the myth was set to explode.

FOUR

Retelling the Story

It is singular among all the poetry Wallace has given rise to how little there is of intrinsic merit. Blind Harry the old rhyming Minstrel beats the whole of them. Then as if it were not that he was murdered by Edward I, he has been murdered on the stage about a dozen times. I intend to read *Valliados* in order to discover if it forms any exception to the general rule.[1]

There was one major revision of Harry's *Wallace*, and that was Hamilton of Gilbertfield's abridgement in 1722. Apart from that, the thirty and more editions which appeared from the presses of a range of publishers were remarkably consistent with what had gone before. It has been pointed out that there has been little change to the vernacular of the *Wallace* since the 1618 edition published by Andrew Hart.[2] The conclusion reached in the last chapter emphasised the role of patriotic belief to sustain unwarranted and dangerous assumptive arguments made to sit alongside more reasoned judgement and usually within the same text. Even the best of historians such as Patrick Fraser Tytler and John Hill Burton were caught in this patriotic/corroboration nexus. Perhaps this can be likened to Sir Walter Scott's pairing of a unionist heart with a Jacobite heart, maintaining a hybrid loyalty. Yet Scots should not be too wary of the patriotic narrative being faced by reality's cold stare: it is how national identity and nationalism are formed in other nations too. It was a will to believe it true, despite acknowledgement of its historical inaccuracies, which sustained the *Wallace* as 'the most treasured of cottage classics'.[3] Writing in 1821, Robertson claimed that there can still be found many who can repeat 'the greater part' of the verse, and 'rare indeed' is it to find someone who is ignorant of the more interesting and remarkable scenes from the

51

poem. The first part of Robertson's claim is clearly an exaggeration, but the knowledge of key scenes is probably correct. It is not patriotic belief sustaining this particular assumption, but rather the outcome of a survey of the many chapbooks and other literary forms which retold Harry's story from the late eighteenth century to the early twentieth century, with a few notable examples beyond even this wide period.

The period encompasses a decline in the number of reprints of Harry (see chapter three, pp. 38–9). According to Goldstein, the poem's reputation was never to recover from the criticism it received in the nineteenth century, quoting one Victorian critic's opposition to its 'rude embodiment of popular feeling', being barbarous in taste and mixed with 'ludicrous prejudice' and 'fierce vulgarity'.[4] But such criticism was not to destroy the narrative, rather it was to stimulate a new generation of authors to retell it, to update it, to smuggle it into their own agenda. The enduring power of the Wallace story was the theme of the valorisation given by Lord Rosebery in 1897. Promoter of the Bill to establish the Scottish Office in 1885, prime minister in 1894–5 upon Gladstone's death, and Scottish Secretary, Rosebery has occupied a curious position in the debates on Scottish nationalism. He was no great supporter of Home Rule for Scotland, preferring instead reform of the Westminster structure.[5] But despite his commitment to the Union, he sustained a strong interest in all things Scottish. Most notably, he accepted an invitation to mark the six-hundredth anniversary of the Battle of Stirling Bridge at a public banquet for 300 gentlemen.[6] He refused to discuss the historical facts on 'so thorny a subject as Sir William Wallace', dismissing the debate on the patriot's Welsh origins or worries over the veracity of the many legends which have grown along with the history. He was convinced that Wallace must have been the greatest of heroes because his imprint on Scottish national consciousness throughout the generations, when so few actual facts are known, had been so profound. He quoted Fordun that Wallace 'lifted his head up from his den'.[7] His narrative then homed in on the notable events known of the patriot: the Battle of Stirling Bridge, the defeat at Falkirk, Wallace's flight to France, then his capture and execution.[8]

Rosebery's approach has been taken by others as the medium for the story to be retold. Rarely would anything original be said, except by those who sought to discover anew what sources remained extant, but such investigators were rare. The majority confined themselves to rewarming the story and spreading it rather thinly. The paucity of evidence contributed to the structure of the re-writes being repetitive. Hume Brown, for example, was typical in that he compressed Wallace's historical contribution to the battles of Stirling Bridge and Falkirk, his resignation from the guardianship and his execution, with, by interesting contrast, not much space, but certainly a little more, afforded to Robert Bruce.[9] Another typical example comes from an anonymous account published in Jedburgh in 1845. It was as authoritative as it was mistaken:

> This history of Sir William Wallace was written in Latin by Mr John Blair, chaplain to Wallace, and turned into Scots metre by one called Blind Harry in the days of James IV, and is succinctly narrated in the following chronological memoir.[10]

By not questioning the existence of Blair's Latin biography, it gives authenticity to Harry and adds glamour to the story (from the belief that Wallace's confidant, writing in 'secret' Latin, was to be translated into Scots by a blind, mysterious patriotic minstrel and now we are let into the secret through the use of modern English). It is this sort of unquestioned history, coupled to easily read and shortened prose, which took the Wallace story to places beyond even the ubiquitous editions of Hamilton of Gilbertfield's paraphrasing. Six stories tend to form the basis from which all other analysis then flows in these portrayals: the physical size of Wallace; the events at Lanark; the battles of Stirling Bridge and Falkirk; Wallace's betrayal and his execution.

Big Man

We like our heroes big, certainly in Britain. Napoleon was a bit small, at least in comparison with Wellington. English culture was formed around the oak-like identity of its heroes.[11] Wallace, too, was reputed to be a massive man. The incongruity of a slightly diminutive five foot ten inch Mel Gibson, playing a, possibly, six foot nine William Wallace, was not lost on some observers of the *Braveheart* phenomenon.[12] That Wallace was physically imposing came most firmly from Harry:

> Nyne quartaris large he was in lenth indeid,
> Thryd part lenth in schuldrys braid was he,
> Rycht sembly, strang, and lusty for to se;
> Hys lymmys gret, with stalwart paiss and sound,
> Hys browys hard, his armes gret and round;
> Hys handis maid rycht lik till a prawmer,
> Off manlik mak, with nales gret and cler;
> Proportionyt lang and fayr was his wessage;
> Rycht sad off spech, and abil in curage;
> Braid breyst and heych, with sturdy crag and gret,
> Hys lyppys round, his noyss was squar and tret,
> Bowand bron haryt, on browis and breis lycht,
> Cler aspre eyn lik dyamond's brycht.
> Wynder the chyn, on the left syd, was seyn,
> Be hurt, a wain; his colour was sangweyn.
> Woundis he had in many diuerss place,
> Bot fayer and weill kepyt was his face.[13]

In *The Tragedy of the Valiant Knight* (*c.* 1815) Wallace was 'endowed with gigantic strength of body, with heroic courage of mind, with disinterested magnanimity, with incredible patience and ability to bear hunger, fatigue, and all the inclemencies of the season'.[14] Alexander Keith's text, *Several Incidents in the Life of Sir William Wallace* (1844), concentrated his story within the 'romantic scenery' of Lanark. But his conclusions upon Wallace were generalisable: 'He was possessed of irresistible bodily strength, and endowed with the virtues of piety, generosity and patriotism in the most eminent degree'.[15] He had 'gigantic strength of body' argued the Revd Watson in 1861, a champion in the defence of justice.[16] Not only was he big, but all his

1. Scotland's Liberator from the *Stirling Observer*, 25 December 1937, was used to advertise an exhibition celebrating the 700th anniversary of the Battle of Stirling Bridge at the Stirling Smith Art Gallery and Museum from 27 March to 15 December 1997. (*Stirling Smith Art Gallery and Museum*)

2. The statues of Wallace (on the right) and Bruce at the entrance to Edinburgh Castle were unveiled in 1929. Each year these patriots from the Wars of Independence against England witness the celebration of Scotland's contribution and loyalty to the British Army, the Royal Military Tattoo. (*Author's collection*)

3. The plaque outside St Bartholomew's Hospital, London, marking the point at Smithfield where Wallace was executed in 1305. (*Author's collection*)

4. The Elderslie Wallace
Monument, completed in 1912.
(*Author's collection*)

5. The inscription on the
Elderslie Wallace Monument.
(*Author's collection*)

6. 'Quham "Thowis" thow, Scot?' The head of Blind Harry, in plaster of Paris by Alexander Stoddart. (*Stirling Smith Art Gallery and Museum*)

7. The head of Robert the Bruce, by Tim Pomeroy, in sandstone. (*Stirling Smith Art Gallery and Museum*)

8. The National Wallace Monument, Abbey Craig, Stirling, inaugurated in 1869. (*Author's collection*)

9. James Thom's statue of the patriot in the Wallace Tower in Ayr, rebuilt in 1833. (*Author's collection*)

10. A stained glass window of Wallace as Samson in Paisley Abbey, the result of money raised by the Glasgow St Andrew's Society in 1873. (*Author's collection*)

11. The Wallace statue in Newmarket Street, Ayr, was unveiled in 1819. The legs on this statue were shortened to fit the niche, a rival to the wee Wallace of Stirling! (*Author's collection*)

12. Letters in support of the National Wallace Monument, 1868, written by the Italian patriots Mazzini and Garibaldi, the Hungarian revolutionary Kossuth, the German political agitator Blind and the French socialist Blanc. They are framed in the Wallace Oak of Elderslie. (*Stirling Smith Art Gallery and Museum*)

virtues were equally colossal. A.F. Murison (1898) held Tyler up to ridicule in his claim that 'Wallace's make, as he grew to manhood, approached almost to the gigantic; and his personal strength was superior to the common run of even the strongest men.' For Murison this was a view of the romancers, not of the serious students. Yet, even this critic could not be swayed from belief that Wallace was a big man: 'in an age when warlike renown depended so essentially on personal deeds of derring-do, the astonishing thing – the incredible thing – would be if Wallace was not a man of pre-eminent physical strength and resourcefulness in the use of arms.'[17] Nor did he stop there:

> Ajax was taller than Agamemnon; and Jop may have stood a head taller than Wallace. But the substantial fact of his impressive physique is not to be denied. The romancers exaggerate, of course; but on this point even Harry scarcely outdoes Major or Bower.[18]

The Revd James Barr, in 1921, described his hero as 'A man of rock, fixed as the strong mountains of his native land, firm as the Stirling Rock at Abbey Craig . . .'.[19] Wallace was celebrated for the 'highest heroism' in 1933.[20] David Ross' text for a short children's book, *The Story of William Wallace* (1998), starts with the purified story of his youthful strength and fearsome physical presence when out-numbered in a fight with English soldiers (while adding conversation in the text that can only be guessed at):

> 'You can have some of my fish,' said the young man [Wallace].
> 'We'll have it all,' they [the English soldiers] said, and one of them tried to grab the basket.
> 'Oh no, you won't!' The young man raised his fishing rod and struck the soldier's arm away. Then he drew his sword. At this the soldiers fled away, and he went home with his basket of fish.[21]

The 700th anniversary of the Battle of Stirling Bridge was marked by the slogan 'Big Man, Big Sword, Big FUN'.[22] We can perhaps sum this up in Simon Schama's claim in the BBC 'History of Britain' series, in Autumn 2000: 'Wallace had hamstrings from Hell!'[23]

Lanark

Clear contemporary evidence of Wallace's actions are found for the first time with the attack on Heselrig (Hezelrigg) at Lanark.[24] It is one of his most notorious attacks, specified in the indictment at his trial and taking place just months before the set piece battle at Stirling Bridge. The event gains its significance because it has been presented as a revenge attack for the murder of Wallace's mistress. However, it was not just personal revenge that was achieved, the event has been used as a device in the narratives to explain how the higher motivations of love for a women were replicated in his ultimate sacrifice, made for love of his nation. Many, then, have marked the murder of Marion as a key motivation in Wallace's actions against the English, usually as justification for the excessive brutality of his revenge:[25] 'for the sake of her that's murdered, ten thousand shall die!'[26]

> . . . with a queen-like heroism [she] stretched herself to the full height of her noble person, confronting the wretch direct, and throwing her arms abroad, well knowing that her death had been determined upon. Cried aloud, 'Strike if thou darest!' As the poor maiden uttered the last words the infuriate beast rushed upon her, piercing her to the heart. Not a shriek escaped the murdered one's lips.[27]

Gabriel Alexander, in 1903, was not alone in fixing the rationale for Wallace's motivations to this event: 'Whilst brooding in secret over his country's wrongs, an event occurred which stimulated the powers of his mind and body into active existence . . . the death of his sweetheart by the English Sheriff.'[28] The remarkable, long-standing selling success that was *The Scottish Chiefs* based its narrative entirely around this murder.[29]

When turned into a drama, then, there was greater opportunity to develop the characteristics of the dramatis personae of the key events. In one children's play, produced in 1822, Wallace's wife/mistress, Lady Marion, fights for his affections against a love rival, Lady Helen.

Marion finally secures a ring for her finger just as Wallace has been betrayed by Menteith.[30] Ignoring the evidence which is consistent in fixing Marion's death at the hands of Heselrig in Lanark in 1297, well before the act of betrayal in 1305, and the suggestion (although false) from Donaldson that Lady Helen was Wallace's second wife, this play creates depth of characters over historical chronology or accuracy.[31] Writing eighty years later, Macrae had Wallace and Marion secretly married 'so as not to expose her to insult and danger from the soldiers of the garrison'.[32] As part of the celebrations to mark the 700th anniversary of the Battle of Stirling Bridge a two-act play *Wallace's Women* took as its theme '. . . Wallace's mother, lovers, wife and daughter; the woman who dressed his wounds and her daughter who saved his life'. It was 'for those who want to see a different history to the Big Man with the Big Sword'.[33]

Stirling Bridge

Of all the events in Wallace's life, it is his victory in the Battle of Stirling Bridge which stands out, the details of which as recounted in the standard chronicles we have seen in chapter two. To add something new and without the sources to add depth, many historians have tried to find a different angle to structure their narratives. Peter Donaldson's *Life* produced 'from authentic materials of Scottish history' identified the work of the carpenters in weakening the supports which held the bridge at Stirling together.[34] It is not a view taken up elsewhere, but is symptomatic of a (perhaps not unreasonable) obsession with the detail of Wallace's one great victory against Edward's army. P.R. Sawers is another who concentrated on the battle when following in Wallace's footsteps in 1856, before turning his attention to Bruce's stratagem at Bannockburn.[35] Alexander Brunton wanted both to 'disprove the absurd story of the skinning of Cressingham' and to determine the whereabouts of the old Stirling Bridge. Rather than at Cambuskenneth, Brunton indicates that the correct bridge was at Kildean.[36] Patriotic honour was at stake and he was at pains to resurrect Wallace's tactical ability in response to the criticisms by

Lord Hailes.[37] Sir James Fergusson (1938) pointed out the impracticability of Abbey Craig being the exact spot where the Scots waited for the English to cross the bridge. The ground there was too steep and slippery to allow a safe and quick descent.[38] He suspects that more likely they were on the gentler slopes to the north-west. However, both it and the bridge have proved hard to track down. The most thorough search for the real bridge has been carried out by the Stirling Bridge Archaeology Project led by Ron Page at Stirling University.[39] Whatever its correct siting, it was not the bridge filmed in Schama's *History of Britain*.[40]

Falkirk

Stirling was the time of triumph and was followed by a happy terrorising of northern England. The chronicles are the main source of propaganda for what went so horribly wrong for Wallace only a few months after his greatest triumph. The size and determination of the English force and its commanders undoubtedly had much to do with it, but the focus has remained steady on the action – or inaction – of the Scottish nobility. Their failure to support Wallace has been taken as firm fact, it has sustained once more Wallace's position as the people's champion whose success would have continued but for this treachery by his social superiors. For one supporter, Wallace's retreat from Falkirk 'has been justly considered as a masterpiece of generalship'.[41] The Scottish Secretariat's publication of 1955 made plain that 'Despite what has been stated by modern critics, Wallace, apparently taken by surprise, had chosen his position well in view of the enemy's preponderance in heavily-armoured cavalry.'[42] This was a little unusual – it was more common to state that it was the Comyns withdrawal of his cavalry which caused the defeat at Falkirk, as in the history of nationalist David Macrae.[43]

Again when searching for a new voice and when not focusing on betrayal, there can be found a heady mix of glamour and the elegiac in the stories of Wallace's military engagements. In *The Life of Sir William Wallace, the Scots Patriot* (1810), the military achievements of Wallace continued to have modern relevance. Referring to the 'present mighty struggle in which Britain is engaged' what more could be done than 'to publish the history of an unequalled warrior, whose example must animate the brave youth, to whose exertions the eye of the public is directed for the defence of its native shores'.[44] Despite some curious geography, where Stirling Bridge is placed over the River Tay, the book ends with Menteith as the traitor and some of the gory details of Wallace's execution.[45]

Betrayal

If the lukewarm support of the nobility can be blamed for Wallace's defeat at Falkirk, no more hated a noble in these stories is Menteith. It was he who led Wallace's pursuers to their man. Menteith made two attempts at deceiving Wallace, with the second involving a young relative disarming Wallace while he slept and leading in his opponents.[46] 'Fause Menteith' was given £150 for his part in the deception, a point made in the Scots Secretariat's publication.[47] The words of Thomas Carlyle are remembered and used to conclude that nationalist history of Wallace, produced in 1955:

> It is noteworthy that the nobles of the country (Scotland) have maintained a quite despicable behaviour since the days of Wallace downwards – a selfish, ferocious, famishing, unprincipled set of hyenas, from whom at no time, and in no way, has the country derived any benefit.[48]

Execution

Except for those narratives that move straight to Bruce's road to Bannockburn, the stories end with Wallace's execution. The betrayal merely added to his elevation to martyr, which his speech, denying the charge of treason on the grounds of never have given fealty to Edward, has kept his name clear of corruption. Sibbald's chronicle of the Scottish poetry since the thirteenth century, published in 1802, concludes his analysis of Harry with an account of Wallace's execution in London.[49] The Morrison edition (1790) of the *Metrical History of Sir William Wallace* carries an engraving of the execution scene in its frontispiece: Wallace is depicted below the gallows and about to lose his head, while the priest holds up his Psalter before the patriot's eyes. Harry's verse (book VI, line 1400) is quoted: 'He got a priest the book before him hauld/While they to him had done all that they would do'.[50] Jane Porter offered some suitable melodrama:

> As Wallace approached the scaffold . . . and the executioner approached to throw the rope over his victim . . . Helen, with a cry that was re-echoed by the spectators, rushed to his bosom. Wallace burst the bands which confined his arms, and, clasping her to him with a force that seemed to make her touch his very heart, his breast heaved, as if his soul were breaking from its tenement; and, while his head sunk on her neck, he exclaimed, in a low voice, 'My prayer is heard! Helen, we shall next meet to—'. He stopped: he fell, and the scaffold shook to its foundations.[51]

There was no mention here of the disembowelling while alive, the drawing or the quartering, and the story immediately then shifts to the heroics of Bruce.[52] The emotion of betrayal and execution are so vital to the story. Sir James Fergusson ended his description of the trial with one of the most evocative juxtapositions of its momentousness and horror:

> The dead eyes stared down upon the ships in the Thames, the tall wooden houses, the hurrying, many coloured crowds, and the sea gulls wheeling about the piers of the great bridge. Seven years before, sea gulls had wheeled with the same grace, the same indifference to the bloody deeds of men, about the bridge of Stirling. Seven months later, Robert Bruce, Earl of Carrick, was crowned King of Scots at Scone.[53]

The execution has sustained so much of the story, giving sympathy and pride to the hero, encouraging the reader to avenge his cruel torturers, making it easier for the patriotic pilgrim to walk its path.

In itself, it has opened one further aspect of the myth-creation: that Wallace be elevated to sainthood. Martyrdom overcomes the lack of two authenticated miracles for such exaltation and it has surfaced in the arguments in favour of Wallace's sainthood by a self-styled 'Catholic historian' in October 2000.[54] McDiarmid has demonstrated that Harry transferred Saint Andrew gifting his sword to Scotland, to Wallace receiving the vision.[55] Others present Wallace as a child being singled out in a vision telling of his destiny.[56] Political martyrdom has, for some, been just the start of some higher claims to his soul.

These are the six themes which structure the stories and in many ways they are little different from the chronicles or from Harry. Constrained by the limited sources, how else could the story be told? Except for the spin and the media employed, the parameters are too limited. Yet new voices have engaged continually with the narrative. Carrick, who produced some of the most balanced work on Wallace, pointed out that since Hamilton of Gilbertfield's text has lost its place in popular reading, it has been taken by *The Scottish Chiefs*, 'a romance which, under the circumstances, may be said to have assumed the position once occupied by the Minstrel'.[57] Jane Porter's version was especially successful in North America. Walter Scott had claimed he would have written his own version of Wallace's life if not for Porter's work in the early 1800s.[58] Its glamour, its romance, its colour pictures (at least in the *c.* 1880 edition), made it a point of inspiration. It is an easy read, it is a good read. Marinell Ash quoted the American folklorist J.F. Dobie on its influence:

> One Christmas we got Porter's *The Scottish Chiefs*. I read it to myself, and at night as we sat by the fireplace my father read it aloud by the flickering light of a kerosene lamp. What heroes to emulate Bruce and Wallace were! My blood still stirs at mention of the mere title.[59]

The dissenting voice of Traquair has suggested that such romantic history has not been kind to Wallace, subjecting him to 'a life of tragic heroism' something which Porter did so much to perpetuate.[60] However, no matter how awful much of it has been, murdered on stage at least a dozen times, according to Walter Scott, chivalric romance has been a major pathway in the spread of the story and its repetition through the ages.

The danger of so explicitly romanticised and melodramatic an approach is to cover up many of the cracks in the story. As well as doubts over who exactly Harry was, doubts have also arisen and impacted upon the historical content of the *Wallace* and of sources more generally. Fergusson sums up the problem:

> To try to write a biography of William Wallace from historical sources only as distinct from traditional ones is like trying to restore a very old family portrait which several painters have tried to improve. It hangs in the place of honour in the dining-room, and all strangers are taken to see it as a matter of course. Most of them are suitably impressed by it. A few, franker than the rest, comment that it is not a very lifelike portrait, and this we are inclined to admit. The truth is that the original portrait, which family tradition tells us was a very fine piece of work, has been invisible for generations, and none of us has ever seen it.[61]

Fergusson's eloquence, here, is difficult to match. Its accuracy, too, is spot on. As has been shown, debate has surrounded the historical accuracy of Harry, as well as the level of plagiarism which permeates the text. A.F. Murison pointed out that apart from the slaying of Heselrig at Lanark and of Selby, when Wallace was a young man, the chronicles offer little or no background information on Wallace's rise to a position of influence and 'plant Wallace at Stirling Bridge almost as if he had just started from the ground, or come down from the clouds, ready to command an army in the field.'[62] The historians have struggled to get beyond all save a few key facts, but this has not stopped the construction of Wallace's biography, profiling the personality of the man. From the caustic rejection of Harry's literary as well as his historical worth by Lord Hailes, others have followed: the *Encyclopaedia*

Britannica in the nineteenth century declared that the *Wallace* 'possesses no poetical merit except a certain rude fire and energy, and as a literary production its place must be reckoned a very humble one.'[63]

From the same source, Taylor's *Pictorial History of Scotland* (1859) doubts the veracity of Harry's evidence.[64] The Victorian distaste for Harry's anti-Englishness, of which we have already seen much evidence, is best summed up by Craik, perhaps with his tongue in his cheek: 'Of the fighting and slaying, which makes up by far the greater part of the poem, it is difficult to find a sample that is short enough for our purpose'.[65] Others have searched for supporting evidence. Joseph Bain used the discovery of new documents to both criticise and to support Hailes.[66] Errors in Harry were compensated for and justified by new 'facts' in Stevenson's work for the Maitland Club;[67] the inconsistencies and the blood-thirsty language in Harry made a 'pantomime' of Wallace, argued Henderson, yet 'there are facts there not to be found in Wyntoun or Bower'.[68] Hill Burton accepted the mixture of fact and legend because 'some morsels turn up to confirm the fundamentals of some of his stories'.[69] Craigie, indeed, supported Harry as a poet over Barbour, but acknowledged that he did so in the face of 'the fierce blasts of the historian, and as if afraid of being caught resetting such dubious goods'.[70] Alexander Brunton dedicated the third part of his study to refuting many of the 'critical remarks of the English History'.[71] The Rector of Aberdeen Grammar School, James Moir, with what appears to be an unintentional pun, was aware that his work for the Scottish Text Society would 'offend all those who blindly believe that the Minstrel's story is veritable history' yet he wished 'to clear [Harry's] memory from the attacks made on him by some of our historians and literary critics'.[72] Both authors, and James Paterson from earlier in the nineteenth century,[73] described Harry as the biographer of Wallace. In the twentieth century we have Fisher's rejection of Harry's 'embroidery'[74] and Jones, although being far from doubtful, refers to Harry's epic as more historical novel than accurate history.[75]

EX-PAT WALLACE

There is truth in Harry, but this should be no surprise. His use of Fordun has already been identified. However, with his claimed authentic source but a manufacture, with so many errors of fact and chronology along the way, it is poetry not history which is his real worth. Is it best to stick to romance, then, and forget any pretence for historical truth? It does sound like the safest option and perhaps it is the best explanation for how the myth has spread so widely and so easily with so little historical material to support it. Is it fair, now, to link romanticised Wallace to an explanation for his continued popularity among Scots communities overseas? The expatriate view is tainted as one that continues to be rose-tinted. This facile observation is too often assigned to these communities, but it is rooted in the style with which the Scottish imagination is summoned up. Work by Tara McDonald, for example, has emphasised how it has been a Highland rather than a Lowland identity which has been preferred consistently through the centuries.[76] In part, of course, this reflects the geographical spread of the migrant population, but this is only a partial explanation. As a result of migration, Scottish culture spread widely, but within narrow parameters. Despite the Highland cultural hegemony, Wallace, forever attached to Ayrshire and Renfrewshire and the central belt of Scotland, has maintained a strong profile.

In their generic form, Caledonian societies are gatherings of Scottish emigrants and exiles which act as the focus for the perpetuation and the celebration of specific aspects of Scottish national character. The Caledonian Society of London was formed in 1837 to partake of food, drink and fine company, and to do so wearing the clothes of 'Old Gaul'. The London Highland Society was concerned with promoting the tales of Ossian, certainly until 1801 when it then became much more utilitarian and explicit in the promotion of the military Highlander.[77] Wallace and Bruce societies were prominent among a range of Gaelic, Highland, Celtic and St Andrew's societies which formed in many of the places where Scots settled from the mid-seventeenth century onwards, but with a notable expansion in the 1880s. The St Andrew's Society of Montreal was founded in 1834 after parliamentary elections had 'caused revival of that national feeling which is to some extent natural to all men, and is said to exist in an eminent degree in Scotchmen'. Their St Andrew's day dinners were chaired by leading Scots merchants and made a point of gathering together images of William Wallace, John Knox, Walter Scott and Robert Burns, as well as some symbolic heather, thistles and a 'small cask of genuine mountain dew specially sent over for the occasion'.[78]

As part of the Kailyard expansion, which saw so much interest in Scotland's (Highland) rural idyll, there was renewed interest in the clan societies. No longer were they voluntary organisations to help the education and the welfare of the those with their surname, now there was interest in the clan history and in genealogical excavations.[79] The Order of the Scottish Clans (1878) and the Daughters of Scotia (1898) were part of the late nineteenth-century revival in clan interest in America. Wallace is found among a range of Scottish surnames in New Zealand's South Island, for instance.[80] The Caledonian Society of Waipo (1871) aimed 'To keep the customs, traditions and language of the Mother country, Highland dancing, music, games, etc., and to assist any immigrants from the Highlands of Scotland or from Nova Scotia who settle in Waipo and are in need of help.'[81] The Ballarat Caledonian Society in Australia unveiled the then only statue of Wallace outside Scotland in 1889 and laid on a special train to bring the citizens of Melbourne, dressed in tartan, to the unveiling ceremony. The Scottish Home Rule Association welcomed the support it received from the Caledonian Club of Fort Wayne, Indiana, in the United States, and endorsed a report in the *Melbourne Argus* of a meeting to inaugurate a branch of its organisation in Victoria in 1891.[82]

Andrew Carnegie's claim that 'America would have been a poor show if not for the Scotch' provides some respect for a group so prepared to perpetuate their ethnic identity in the land of prime Tocquevillian freedom.[83] The opportunities of this new democracy (of civic nationalism) were still not enough to forego reminders of older ethnic identities.[84] Ex-pat Wallace is identifiable with romantic Wallace of the prose and this is no great surprise. It has kept the story alive among those who left Scotland's shores and provided a point of contact for the Scottish tourist who, to use the language of that industry, is categorised as visiting friends and relations (VFR) – a group who stay with relatives, not in paid-for accommodation and accentuate the idea of the community across the sea (and link Scotland's national culture, too). The Gaelic Society of Cape Briton has done much since the 1960s to promote the cultural development of Gaelic to counter its decline as a language of the everyday.[85] Indeed Gaelic tourism has come into its own in the 1990s, along with Tartan Day in North America.[86] The first Gaelic edition of the *Wallace* was not published until the 1920s, and there are claims that this was the language spoken by the patriot.

THE BALLADS AND THE POETRY

It was not just in the prose literature that the retelling of the Wallace story found strength. It appeared notably with many embellishments among the immensely abundant balladists and in the recovery of seemingly lost songs, a move which took off throughout the second half of the eighteenth century. Renewed interest in collecting this verse in the nineteenth century saw Hogg's two-volumed *The Jacobite Relics of Scotland* (Edinburgh 1819–21), Motherwell's *Minstrelsy: Ancient and Modern* (Glasgow, 1827) and Child's *English and Scottish Ballads* (Boston, 1859). The earliest preserved ballads are of doubtful antiquity and refer to the murder of Marion in Lanark.[87] The first is ninety-eight lines in length and emphasises Wallace's brute strength:

> He slew the captain where he stood,
> The rest they did quack an' roar;
> He slew the rest around the room,
> And ask'd if there were any more.[88]

The ballad entitled 'Sir William Wallace' is over one hundred lines long and Child's version came 'from an old gentlewoman in Aberdeenshire'. The first quarter of the poem shows the romantic Wallace bold in the face of capture, taunting the English soldiers:

> Wo'd ye hear of William Wallace,
> An' sek him as he goes,
> Into the lan' of Lanark,
> Amang his mortel faes?
>
> There was fyften English sogers
> Unto his ladie cam,
> Said 'Gie us William Wallace,
> That we may have him slain.
>
> 'Wou'd ye gie William Wallace,
> That we may have him slain,
> And ye's be wedded to a lord,
> The best in Christendeem.'
>
> 'This verra nicht at seven,
> Brave Wallace will come in,
> And he'll come to my chamber door,
> Without or dread or din.'
>
> The fyften English sogers
> Around the house did wait,
> And four brave Southron foragers
> Stood hie upon the gait.

At this point, his lover repents for helping to set a trap: 'And for the ill I've dane to you, Let me burn upon a hill.' Wallace then disguised himself in women's clothing, but 'yon lusty dame' was uncovered. The verse, however, would not allow his defeat:

> Then all the Southerns follow'd him,
> And sure they were but four:
> But he has drawn his trusty brand,
> And slew them pair by pair.[89]

Of the published poetry, one of the earliest mentions comes in 'Symmie and his Bruther': 'Thair is no story that I of heir/Of Johnne nor Robene Hude/Nor zit of Wallace wicht but weir/That me thinks half so gude.'[90] It links Wallace to the outlaw tradition: it was through the ballad that the myth of Robin Hood was first created and transmitted.[91] In one undated eighteenth-century account, probably from the 1740s, the Duke of Perth was reminded of the freedoms Wallace secured:

> Design'd from Mankinds loyal nameless Crowd
> To raise the Humble, and to check the Proud,
> To stop the baseful Growth of lawless Power
> And render injur'd Innocence secure.[92]

In another published in Edinburgh around 1745, the admiration for his physical prowess in a fight is again made explicit:

> Then Five he sticked where they stood,
> And Five he trampled in the Gutter,
> And Five he chas'd to yon green Wood,
> He hang'd them all out o'er a Grain
> And 'gainst the Morn at Twelve o' clock
> He din'd with his kind *Scottish* men.[93]

The verse conforms to the 'big man' theme of the narratives, but this time concentrating on this everyday physical prowess rather than the set piece battles. They are bloodthirsty, they indicate cunning over tenacious and cruel opponents and always Wallace's ability to overcome superior numbers is stressed. It would only be betrayal, not physical or military defeat, which brought about his end. Once that happens, the verse tends to dramatise the emotions of his execution: 'He got a priest the book before him hauld/While they to him had done all that they would do.'[94] That edition of Harry from the 1790s includes at this point William Birrell's engraving of the execution scene. Others use key identifiers on which to hang their verse: the sword symbolises his political struggle, his martyrdom and his spiritual inspiration. For example, *The Sword of Wallace* (1802) verse one:[95]

> Thou Sword of true valour! Tho' dim by thy hue,
> And all faded thy flashes of light
> Yet still my mem'ry thy sight shall renew
> The remembrance of WALLACE that night!

The final verse of *The Shade of Wallace* (1807) made a plea for Wallace's continued life in heaven:

> When I throw off this mortal coil,
> Fly from a world of wrongs and toil
> Where me themselves in cares embroil
> Grant me this solace
> Once more, on heaven's exalted soil,
> To see great Wallace.[96]

Despite such compassion in his death, baseness could be as much an excuse for poetry as spiritual advance. Holford's *Metrical Romance* (1809) was described by Walter Scott as not one to please the Scots because Wallace is a character not suited to poetry, although he suggested it would be better appreciated in England.[97] It was poetry reminiscent of Harry's gruff style:

> A king in chains – a trampled land;
> Our chiefs, a pale, desponding band;
> A people, wrong'd, despoil'd bereft
> Nor courage, zeal, nor honour left!
> Stewart I scorn to boast – ''Twas I'
> I rallied around her banner'd tree

And there were examples of anti-Englishness being maintained, most notably Burns' *Parcel of Rogues*, which he never owned up to in his lifetime, and, much less well renowned, *The Tragedy of the Valiant Knight Sir William Wallace*, from 1815:

> *Parcel of Rogues*
>
> Oh would, or I had seen the day
> That Treason thus could sell us,
> My auld grey head had lien in clay
> Wi' Bruce and loyal Wallace!
> But pith and power, till my last hour
> I'll mak this declaration;
> We're bought and sold for English gold-
> Such a parcel of rogues in a nation!
>
> *The Tragedy of the Valiant Knight Sir William Wallace*
>
> Behold! Who tramples on the Lion bold?
> A patriot greater than the heroes of old:
> Treach'ry alone o'er him gave England pow'r
> In death doth Edward's spite show to this hour.[98]

During the Napoleonic Wars loyalty to the idea of Britishness is found. The construction of a tower in the style of Nelson's upturned telescope as a tower on Calton Hill in Edinburgh and the unfinished National Monument for a neighbour are examples of this.[99] *Wallace and Bruce, a poem* (1825) was published about ten years later and just after George IV made his high-impact jaunt to Edinburgh, acclaimed for doing much to make the Hanoverian monarchy acceptable – and later loved – in nineteenth-century Scotland:

> While amply broad the firm foundation lies,
> And rare devices ev'ry side emblaze
> For shall the top ascend the yielding skies,
> The statue, stern, sublime in air to raise,
> And strangers oft will come, in future days,

Here to contemplate Scotia's Patriot Knight,
Whose glorious aim (that yet commands our praise)
Was always to secure his country's right,
By wisdom in debate, by valour in the fight.[100]

His country's right was now peace with England. Wallace's fight for freedom could also be romanticised in Scotland, as in J. Morrison Davidson's biography of patriotic Scots published at the beginning of the First World War:

Of 'Wallace' to be found, like a wild flower,
All over his dear country; left the deeds
Of Wallace, like a family of ghosts
To people the steep rocks and river banks
Her natural sanctuaries, with a local soul
Of independence and stern liberty.[101]

The set piece events, the romanticisation of his motivations resulting from the murder of his wife or mistress, and his fight for his country's freedom, permeated poetry, ballads and prose that could be passed on through listening and recitation. The impact of the Wallace myth is confirmed by its use in the wider politics of the nation, confirming the story as central to the national psyche. If the myth was evoked at 'non-Wallace' national occasions, then it is clear that the story – the collective national memory – is of the first order. Two examples can be found. In the fight for reform of the franchise in 1832, political songs and squibs used Wallace to make their vitriolic point:

CHAM'ER LILT[102]
NUMBER 1
BEING A SOUGH FRAE THE ADDRESS
TUNE. – 'Scots Wha Hae.'

Tories, – Friends of Bill D—s,
Sycophants of every class,

Rats, we're sore beset, alas!
Whisk your tails round me.–

Now's the day, an' now's the hour,
See her frown Britannia's lour,
See approach Truth's awful power,
Honour and Honesty.

Only the first two verses are presented here, but it shows an important part of the nation's cultural creation, where some form of association with the patriot permeates the everyday and sustains wider political objectives. At the failure of the first referendum on devolution in 1979, a similar use is made of the song and tune. From the fallout of that event, splits appeared within the Scottish National Party. In response, the following lament was penned and published in *The Scotsman*:

Wha will find the Labour knave,
Infiltratin' oor conclave?
'For God's sake, man. Come on! Behave!
'A socialist? No' me!'
Tell the workers no' tae mourn;
Freedom's cause is no' forlorn!
Maybe no' the morn's morn,
But in Eternitie![103]

It is a good example of cultural transmission: juxtaposing Burns, Wallace and contemporary politics, and the satire is clear in each example, bringing the non-literate or the non-political into the ring. It helps the people to touch the myth of Wallace, just as the chapbooks offered cheap publications for the growing consumer public.

FIVE

Heritage Wallace

Pageantry and ceremony have always featured strongly in BTA and national tourist board promotions, films, videos, posters and direct marketing. Re-testing of traditional images shows traditional events, such as the Royal Braemar Gathering and Royal Ascot, palaces, castles and troops in ceremonial dress still prove effective in certain markets, such as North America.[1]

See when you come doon tae it! Your country's like your own fizzer, intit? It might be a pock-marked, drink-ridden eyesore, but you're stuck with it. So you may as well try and love it.[2]

A fair number of the publishers of the histories and com-memorations of Wallace were English based. For so anti-English a patriot, this seems remarkable, even if it does reflect in part the economics of the publishing trade. Apart from a plaque marking the spot in Smithfield where Wallace was executed, one would be hard pressed to find any tangible mark of Wallace's life south of the border.[3] Indeed, statues to the patriot are much more common overseas, but none of this should be surprising. Unlike the retelling of the story, heritage Wallace is a home-grown creation. It is a local tour, typified by David Ross, historian to the Wallace Clan Trust, whose beloved motorbike has taken him on the hunt for places linked both to Wallace and Bruce.[4]

Even without these two medieval patriots, Scottish history resembles a cocktail of myth and mythology. It is a potent and heady combination which borders on the exotic. In a country which cannot guarantee its visitors sunshine, there are rich pickings to be gained from marketing the Scottish past. In Scotland, tourism and heritage have always been partners, working together to convert patriotism into pounds. The colourful chaos of Scotland's past is a powerful magnet which draws visitors from elsewhere in Britain and from all over the world. In 1997 5.2 million English tourists visited Scotland. In addition, there were 2.01 million overseas visitors to Scotland. Of these 429,000 were from the US; 239,000 from Germany and 149,000 from France.[5] In 1998, spending by overseas visitors to the UK reached £12.8 billion, of which £948 million was spent in Scotland, an increase of 10 per cent on 1997. UK residents spent more than £14 billion on staying visits within the UK and day-visiting in the UK added a further £22 billion to this figure.[6] There are, after all, more museums per head of the population in Scotland than in any of the other nations in Great Britain and Britain has a lot of museums.[7] Indeed, according to the BTA, visiting heritage sites is the most popular pastime for overseas holidaymakers in Britain. Top of the list in 1998 was the Tower of London, visited by 2,551,000 tourists, the next most popular was Windsor Castle with 1,495,000 visitors; in Scotland, the most popular royal attractions include the Palace of Holyroodhouse (288,000 visitors) and the former Royal Yacht *Britannia*, berthed at Leith in Edinburgh, which received over 160,000 visitors in its first year of opening, in October 1998, with 300,000 expected during the 1999 season, although preliminary estimates were disappointing for 2000.[8] By contrast, in the post-*Braveheart* glow, Stirling Castle has seen visitor numbers jump from 250,000 in 1991 to more than 430,000 in 2000.[9]

The heritage industry is a modern phenomenon and is uncaringly ironic with it. It grew out of a desire to protect historic buildings after the Second World War. To control the spread of urban areas and industrial activity, the Town & Country Planning Act of 1947 was passed and instead access to the countryside was managed and delimited. Complementing this Act, the National Parks and Access to the Countryside Act of 1949 was inspired by a vision of the countryside as an area to be preserved for all. This was partly in terms of the production of food and the extraction and processing of raw materials, but it was also part of an ideological vision of the land as national heritage.[10] For the heritage industry the 1980s marks a divide with what had gone before, because it encompasses a greater number of houses and sites than ever imagined. It attracts significant numbers of visitors and includes private charities, entrepreneurs and governments. It is its ideological importance which is the most crucial aspect of this industry. The writings of Hewison, Wright and Samuel have had an immense impact, through their reflection on the state of the English nation and its use of heritage to cling to during industrial decline. Heritage adhered to both right- and left-wing agendas, although the former appears to have the ascendancy in the profile of houses and attractions.[11] Roger Scruton phrased it thus:

> In every English village there is one object that stands out as the prime focus of the traveller's attention, and the fitting representative of stable government beneath whose mantle he journeys. This object is the telephone booth: a cast iron structure in imperial red, classical in outline, but with an interesting suggestion of the Bauhaus naughtiness in its fenestration . . . The door, divided into three parts by its mullions, has a brass handle, set into the cast iron frame, and above the cornice a little crown is embossed, symbol of national identity, and promise of enduring government. So suitable has this form proved to the streets, countryside and villages of England that it now appears on Christmas-card snow scenes, beside the Gothic spire, the gabled cottage and the five-barred gate.[12]

The powerful counterpoint analysis from McCrone, Morris and Kiely demonstrated the distinct orbit of Scotland's own heritage industry. It is a debate about the kind of history used to define the nation from within. It includes awareness of the influence of other nations and émigrés on Scotland, yet it stands in distinction to the 'new British history' – history without borders – which Pocock ignited and which developed its Atlantic perspective as the history of 'Greater Britain'.[13] It is also rather different from the situation in England where, as Neal Ascherson has convincingly argued, 'there is still an assumption that "our" history can only have one focal point, one perspective', and in which the past, although venerated and idealised, stands firmly behind the present, as something which is essentially over.[14] A recent guide to cultural identity in Britain started its explanation with 'traditional Britain':

> Broadly speaking, Britain has a historical heritage of whose gross features everyone is aware: colonised by the Romans; last invaded in 1066; a rural country up until the eighteenth century; unprecedented industrial growth in the nineteenth century; the largest empire the world has known; postwar decolonisation, and economic decline.[15]

This is English history and a very particular one at that. Its inapplicability for the histories of Scotland, Wales and Ireland is profound, as it is to the boundaryless of the 'new British' historians. Being a 'stateless nation', dominated politically throughout the ages of modern nationalism, has forced the presentation of Scotland's history to be circumspect – to debate from within, but without insularity.[16] The Union of 1707 with England and the focus upon Union when nationalist sentiment is mobilised, has projected history as a barometer of Scottish national identity and as non-neutral political material. The situation in Scotland, Ascherson explains, is more like that in France where it is assumed and indeed expected, that any account of French history will reflect the political leanings of the narrator. Thus a Republican version of French history will be inherently different to that of a Communist or a Catholic monarchist.[17]

Unlike the singular approach to 'traditional Britain' and historical England the importance of debating how the (national) past is remembered has not been lost on theorists of English heritage. Michael Crang has argued that 'it is insufficient to appeal to an "authentic" history against an "ideological" one'.[18] He argues that the rise of heritage as the purveyor of the historical past has made plain the multiple interpretations of the past which exist, to an extent that makes them seem real to us today: 'The organisation of such histories into heritage has political implications. Heritage and its organisation of tradition are fixings of a history. They make an apparently immutable history present in the now of society – as a logic of the concrete.'

Popular knowledge of history is part fact and part myth, that much is well known. Popular understanding of the past 'embraces all modes of exploration', argues Lowenthal, so we should expect history to be only one source of information.[19] Such understanding, transmitted most completely through what we know as 'heritage' is not the rival, but the first cousin of scholarly history.[20] To quote Samuel: 'the sense of the past, at any given point of time, is quite as much a matter of history as what happened in it.'[21] To capture the historical past, we must follow the path of the polymath: 'The signs which represent episodes from the past can be found in historians' scholarly texts as well as at heritage sites'.[22] The argument being proposed here is that heritage is the key conduit in mixing myth and the historical past; it dominates popular understanding of 'who we are as a people' as well as the signposts to Scotland as a tourist destination.

Of the many uses of the term over the last century, both to promote the countryside or to extract funding for urban regeneration, 'heritage' is increasingly crystallised into a debate about the national past both in England[23] and in Scotland.[24] This is a trend which has matured to reposition the nation-as-locality in the 'global age'.[25] The historiography of Scotland is not just about book reading. It is now increasingly – since the mid-1970s – a matter of passive consumption, promoted through the 'tourist's gaze'.[26] Here myth is readily promoted through heritage: and as consumers of tourism, we exhibit 'the tremendous desire to turn fragments into mysteries and signs; lore is not so much passed on or transmitted as made up and amplified, until there is not a stone without a story attaching to it'.[27] It is a promoted history: one to sell, to maintain jobs and local economies, estimated at 180,000 people, or eight per cent of the Scottish workforce in 1999–2000, adding over £2 billion each year in the Scottish economy.[28] In a study of tourism in Orkney, it was found that having its own Area Tourist Board and Chief Executive, who was committed to the type of rural and agricultural tourism which dominates the area, did much to compete with other more central parts of Scotland for visitor numbers.[29] Heritage is there to be packaged and promoted. Myth is everywhere in our tourism, and what is increasingly acute is the interplay between myth and history in the heritage industry and the effect it has on Scotland's political national identity.

Nor has the Wallace story escaped commodification in the new world of heritage. The almost surreal debate that engulfed the extended Museum of Scotland, as it contained no mention of Sir William Wallace, has already been discussed; but it has been in stone that the Wallace heritage trail has been best created. The National Wallace Monument was opened in 1869, the culmination of the work headed by Charles Rogers, co-secretary with Thomas L. Galbraith and the National Wallace Monument Committee. The Duke of Montrose and the Earl of Elgin and Kindcardine were the joint presidents of the Acting Committee organising the subscription.[30] The choice of design was not without disagreement, as they had to build the myth of Wallace 'correctly'. William Stirling feared that 'It was most discreditable to the taste of Scotland, if, in the year 1859, Wallace and the Abbey Craig, were to be . . . pilloried in the fashion which, early in the century, befell Nelson and Calton Hill'.[31]

The Glasgow lawyer William Burns was convinced of the propriety of the people of Glasgow taking part in the erection of a 'Great National Monument to the memory of Sir William Wallace'.[32] The organisers were keen that 'a special resolution for working men' be added to the programme to commemorate the laying of the foundation stone.[33] Indeed, the penultimate resolution, by Revd Alexander Low, Minister of Keig in Aberdeenshire, stated: 'That the chief supporters of Wallace in his struggles for independence, being the Scottish peasantry, it is fully expected that this Class will cordially unite with their fellow countrymen in the present movement'.[34] It was the case that the lists of subscriptions from around the Glasgow area showed many small amounts and that a number of the lists were published as posters.[35] At that ceremony – scheduled for the anniversary of the Battle of Bannockburn (not Stirling Bridge!) – there were five or six amateur (not professional!) bands playing 'Scots Wha Hae' and many wore 'the garb of the auld Gaul'.[36] Introducing the second resolution, Sheriff-Substitute Henry Glassford Bell declared that: 'Scotland and England are now one. Any Scotchman who now entertained animosity towards England, or any Englishman who entertained animosity towards Scotland, would be set down as simply insane (hear, hear)'.[37]

Support for the plans to construct a monument prefaced a number of the chapbooks. Buchanan offered his best wishes for the Abbey Craig plan, while Hutchison celebrated the recent construction of the Barnweill monument.[38] The celebrity nationalists Giuseppe Mazzini (1805–72), Giuseppe Garibaldi (1807–82) and Louis Kossuth (1802–84) all signed letters of support for the construction of the National Wallace Monument.[39] Garibaldi was the greatest icon, described as the 'Wallace of Italy' who inspired many Scots to sign up for the British Legion to support his cause mid-century.[40] *The Scotsman* reported in July 1869 Garibaldi's plans to visit Scotland 'which had been intimated to a friend in the north of England', an indication of that patriot's appeal.[41] The chosen design was that from the architect J.T. Roachead.[42] Upwards of 50,000 were said to have attended the laying of the monument's foundation stone and they were treated to much music and statements of the peace that Wallace and Bruce had instigated for their people.[43]

After the usual delays resulting from increased costs and insufficient funds, the monument was officially opened on 11 September 1869 with a formal ceremony lasting only half an hour and with it the monument was then put in the custody of the Town Council of Stirling.[44] On that Saturday morning a portrait was presented to Mrs Rogers representing her husband Dr Charles Rogers who would not attend.[45] Rogers was accused of taking for his own expenses the subscription to the monument given by the Alloa and Tillicoultry Weavers, and he resigned his chaplaincy in 1863 and removed himself to London.[46] It was a sad moment for one of the great Wallace enthusiasts of the nineteenth century.

Once opened, the monument became a successful visitor attraction. The *Stirling Observer* in 1887 expressed concerns over *too many* of the wrong sort of people being attracted to the Abbey Craig for the view, with a bottle of the hard stuff in their hand.[47] Inside the monument there is to be found the so-called Wallace sword. Charles Rogers had affirmed that 'this great blade' was found on Wallace's pillow the night of his capture in Robroystone in August 1305.[48] We know this to be no more than a story, but it has obvious symbolic importance, reputed therefore to be the only known Wallace artefact. On the evening of Sunday 8 November 1936, four men used force to steal the sword from the monument. At the time of the Custodians' Committee the next month it was still at large.[49] Despite many pointing out at the time that the sword was a fake, concluding that it was not made until the second half of the sixteenth century,[50] there was much concern raised until its return (as there was in 1972 when it was again recovered after its theft).[51]

In the twentieth century the National Wallace Monument acted as the key focus for much of Scotland's nationalist sentiment. Although figures showing revenue raised at the monument have been known since its opening, visitor figures were not kept until the turn of the century. Between 1900 and 1905, numbers fluctuated between 22,111 and 25,113 which were healthy, if not overly profitable.[52] The lessee in 1906, Mr Middleton, wrote to the railway companies to ask them to reduce fares on excursions to Stirling in an attempt to get more to climb the Abbey Craig.[53] If only Middleton had had access to the 'Braveheart effect' he would have had no need to pressurise the railway companies. The annual number of visitors to the Wallace Monument rose from 50,173 in September 1994 to 128,638 in August 1996, reaching over 200,000 in April 2000. Part of the growth can be attributed to the earlier refurbishment of the monument over eighteen months, at a cost of nearly £1 million, before being reopened in May 1993.[54] In any event, it put the revamped site – with new audio-visual displays – in a strong position to grasp the market opportunity *Braveheart* afforded two years later. Neither at the beginning nor the end of the twentieth century do the figures include those who climbed the Abbey Craig for free to admire the view – the tourist-pulling power of the monument can only be underestimated.[55] Keen to take advantage of this marketing opportunity which the Hollywood film inspired, Stirling temporarily dispensed with the bureaucratic appellation of 'Central Region' and plumped for the rather more romantic 'Braveheart County' instead.[56] This has not always been successful in the past, as McCrone, Morris and Kiely show, when the Conservatives gained control of Stirling District Council in 1992 and reassessed the value of the council's branding: 'A knight on horseback does not give the impression of an open accessible council that cares about its customers'.[57] But with a bandwagon to jump upon, others left such reticence behind.

WALLACE MONUMENTS

Wild scenery, historic and cosmopolitan cities, rich culture, romantic islands, royal connections and whisky distilleries are only a few of the attractions . . . something to offer in all four seasons.[58]

The Scottish Tourist Board may have had to deal with falling visitor numbers in 2000, but it is not usually wrong on the appeal of Scotland, despite its weather. The physical remains of its medieval history, as well as its commemoration by later generations, are great magnets to tourists. The monument at Abbey Craig has captured much of Scotland's Wallace tourist trail, but it cannot be taken in isolation. As part of the 650th anniversary of Wallace's death a range of commemorations took place in 1955, including a demonstration at Elderslie, a Wallace Memorial Service at Paisley Abbey and a range of 'prominent Scottish Nationalist speakers', with music and a pipe band, at the Ross Bandstand in Princes Street Gardens in Edinburgh.[59]

There were also a number of other monuments built before and after this one. The first statue of Wallace was commissioned by David Steuart Erskine, 11th Earl of Buchan in 1814.[60] It was designed in red sandstone by John Smith to stand twenty-one and a half feet high with the likeness taken from a watercolour in Buchan's possession.[61] It was restored in 1991, during dramatic, high winds on the exposed site.[62] As the *Glasgow Herald* put it: 'His threatened downfall now is not in the hands of the English . . . [but he] is suffering from another relentless enemy – the elements.'[63] Similarly, the next in a line of monuments inspired by Buchan's creation has also required restorative attention. St Nicholas Parish Church in Lanark is the location for a statue of Wallace which was put in place in 1820.[64] Its restoration, by Ainsworth, was carried out in 1993 at an estimated cost of £15,000: both monuments, it should be noted, were restored before the *Braveheart* mania began in earnest with the film's release in 1995.[65] Much of the appeal for funds was directed to the Wallace Clan throughout the world, rather than from home sources. As the historian A.A.M. Duncan stated at the time: '[The government] feel a bit uneasy when Scotland celebrates the life of a hero who defeated the English in battle.'[66] It was in the places most associated with Wallace that statues were placed. There were two built in Ayr town centre: the first was a statue of Wallace placed in a niche in Newmarket Street in 1819. The second was raised to note where Wallace was supposedly imprisoned in Ayr and the Wallace Tower could be named after him, or, much more likely, his namesake who owned the structure.[67] It makes quite a difference, but there is a Wallace statue which is part of the Tower, which was first built in 1831, but rebuilt two years later at the cost of just over £2,000, following the discovery of a fundamental weakness in its foundations. The sculpture of Wallace was made by James Thom and is placed high up in the 113 feet tall tower.[68]

The Barnweill Monument in the Ayrshire parish of Craigie was the outcome of an appeal started in 1837 and was completed just over a decade later.[69] The nationalist Lewis Spence ended his biography of Wallace with the quotation inscribed upon the tower:

Centuries have not diminished the lustre of his heroic achievements; and the memory of this most disinterested of patriots shall, through all ages, be honoured and revered by his countrymen. . . . Ever honoured by the memory of the matchless Sir William Wallace. . . . From Greece arose Leonidas, from America Washington, and from Scotland Wallace, names which shall remain through all time the watchwords and beacons of liberty.[70]

Its site marks the point where Wallace and his associates set fire to a barn full of sleeping Englishmen and supposedly shouted: 'the barns of Ayr burn well', so giving the area its name.[71] Barrow is not alone in disagreeing with this story, however.[72] There is a stone pillar at Wallacestone above Falkirk (from 1810),[73] interesting for marking a point of defeat. Wallace and Bruce vie for commemoration in Stirling. Bruce's heart is now in Dunfermline and the National Wallace Monument overlooks Stirling Castle with its renowned statue to Bruce at its entrance.[74] In Stirling itself, on the corner of Baker Street and Spittal Street and sculpted by Handyside Ritchie in the 1880s, is another Wallace statue. It was paid for by William Drummond,[75] and provides a more imposing commemoration than the statues of Wallace and Bruce on the municipal buildings (1855) in the town.[76] A picture of the Aberdeen statue to Wallace, with a historical description, comprised the 1951 Christmas card from the Lord and Lady Provost of Aberdeen.[77] It tells the history of the statue which was constructed with money donated in the will of John Steill from Edinburgh. A competition which secured twenty-five models was won by W. Grant Stevenson and depicts Wallace sending the English homewards immediately prior to the Battle of Stirling Bridge.[78] The monument at Robroyston, marking the spot where Wallace was betrayed by Menteith, has been more controversial. Unveiled in 1900, David Macrae linked the betrayal of Wallace to the betrayal of the aristocracy and such rhetoric was part of a range of contributions to the letters page of the *Glasgow Herald* on the same theme.[79]

Edinburgh had to wait until the twentieth century to get its monument to either Wallace or Bruce. This was despite the council advertising in 1882 'a public competition for a Wallace and Bruce memorial under the terms of a bequest left by Captain Hugh Reid'. It was remarkably successful, in that £2,000 was made available for the construction, yet nothing materialised.[80] It was not until 1929 that statues to the two heroes were unveiled on the Esplanade of Edinburgh Castle[81] by the Duke of York, later King George VI, on the 600th anniversary of the city's Royal Charter of 1329.[82] The Lord Provost Sir Alexander Stevenson proclaimed that Bruce had completed what Wallace had begun. The Duke of York wore the uniform of the Cameron Highlanders and accepted the words of the Lord Provost, stating that 'it is always a source of pride to us that we [himself and his wife] are both descended from Robert the Bruce'. He framed the patriots in the recent experience of war:

> Six hundred years have passed away, and those two countries, who were then the bitterest of foes, have become sister nations, linked together by the closest bonds of blood and affection, bonds which have been cemented by the most enduring tie of all – comradeship in war. Animated by the same spirit and ideals which inspired those two heroes of old, Scotsmen and Englishmen fought side by side in the Great War for justice and liberty; and side by side they endured hardship and suffering until victory had been won.[83]

The unveiling ceremony was two days before the general election, so precluding a number of notables. Ramsay Macdonald blamed either Bruce or Baldwin for the closeness of the dates preventing his attendance. Lloyd George was similarly absent, but offered his congratulations to the Scottish capital from 'one of another people within the family of British races'.[84] A rendition of 'Scots Wha Hae' followed the speech by His Royal Highness.[85]

The twentieth century failed to live up to the nineteenth century in all forms of monument building, yet there are some worth mentioning. The first is Sandy Stoddard's representation of Blind Harry which so impressed the visitors to the Brave Art Exhibition at the Stirling Smith Art Gallery and Museum in 1997. It brought new authority to the poet's place in history. The second is the bust of Wallace presented to the National Wallace Monument in 1998. It is a likeness of Mel Gibson. To quote the website from which this story is promoted: 'Tom Church, after a heart attack, watched the film *Braveheart*. So inspired was he by Wallace's patriotism and determination, that Tom resolved to produce a sculpture that would capture the spirit of one of Scotland's greatest heroes.'[86] We have no true likeness of Wallace, so who can cast the first stone of objection?[87] All the sources indicate that Wallace was a very large man and Mel Gibson is a little small to be physically imposing in warfare, but when did size ever matter? There is plenty of scope for satire here, but it is more evidence of the capacity of the myth to grow, to take on new clothes, new faces. That the National Wallace Monument can add this Gibson/Wallace to its almost century and half of heritage, plus its Wallace sword dating back at least to the early modern period, is remarkable. Whose myth? A'body's myth. We all make it so.

THE WALLACE HERITAGE TRAIL

These monuments and sculptures are specific foci of commemoration, but there are many other places that have been touched by the Wallace myth throughout Scotland. At the height of mid-nineteenth century Wallaciana, a survey carried out by Patrick Yule claimed there were over fifty sites ranging from caves and trees to wells, cairns, hills and waterfalls.[88] However, that survey was far from exhaustive. There were also a portrait, chair and quaich at Bonnington in Lanark, a spring well – Wallace's well – situated about a quarter of a mile to the north-east of Robroyston,[89] a cleft in a rock at Garleton, East Lothian, is known as 'Wallace's Hole' or 'Cave', Loudon Hill is the location of Wallace's Know[90] and 'Wallace's Butts' is located in the Lamond Hills.

Numerous other caves, camps, chairs, seats and stones named after Wallace and identified as such by various nineteenth-century commentators have been found.[91] Those listed by Donaldson and Morpeth show 'Wallace's Beef-Tower', at Bothwell Castle; 'Wallace's Larder', referring to the Dungeon in Craig's Castle, Ardrossan, where William Wallace is said to have thrown the bodies of the defenders after he captured the castle; and 'Wallace's trench', which is sixty-three feet in circumference, near Blair Drummond.[92] Elspeth King identified eighty-three places named after Wallace from modern maps, rightly indicating that many more references could be found in maps from earlier years. All but seven or eight of these sites are in the central belt or borders of Scotland.

Looking through the references to Wallace logged by the Royal Commission on the Ancient and Historical Monuments of Scotland (RCAHMS) produces a bewildering variety of hits, some more tangential than others. Crosbie House is associated with Sir Reginald

Crawfurd, an uncle of Sir William Wallace, although little remains. The ruins of an old castle called 'Gascon Hall' which, according to the RCAHMS, 'is said to have been the place where Sir William Wallace encountered the ghost of Faudon, as narrated by Blind Harry. The real Gascon Hall is said to have stood about a mile and a half to the north-east, among the present woods of Gask.' Since *Braveheart*, David Ross has done most to map this trail and despite his avowed patriotism, he offers a review of the claims of association he finds on his travels.

There are places associated with the events of Wallace's times, rather than directly with the man himself. Paisley Abbey is where the patriot may have been educated, which contains the Wallace Memorial window (1873) with Wallace cast as Samson.[93] Cambuskenneth Abbey may be where one of his arms is buried, but otherwise any link is through his uncle only.[94] This heritage trail makes the spread of the ordinary Scots' association with Wallace all the wider. National monuments and other statues are especially good for heightened moments of nationalist expression and these geographical and physical sites across the country provide a tangible link to the local communities, giving people a sense of personal attachment to the story.

THE WALLACE SOUVENIRS

It is possible to identify a range of souvenirs which have been produced to commemorate Wallace and allow some entrepreneurs to make a living. The construction of souvenirs started early. The Goldsmith Company of Edinburgh presented a snuffbox made out of the wood from Wallace's oak to the Earl of Buchan. To highlight his republican sympathies, Buchan passed the gift to George Washington in 1790.[95] A musical box was produced for George IV on his visit to Scotland in 1822: '. . . the root of that oak which had preserved the houseless patriot when outlawed by the enemies of his country has gone to the legitimate descent of that race of kings for whose right he so nobly contended.'[96] How ironic that the Hanoverian monarch should be honoured with a souvenir of Scotland's struggle for independence. The same could be said for the Wallace chair presented by Joseph Train, in 1820, to the Tory and arch-Unionist Walter Scott.[97] The chair was constructed from wood taken from the barn where Wallace was captured; today the owner of Harrods and keen pursuer of British citizenship, Mohamed Al Fayed, has a Wallace Chair on his Highland estate. The shooting trophy, the *Caledonian Challenge Shield* from 1863, is an incredibly impressive structure: 9 ft 6 in by 6 ft and made of oak. Wallace and Bruce are there, with Scotland's motto: *Impure Lacessit Nemo Me*. The national monument itself became the focus for the trade in souvenirs: Wallace pin cushions,[98] table centres, cups, saucers and spoons,[99] the Wallace sword brooch,[100] or, by 1936, the specially erected Tea Pavilion.[101] This latter was not a souvenir, but a place of consumption. The Tea Pavilion, situated in Pine Woods adjoining the monument, offered tea, cakes and scones at town prices.[102] R.W. Salmond sold it to the Custodians of the Monument in 1937 for £60 at the end of his time as lessee in January that year.[103] For £70 or $115 one can now purchase, over the internet, a model of the National Wallace Monument in miniature, specially commissioned by Loch Lomond, Stirling and Trossachs Tourist Board.[104] Braveheart Warriors Tours are advertised by the Clan Centre and Braveheart Trading Post, part of the Clanranald Trust, which plans to build a Scottish Fort and working Highland village, enact fight displays, offer guided tours and invites tourists to be photographed dressed like William Wallace or Murren from *Braveheart*.[105] Don't just believe the myth; be the myth. Role play your way to a new depth of understanding.

MODERNITY'S 'MYTHSTAKES'

Such is the proliferation of different media, we should not be surprised to find the Wallace story permeating our culture in new ways and corrupting the story into new permutations. Heritage is not just about places to go or places to see. Like the use of 'Scots Wha Hae' as a tune for all political occasions, heritage Wallace has infiltrated the popular consciousness in a variety of ways. Exhibits A to E are some favourite 'mythstakes':

EXHIBIT A

CANADA 3,000 IN-FLIGHT MAGAZINE

The Wallace monument at Sterling (sic) marks the spot where Wallace Simpson camped in 1297 before defeating the English in an encounter made famous by Mel Gibson in the Oscar-winning film *Braveheart*.[106]

EXHIBIT B

BRAVEHEART TO BLAME FOR DANGEROUS PASSIONS IN THE DEEP SOUTH

'The American South can rise and be a nation again!' claims the LEAGUE OF THE SOUTH. Its supporters are descended from an influx of radical Scots in 17–19th centuries: 'William Wallace stood up to Longshanks army because it was right. He didn't think of the consequences'.

It was an event with a conspicuous absence of black faces.[107]

These days the film's capacity to be mobilised by ultra-reactionary groups has reached frightening proportions. A recent article in a Glasgow newspaper outlines how in America Christian fundamentalist, white supremacist, Southern nationalists and armed militia groups are increasingly claiming kinship with what they imagine to be ancient Celtic, particularly Scottish, traditions. Within this, *Braveheart* is assuming a central recruiting and rallying role.[108]

EXHIBIT C

TARTAN DAY
(the T word)

6 April, the day the Declaration of Arbroath was signed in 1320 – and its philosophical links to the American Declaration of Independence were stressed. There were 260 Highland Games in the USA to mark it and Tartan Day was celebrated by an academic symposium in the Smithsonian Institute on the historic links between America and Scotland.[109]

AWARD FOR CONNERY

The US will honour Sir Sean Connery next year when he is presented with the William Wallace award in recognition of his contribution to America. The award will take place on 6 April, the anniversary of the Declaration of Arbroath, and will be the highlight of Tartan Day, the annual American public holiday that marks Scotland's contribution to the US. Sir Sean will be presented with the award on the steps of Washington Capitol Hill.[110]

EXHIBIT D

. . . the curse of Mel is hard to shake off.

The Dryburgh statue, built in 1814, supposedly on a likeness of Wallace: 'Whatever his [the sculptor John Smith's] model, the resulting sandstone edifice has a sort of hollow-eyed classical look about it, with its beard and gladiatorial helmet. In fact it resembles nothing so much as one of special-effects wizard Ray Harryhausen's giant stop-frame figures from *Jason and the Argonauts*, or some such epic. . . . At least it doesn't possess the features of Mel Gibson, whose phizog adorns a more recent statue of the Guardian of Scotland, erected at the Wallace Monument in Stirling in 1997 to mark the 700th anniversary of the Battle of Stirling Bridge. Its sculptor, Tom Church, carved it as 'therapy' after a heart by-pass operation, and justified his modelling it on the blue-faced actor by claiming: 'When we think of Wallace we see Gibson in full battlepaint crying out "Freedom"'. . . .The curse of Mel, however, is not warded off too easily. Near the foot of the Dryburgh statue is a sort of American-style mail box, within which a small and dog-eared notebook serves as a visitors' book. A cursory glance reveals the last entry, made by some wag from the US. And it reads: Freedom![111]

EXHIBIT E

'Braveheart takes a hand in the Comeback for Celtic Weddings'.

Nineteen Celtic weddings in 1999, for a practice all but died out.

Mr. Porter, 37, a janitor in Aberdeen's Academy shopping centre, said: 'When we watched *Braveheart* together, Tracy turned to me and said, 'I want it like that'. I'm proud to be Scottish, so I thought, 'Let's go for it'.

Ms. Sutherland, 28, a chef, said: 'It's a true Scottish wedding. I am Scottish through and through and this is how I always wanted it. The way we are married is a very important thing.'[112]

There appears to be no end to the uses and abuses of the Wallace myth. The confusion in Exhibit A, from the in-flight magazine, merely demonstrates the willingness of other cultures to mention Wallace. Tartan Day is to rival St Patrick's Day, to celebrate Scotland's cultural influence in America and the rhetorical influence over its constitution: is Connery the new Wallace?

Tartan Day is spreading to Australia too.[113] Exhibits D and E bring the culture back home: is Tom Church's creation, with Mel Gibson as Wallace, any different from the new-found heritage of the Celtic wedding? Scan any local newspapers for the wedding photographs or graduation day smiles. If tartan is not displayed from Rangers, Celtic, Aberdeen or one of the other football club-created weaves, then it is the garb of old Gaul which predominates. The bonds of marriage bind Wallace to Scotland's culture with no imminent danger of divorce papers being filed.

Of these somewhat diverse examples, it can be said that Harry's romantic verse has found its patriotism taken around the world through film, sculpture and the internet. It is not merely some ad hoc response by bedroom-bound enthusiasts through their terminals. There have been concentrated efforts to make money out of 'Wallace's freedom', as these examples have shown. The Wallace Clan Trust claims to be in the business of attracting film money into Scotland and to focus on the Clan Lands, an activity that was receiving 150 enquiries a week in 1997. Because of this, it claims it supports indigenous peoples rather than nation-states[114] and its international profile is high. Forth Valley Enterprise, Stirling Council and the European Regional Development Fund donated money for Stirling's 'Battle of Stirling Bridge office' to mark the 700th anniversary.[115] The brewers Maclays of Alloa helped fund the Stirling Smith's exhibition and events.[116] Wallace has value as an international brand name. Drawing from the insights of Baudrillard and the theory of semiotics, Nuala Johnston suggests that signs are all that we consume and that we do so knowingly. The signs which represent episodes from the past can be found in the scholarly texts of the historian as they can be found in the productions of the heritage entrepreneurs.[117] The 'mythstakes' mix the funnies with falsity; the historian is there to debunk, but what good is that in the face of the nationalist narrative? The heritage industry and the historian are part of the same process. The myths are strong and hard to dismantle. Heritage is now the carrier of the nation's imagination as never before.

SIX

Proletarian Wallace

She said they were ' a' very ta'en up wi the picture'. He [her husband] liked to look at it, and she had moved his bed that he could see it when he wanted without moving his head. 'I whiles stand an' look at it mysel' when I'm reddin' things up, and I've seen us talkin' aboot thae men and what they're efter.' She pointed to the two debonair gentlemen, with their backs to the dejected room of the poor Scots family, mounting the glimmering marble steps to move through the palace with the broken arch, and out by boat to the golden island with the castle in the bay. 'The bairns are gey ta'en wi' it, too. I've catched them sitting by the fire at the night makin' up stories aboot thae men.' 'What sort of stories?' 'Oh just a' havers like. I heard the wee yin saying that the yin wi' the lang legs was Wullie Wallace. But they'll no let me hear them, and 'deed I dinnae gie much heid to what they say, but whiles they're on talkin' and talkin' aboot them the rest o't till I send them aff to their bed.'[1]

The creation of the Wallace myth has come a long way from Harry, Hamilton and Jamieson. The vernacular has been transposed in each of these creations and has allowed new market penetration of the story. The chapbooks, romances, poems and ballads focused on key elements of Wallace's biography and took the myth deeper into the national consciousness. The many physical sites associated with the patriot took the story to the regions, creating personalised and community-based points of contact. For every schoolchild – of a certain age – who was educated in Ayrshire, visits to Burns' Cottage were as regular as the changing of the seasons. So the local association with all things Wallace acted as an essential conduit. An argument against greater

European integration, for example, through the spread of a European citizenship, is premised on the profusion of monuments which litter the European nations and mark the wars between them.[2]

The Wallace trail in Scotland has taken the myth to the people. This was not to divide the Scots, as in the European analogy, but to thicken the web. It deepened the mythic touch of Wallace, but no matter how intricate it has become, the story remains segmented. Not all sides of Scottish society have been equal at all times in the mythology. Much of the historiographical literature has taken Wallace as the people's champion, who achieved what success he did in spite of the jealousies of the nobility. He was turned in, too, by an ignoble noble, so there is plenty of material for those who may wish to make Wallace Scotland's first working-class hero: a rebel with a big sword.

Marinell Ash made some of the clearest statements in support of this narrative. She argued that as the myth is understood in the late twentieth century, Wallace 'was a victim of the class conflict and the conspiracy theory of historiography'.[3] It is a nice idea: proletarian Wallace, socialist Wallace, fighting to clear his name from the (right-wing) writers of history. The socialist home ruler and later Secretary of State for Scotland, Tom Johnston, writing in 1920, made much of 'the serfs' who fought under Wallace and Bruce. These poor people had associated with men of the towns, discovered what freedom meant, and 'developed on the battlefield a consciousness that they were the equals, in the last resort, of the knight and men at arms they speared at . . . it was unthinkable that when Bannockburn was fought and won they would go back to the old settled slavery'.[4] Agnes Mure Mackenzie (1936) quotes Fordun who claimed that 'all who were in bitterness of spirit and oppressed by the weight of intolerable sovereignty of the English dominion' flocked to Wallace.[5] In contrast to the language of slavery, the Whig historians of the nineteenth century looked only for steady progress – of reform – as the triumph of civilisation, of modernity.[6] Wallace, it appears in this line of argument, got so far, but then the big boys – the legitimate rulers – took over. It was they who saw Scotland safely home, to constitutional monarchy and democracy.[7]

What is the interplay between the two narratives? Was Wallace the proletarian hero or the hired muscle for the constitutional reformers? No easy question, yet the theories of nationalism warn us to expect such dualities. Nationalism is a delicate mix of the modern and the pre-modern, the official and the peripheral. Nation-states are modern creations and their ideology, their nationalism, followed in quick time. It is nation-states that make nationalism, as the thrust of Gellner's argument would make plain. A predominant form of nationalism is a movement led by the bourgeoisie, a group usually from the towns. But the *appeal* of nationalism – its plea to its people – is of older loyalties, of the pre-modern land, the fatherland and the motherland. As King has put it, '[n]ationalism is an urban movement which identifies with the rural areas as a source of authenticity, finding in the "folk" the attitudes, beliefs, customs and language to create a sense of national unity among people who have other loyalties'. He develops his argument by placing this ideology within the boundaries of the community and in distinction to foreign ideas.[8] The Wallace heritage trail has given the patriot his folk roots, but his political legacy is up for grabs. The first source of this duality is one in part already dealt with: his relationship with Scotland's nobility. It flows from his coupling with Bruce, contrasting the two. The second comes from a political ideology associated with those times, that of the community of the realm.

The following two extracts from the lexicon of Wallace stories are a century apart. Both refer to the aftershock of defeat at the Battle of Falkirk:

. . . that the cause he headed was a great popular cause. The natural leaders of the people had either failed them, or betrayed them, or forsaken them, and so fierce were the internal divisions that raged between the leaders of the people that one of them, Sir Richard Lundin, went over to Edward, justifying his defection by the declaration, 'I will remain no longer of a party that is at variance with itself'. The People turned to the new man with a new hope and a new expectation; and as he was deserted by the aristocracy and the priesthood, he became essentially the man of the people.[9]

Robert the Bruce lifted his face. He saw Wallace escaping. All around him were dying Scots. The Bruce lowered his eyes to the earth, muddy with the blood of his countrymen.[10]

Here Robert Bruce realises his failure. It is not Scotland's – the people's – failure, it is a failure of Scotland's leadership. By not supporting Wallace at the time of his greatest military defeat, so Scotland was let down by its nobility. It is from Falkirk that Wallace's martyrdom begins.[11] Many examples could be taken from the histories written before and after these two extracts, and some have already been cited in earlier chapters. But where this narrative crystallises around his nemesis, Robert Bruce, the cloth cap of the proletarian begins to fit all the tighter around Wallace's head. If the history and literature of Scotland can be described as the polar twins,[12] then I think we can be justified in likening Wallace and Bruce to two old rockers, such is the tempestuousness of their relationship: the Glimmer Twins is, I think, a more than serviceable epitaph.

THE GLIMMER TWINS OF SCOTLAND'S NATIONAL PAST

A great man rose with the promise of freedom again, to die in torment with freedom farther lost: the last thought of Wallace may well have been despair. Then another took the broken sword and reforged it, reforged the nation, won through nearly a quarter-century of war against odds more impossible than those confronting St Joan or Garibaldi, worked one of the miracles of history, and died Robert, King of free Scots, by the grace of God.[13]

Populist history still struggles to get beyond Bruce as much as it does Wallace. Bonnie Prince Charlie and Mary Queen of Scots do, of course, get more than a look-in, but the coupling of these two warriors, fighting their battles of destiny, is heady stuff and easily digested. The world may claim a Great War, but it is nothing compared to the Wars of Independence. Evidence which indicates that the impact on politics at the time might not, in fact, have been that decisive is not a view that can be countenanced. Their ideological symbolism remains too great. In identifying the key national icons of Scottish nationhood, Jonathan Hearn describes Wallace as 'the rebel military leader from a knightly family' while Bruce was the 'defender king'.[14] The contrast between rebel and king is interesting and all the more so because it is used to contextualise an anthropological study of the movement for home rule as it developed in the 1980s and 1990s. The symmetry is just remarkable and it mirrors the binding of Harry's *Wallace* with Barbour's *Bruce*. The appeal of Wallace to the people is captured in the political concept of the 'community of the realm'. It is a contentious and sometimes excessively optimistic idea, but it carries the name of the people shoulder high into the rite of king-making.

Commentators have made much of the supposed symbiosis of people, government and crown. It is the people who are at the heart of the Declaration of Arbroath, where the king pays fealty to the people: 'So long as one hundred of us stay alive.'[15] N.H. Reid has argued, however, that the Declaration is again more a totem of later generations than showing a dramatic change in contemporary politics. Reid's analysis of legislation of the time indicates that the declaration was more continuation than break in governance, but still it, and the political manoeuvring about it, marked an important period in the interdependence of the community and Bruce. Geoffrey Barrow is the leading historian to have fixed the community of the realm as central to thirteenth- and fourteenth-century political theory. At its most inclusive, the concept gave influence to the 'the totality of the King's free subjects'. It was Bruce's innovative evocation of this concept which helped secure him the crown over Comyn. There are, of course, those who see the community of the realm as a concept that was, in theory and in practice, less than complete. Archibald Duncan is one historian who has argued that despite contemporary rhetoric, there are clear doubts as to how open this political principle was in reality. Edward Cowan has also warned against taking such an all-encompassing view.[16] And the Declaration has had a mixed commemoration. Its 650th anniversary was marked with a commemorative stamp, but not a public holiday to match that which had been granted for the Magna Carta.[17] In more recent years, the Declaration has become a totem of Scotland's contribution to world democracy (the American Declaration of Independence now thanked during Tartan Day) and a poster, framed or otherwise, in many a home.

The theme of Scotland's democratic heritage can be found in the interpretation of the usual suspects from the Wars of Independence. Young, for example, presents a powerful corrective account of the Comyn family, the rivals to Bruce. This work unearths the construction of the Bruce and Wallace myths in the chronicles of John of Fordun, Walter Bower and Andrew of Wyntoun and contrasts their linguistic construction through which John Comyn was undermined, subsumed within the over-patriotic chronicles which accuse him of siding with Edward I against Robert I.[18] Such rhetoric has been important. Fiona Watson has shown the attractiveness to Bruce of the potential contained within the patriotic well. It was a suitable medium for him to channel his power, she argues, in a number of different ways.

The other side of this, of course, is the attractiveness of Bruce to later generations of nationalists, and it is this which flows from the biased history unearthed by Young in the chronicles.[19] That Bruce harboured his own doubts about changing sides – such as his anxiety over joining in with Edward in 1302 – a point made in documentary researches by Stones – is not a narrative that sits comfortably with the creation of proletarian Wallace against opportunistic Bruce.[20] When Tom Johnston coupled the two together, he proclaimed their inspiration to ordinary Scots, but if the integrity of Wallace was to be overshadowed by Bruce, then he offered a terse corrective: 'In truth, the "Good King Robert" of our school books played a most despicable, vacillating, and traitorous part in the by no means clearly defined drama of the times.'[21] He confirmed this by listing the many occasions Bruce had changed sides, offering loyalty to Edward, undermining Wallace and, it has even been suggested, witnessing his trial.[22] This sustained the Glimmer Twins in Scotland's national history, with their supposed meeting after the Battle of Falkirk or in the chapel in Dunipace essential to setting the relationship between the two patriots. Craigie has described these meetings as 'perhaps the most dramatic scenes in the whole of old Scottish literature'.[23] Alexander Brunton dipped into the world of Blind Harry to protect the integrity of Wallace's military skills: 'If Robert Bruce excelled him in military glory, I do not place him in competition, because the former flourished after William's time', but adds his own editorial retort, that, in any case: 'This is not true. Wallace far excelled Bruce in military glory.'[24] Others have joined in the defence. As a reaction to Maxwell's *Life of Bruce* (1897), in which William Wallace is chastised as 'an outlaw, a thief, a brigand', McKerlie wrote that Wallace was all the greater because he faced such turbulent opposition.[25] In contrast C.S. Terry devoted much more time to Bruce than Wallace and his praise was false: 'History records few instances of so meteoric a rise from insignificance to power, and the achievement records the depth and resolution of popular stirring to which Wallace's obscure personality had given a voice.' Terry then concludes that Wallace's influence was short-lived and, more importantly, that it was Wallace who championed the cause which was to propel Bruce to the kingship. Supporters of Wallace and Bruce each vied to place their favourite in the better light. It served to keep the non-royal Wallace in the public frame of reference by offering a useful and easily understood stage show for the audience to boo and cheer as their loyalties dictated.

FROM STIRLING BRIDGE (1297) TO BANNOCKBURN (1314)

The contrast between the two men kept legitimate interest in a patriot for whom only a few years of activity are known or could even be classed as influential. This worked all the more successfully because the rivalry was channelled into two parallel life courses, which meet in 1305 when, upon the execution of Wallace, Bruce is charged with completing the destiny of the other. Mackenzie summed up the nine years from 1305 until the Battle of 1314 as 'The road to miracle'.[26] A.F. Murison made Bruce walk in a dead man's shoes:

> Wallace had done his work right well and truly, as builder of the foundations of Scottish independence he had sealed his faith with his blood. Probably he died despairing of his country. Yet barely had six months come and gone when his dearest wish was fulfilled. The banner of Freedom waved defiance from the towers of Lochmaben, and in the Chapel-Royal of Scone the Bruce was crowned King of Scotland.[27]

The closing words of one recent children's book considers the death of Wallace as not the end:

> Edward's victory now seemed complete. His control of Scotland was even stronger than when Wallace had first begun to fight back. But after Wallace's example, the Scottish people were not prepared to submit meekly. Less than a year later, Robert Bruce, who had first supported Wallace then changed sides to help Edward, once again defied the power of Edward.[28]

This has become the dominant narrative. The flyer from the National Trust for Scotland (NTS), defining the historical importance of Bannockburn field, makes it official:

THE NATIONAL TRUST FOR SCOTLAND
VISIT
BANNOCKBURN

From this battlefield the Scots 'sent them homewards to think again', when Edward II's English army was soundly defeated by King Robert Bruce. This brought the independence for which William Wallace had also fought.

The Heritage Centre exhibition includes a large model of the Battle of Stirling Bridge, and exciting life-size figures of Wallace and Bruce. It brings to life decisive moments in Scotland's history, including the signing of the Declaration of Arbroath which inspired Thomas Jefferson when he drew up the American Declaration of Independence. An audio-visual presentation tells the dramatic story of Bruce and of the battle, with haunting sounds and images.[29]

From earlier narratives, the betrayal at Falkirk and the cruel attacks on his reputation ensured that Wallace would step out of the shadow of Bruce, with his flat cap waving, while the latter's crown was smuggled out of sight. But now a great feat of political imagination was made to fix Bruce as the source of Wallace's greatest triumph. From antipathy to consummation, the actions of the crown now makes the flat cap gold. The Bannockburn battlefield fulfills the life-plan of Wallace. Its date is one of the few most Scots will know, and revel in the memory of, when a small army under the command of King Robert I defeated a larger English force. The patriotic sentiment tagged on to the history of the Scottish king, Robert Bruce, is central to Bannockburn's importance as a tourist attraction. The battle is the acme of the long-developed military traditions in Scotland.[30] In 1930 the then Earl of Elgin helped to raise funds for the purchase of fifty-eight acres of land at Bannockburn to turn the battleground into a heritage site.[31]

That Bannockburn is in the care of the National Trust for Scotland is interesting for two reasons. Firstly that the site of Scotland's most important battle is not, unlike the battlefields of France and the USA, in the care of the state, but of a voluntary institution,[32] and secondly, the NTS, a body whose ruling council has always had a strong aristocratic and landed presence, is caring for a visitor attraction which is so strongly identified with the aristocratic Robert Bruce and not the National Wallace Monument at Abbey Craig (the responsibility of Stirling Town Council).

The Bannockburn heritage centre is visited by nearly 60,000 people a year. The memorial itself is free and the local council estimate that around 250,000 visit it annually.[33] Its Rotunda was officially opened by the Queen in 1964, as was the statue to Bruce at Stirling Castle. Earlier, in 1814, 15,000 people had come to celebrate the 500th anniversary of the battle.[34] Over time, others used the site for their own ends. The 6,000 Good Templars who descended on Bannockburn in 1897 planned to use the inspiration of Bruce to warn of the evils of drink.[35] Compare this with the failure of the centenary of Culloden to attract any sustained attention in 1846; nor was the attempt to secure a cairn to mark the site following its 150th anniversary in 1896 straightforward.[36]

From the 1950s the Scottish National Party began holding annual rallies at Bannockburn, as they had done in Elderslie, the birthplace of Wallace.[37] While the importance of Bannockburn to the SNP seems obvious, it is interesting to note that the battlefield has become an icon to all Scottish political parties. In 1993 *The Scotsman* newspaper published a series of articles which asked prominent people to identify and explain at which historical event they would most have liked to have been a 'fly on the wall'. Ian Lang, then Conservative Secretary of State for Scotland, chose his location at Bannockburn:

I would have liked to have been on the field of Bannockburn on 23–24 June 1314, to see the most decisive battle in Scottish history: the victory of Robert the Bruce's Scots over Edward II's English army.[38]

Two weeks after *Braveheart* gained its Oscar success, his successor Michael Forsyth was quoted in the media lamenting that Scots were prioritising Wallace over the wealth creators of history. Stirling University's Williamson Memorial Lecture was the occasion for him to argue that the Scots were poor at recognising success and 'That is why the cult of the defeated Wallace eclipses the successes of the crowned Bruce'. It was, he argued, a symptom of 'out-of-date political proletarianism'. Bannockburn is an example of a tourist attraction whose selling power is based on the myth of the heroic patriot king, ignoring the historical reality of Bruce's expedient support for whichever side was most likely to win. It is the focal point in a tourist trail of the many sites associated with Bruce's guardianship and kingship of Scotland, just as those of Wallace's exploits have been documented.[39] The supposed meeting of Bruce and Wallace after the Battle of Falkirk in 1298, despite never taking place, has been promoted as the link between the two heroes – the aristocratic Bruce and proletarian Wallace – giving much needed historical continuity for the nationalist vision of the long fight for independence. A retelling of this myth by Randall Wallace, author of the *Braveheart* screenplay, has been described as 'a mélange of authorial hubris; mystical, quasi-blood-and-soil ideology; and a sensibility of staggering vulgarity and sentimentality'.[40] It was, to quote one review 'History in the faking'.[41] However, the fabricated meeting and the type of language it engenders, appeals to universal notions of freedom.[42] From this it builds tourist appeal. Fact-based myth is more powerful than that which is invented; it sustains the 'living history' that Samuel tells us is so important to the nation's *Theatres of Memory*, yet is so remote from scholarly, historical practice.[43]

BUILDING THE PEOPLE INTO THE STORY

The perpetuation of the story of Wallace's betrayal by his social superiors has been long sustained. The story starts in Fordun, it is embellished by Harry and followed in the nineteenth-century chapbooks, ballads and songs. It was also part of the heritage trail, taking national history away from the royal castles of Stirling and Edinburgh and placing it among the people's heritage. When building the monuments to Wallace, the appeal promoted him as a man of the people. As we have seen, the organising committee of the subscription to the National Wallace Monument made much play from the many small donations and subscriptions they had received from ordinary working people. Early in its progress, it was feared that one of the arguments against even building a national Wallace Monument was that it was offering an opportunity for the aristocracy to shape the memory of the proletarian hero. The mid-nineteenth-century nationalist John Steill denounced the inclusion of the nobility in the commemoration of Wallace: 'The ancestors of these men were the bitterest foes Wallace had to contend against. . . . No, it is the peasantry, mechanics, and the middle classes of Scotland who ought to take this matter into their own hands. They alone fought under Wallace's banner. It is for them he laid down his life.'

Later in the century others embellished this theme. Thomas Carlyle, in a review of Scott's *Tales of a Grandfather*, wrote, 'It is notable that the nobles of the country have maintained a despicable behaviour since the days of Wallace downwards – a selfish, ferocious, famishing, unprincipled set of hyenas, from whom at no time, and in no way, has the country derived any benefit'.[44] The Scottish Home Ruler, Charles Waddie, sent a letter to the *Ayrshire Post* which rebuked the way in which the aristocracy had represented Scotland:

> Their patriotism is of the sickly sentimental kind, reaching no further than singing a Scotch song, playing at golf, and wearing the tartan; but they never lift their little finger to stop the plundering of Scotland or the ruin of our national monuments. It is not to these snobs but to the people – the common people of Scotland – we must look for redress. History in this will but repeat itself. The nobles of Scotland deserted their country over and over again; the common people supported Wallace to free his country from English tyranny and the same people maintained their religious independence in the Covenant.[45]

The theme has lasted in nationalist discourse. The SNP were represented at the Wallace Rally held in Stonehaven in August 1995 by Andrew Welsh MP. The organisers, who were expecting a big increase in numbers attending after the recent release of *Braveheart*, defined their purpose in order to attract support:

> The rally is held annually to commemorate the life of Scotland's greatest hero. At a time when the earls and barons of Scotland either sat on their hands and did nothing, or worse betrayed their country, William Wallace remained devoted to Scotland and led the struggle for freedom and liberty. More than any other person in our history it is to Wallace that we look for inspiration in our aim to achieve independence.[46]

The proletarian myth has also served to support the construction of a popular Scottish ethos, a collective spirit, a greater (than in England) sense of community. Robert Burns, of course, provided much inspiration, but, as Angus Calder has shown in *The Dumfries Volunteers*, the vision of liberty Burns ascribed to had been compromised:

> To thee, I turn with swimming eyes –
> Where is that soul of Freedom fled?
> Immingled with the mighty Dead!
> Beneath that hallowed turf where Wallace lies!
>
> Is this the ancient Caledonian form,
> Firm as her rock, resistless as her storm?
> Shew me that eye which shot immortal hate,
> Blasting the Despot's proudest bearing:
> Shew me that arm which, nerved with drunken fate,
> Braved Usurpation's boldest daring!
> Dark-quenched as yonder sinking star
> No more that glance lightens afar;
> That palsied arm no more whirls on the waste of war.[47]

The Scottish Chartists – in the 1830s and 1840s – placed their political concerns in a historical context which made reference to Wallace. Without the English tradition of the Norman yoke, it was Wallace's victory against Edward which provided the historical inspiration. Heroes like William Tell and General George Washington were placed alongside the Scots patriot as indicators of how future aims might be realised.[48] As Hamish Fraser concludes, 'A usual implication was that what was needed was a great and enlightened leader'.[49] This, he explains, may be part of the appeal of Fergus O'Connor, despite his aggression being too much for many on the moral force side of the debate in Scotland. John Maclean, writing a century after the Chartists, fixed his analysis to the Scottish sense of community in *The Irish Tragedy: Scotland's Disgrace*:

> My plea is that Britain has no right to dominate Ireland with constabulary armed with bombs and with an army and navy considered foreign to the Irish. We Scots have been taught to revere the names of Sir William Wallace and Robert Bruce because these doughty men of old are recorded as championing the cause of freedom when Edward I and Edward II tried to absorb Scotland as part of English territory. All Scots must therefore appreciate the plight of Ireland, which for over seven centuries has chafed under the same English yoke, and now ought to stand by Ireland in her last great effort for freedom; the last because triumph is bound to be hers very soon.[50]

Non-socialists have been equally at home with the sustained narrative of radicalism in the Wallace story. Andrew Carnegie's preference for Wallace over Bruce – the laird over the king – has been linked back to his radical politics and unorthodox religion: protests which inspired his emigration to America.[51] James Barr's *A History of the Covenantors* (1947) tried to tie such radical religious heritage to the democratic cause of postwar Scotland. It was backed by the *Scots Independent* which did much to foster democratic egalitarianism within Scottish nationalist politics.[52] The socialism–nationalism link was frequently a difficult one, however.

At the 1932 Bannockburn Day meeting organised by the National Party of Scotland in the King's Park at Stirling, John MacCormick's telegram of allegiance to the King was met by the many miners who attended, removing their badges and trampling them into the ground.[53] Others added a more ethnic slant: the Scots National League claimed that the Scots were more socialist in their beliefs, linking Celtic culture and Celtic communism, 'from which Wallace drew his inspirations, we who share his convictions and speak his tongue, will use both to work out freedom for our beloved land'.[54] The Home Ruler Lewis Spence, founding member of the Scottish National Movement in 1926, quoted, with approval, Garibaldi's warm sentiments on the international reputation of the Scottish patriot:

> The name of William Wallace has not only a British but a European reputation. Said Mazzini, the Italian patriot: 'Wallace stands forth from the dim twilight of the past, one of the high prophets of nationality to us all; honour him, worship his memory, teach his name and his deeds to your children'.[55]

Others were wary of nationalism undermining the cause of socialism, but could not deny the pull of its own patriotic content:

> [Scottish radicalism] is far more concerned with Bannockburn, Stirling Bridge, Bruce and Wallace, than it is with the dictatorship of the proletariat and Karl Marx. . . . The Scots Labour man sees himself and his party as the living embodiments of the age-old tradition born of ancestral soil. He loves to think that men of his own kin fought in the past for ideals that are now, however changed in outward guise, fundamentally his own. To him the defenders of Scottish freedom on the battlefield, in the Council Chamber, at the state, in the whelming flood, on the misty hillsides, in desolate hollows of the waste, in Tory-dominated Courts, in the mean rows where miners dwell, all these, and more than these, are brothers. And, indeed, though it is probable that a good deal of the historical detail of this view of Scottish history is

107

not very accurate, who can deny the substantial truth of the main inference drawn from it.[56]

The argument cannot be taken too far, despite the rather surprising ways that the countries of the former Soviet Union and others would celebrate Burns and his doctrine of Scottish equality and freedom. In the 1950s Douglas Young recalled Russian, Polish and Esperanto editions of Burns in production.[57] Internationalism was one thing, but local issues tended to be at the forefront of the early proletarianisation of the myth.

In John Stevenson's *A True Narrative of the Radical Rising* (1835), what is described as the most important comment on Scottish nationalism in the insurrection of 1820 is produced:

> John Morrison, who had fought and beat the French often in the Peninsular wars, laughed heartily at the idea of the yeomanry attacking us, he said he would wager his head against a rotten apple, that twenty-five brave fellows like us would rout a regiment of such vermin; he likewise said, that Wallace and Bruce, had often fought and conquered in the glorious cause of liberty, and that he was proud to see free Scotsmen leave their homes to tread in the footsteps of such illustrious men, and if we are to perish, let us do it nobly, our names will be recorded among Scotland's patriotic sons.[58]

But there is little else at this time, despite attempts to make the most of the same rather thin evidence.[59] By contrast, franchise reform was more innovative in its use of nationalist symbolism. A Grand Procession and National Jubilee was produced to celebrate the Parliamentary Reform Act of 1832 which brought the middle classes – the £10 property holders – into the electoral process and which offered the first glimmer of hope for the industrial and industrious classes:

> The business of the day shall be commenced by vocalists singing the grand national anthem of 'Rule Britannia'; after which the

address to the House of Commons and his Majesty's Ministers, on the triumphant success of the great cause of Reform, will be read and submitted to the meeting, the approval whereof will be accompanied by the Band with 'God Save the King' and the business of the meeting being concluded with 'Scots, wha hae wi Wallace bled'.[60]

There were seventy-one delegates at the procession and number fifty-three was the Wallace Youths Society. They carried two yellow banners, one with the Scottish arms, the other with Wallace's arms and the motto 'God Save the Patriot'. A blue flag was carried which displayed Wallace and Bruce supporting the Scottish shield, with the Royal Arms of Scotland and more mottoes on the reverse.[61] The Lord Advocate, chairing the event, declared that 'We confidently anticipate that we shall be able to record that the first popular election in Edinburgh has not been attended with a single act of intrigue, or any accident of a painful nature'.[62] The passage of the second Reform Act in 1868 was also marked by nationalist symbolism. The bird of freedom was depicted to indicate their freedoms and most mixed variations of the Scottish lion rampant with loyalties expressed to Queen Victoria and British constitutionalism. It was to be a respectable gathering – with no bevy – to further the artisans' claims to the franchise.[63]

Other examples from the political left were sporadic. Research on the Independent Labour Party in the 1920s found nothing of significance to report on the ideological influence of Wallace,[64] nor among the legend of Red Clydeside,[65] radical Paisley,[66] nor the history of the Communist Party in Scotland.[67] Yet some evidence can be found in other political corners. 'Scots Wha Hae' was used as a song of independence by the women's movement in its early years and Wallace was used in Scottish suffragette propaganda.[68] In 1909 suffragettes in Edinburgh took part in a mass demonstration with women pipers accompanying the marches and a historical procession picturing famous Scottish women.[69] One explicit coupling of the Wallace myth with women's rights came in 1912. Ethel Moorhead, who had been arrested in London for damaging two windows in March, smashed the glass at the National Wallace Monument six months later.[70] Upon arrest she gave her name as Edith Johnstone, most likely in an attempt to confuse the authorities. Her stated aim was 'to draw the attention of the people to the fact that their liberty was won by fighting'. Moorhead was held in Stirling prison overnight, then Perth prison for seven days, achieving much publicity on her release by complaining about the conditions there.[71] The nationalist position, of the powerless asking to join the top table, offered inspiration to the women's movement. If not Wallace, then General Garibaldi was the firm favourite. Dorothy Pethnick finished her account of the pain and horror of force-feeding in prison in 1909: 'I used to watch the sunset going down the side of the cell – a streak of light – and I always had a very strong feeling of people like Garibaldi, Mazzini and Joan of Arc with me'.[72] Or, on a more upbeat note: 'We must have a thousand women on this deputation. Garibaldi with his thousand set a nation free. Remember, if we have a thousand, it will be impossible for the government to punish any.'[73]

RHETORIC OF THE PEOPLE

These dual themes have sustained Wallace as the people's champion, and evidence of this can be found in a variety of places. Walter Scott described the Galashiels weavers – who were then unable to get to him across the flooded Tweed – as 'like Wallace and Bruce across the Carron'.[74] Scott was Bruce to the weavers' Wallace, and how he must have enjoyed himself. However, the subject of this chapter has been to show how the rhetoric of proletarianism has been used to sustain both nationalism and socialism, not Scott's Tory Unionism, when constructing the myth. As will be examined later, Wallace becomes a symbol of twentieth-century democracy. From kingship in the medieval years, to radicalism in the eighteenth and unionist-nationalism in the nineteenth centuries, Wallace was now a figure of suffrage and social inclusion. The socialist James Maxton used the occasion of the commemoration of Wallace in 1923 to castigate English people for the arrogance of their domination of the Scots as they had dominated India and Ireland.[75] Lewis Grassic Gibbon, in his discussions with Hugh McDiarmid, declared that he supported Wallace as saviour of the poor over the aristocratic Bruce.[76] By the 1930s the image of religious martyrdom, from the previous century, appears to sit uncomfortably and now the hero is downgraded to the curious term 'proto-martyr':

> From this historic spot, dear to all Scotsmen, we launch this appeal. Centuries ago, Wallace, the proto-martyr of Scottish nationalism, laid down his life for an ideal. Throughout his all too brief career he fought, struggled, and lived for Scotland. His ideal was the freedom of our native land.[77]

This 'freedom' has, of course, changed from empowered local councils to federal and devolved parliaments to independence, but it also includes the suffrage rights of the non-property holders and women. Not national, but cross-national issues, Britain-wide disjunctures find inspiration from the Wallace myth. The people developed a new conception of their rights, class and democracy. The narrative is dominated by the demand for freedom and a political spirit is forged. It was made in distinction to aristocratic vacillating Bruce, as much as it was made complete by Bruce's actions on the field of Bannockburn. The politics of Wallace have now been framed and it has been the nationalists who have carried the myth forward.

SEVEN

Nationalist Wallace

I answer, emphatically and without hesitation, that the people of Great Britain have – as far as it was possible for a people immensely advanced in civilisation to do – bona fide carried out the meaning, design, and objects of the Treaty of Union.[1]

> Scotland, a nation! Our dear mother-land.
> Shall only be ruled by her sons
> Nor more shall she brook the slave's emblem and brand;
> The symbols of bondage she shuns.
> She wakes from the slumbers of years in her might,
> To shatter the cankering chain.
> She calls to her children to rise for her right,
> Ah! shall her appeal be in vain?[2]

The flag of old Scottish sovereignty was a rampant lion. For the North British Collies today the appropriate emblem is an old sheep in a starving pasture being fleeced of its last maggoty wool.[3]

The construction of the Wallace myth has offered a detailed example of the power of 'living memory', taking history from the written book and selling it to the visual and the material world.[4] The filming of the Oscar-winning *Braveheart* (1995) by Hollywood sparked a resurgence of curiosity in the story. In recent years the neo-cult of Wallace has travelled beyond Scotland and entered the realms of an international brand name. *Braveheart*'s run at the cinema was long, the video-release much anticipated and to enthusiasts, limited edition copies (at a premium) were offered. Once consumed, it could be upgraded to the DVD edition, launched on 29 January 2001 with the exhortation to let the legend continue. The official *Braveheart* 'home page' on the internet has now gone, but many others offering 'MacBraveheart'[5] and 'William Wallace: the truth', are readily accessible and dedicated 'to keeping alive the spirit of *Braveheart* (the best motion picture ever) and to the interest in Scottish history, culture and politics which *Braveheart* has helped awaken'.[6] Interest in the film gave a boost to Scottish tourism and the National Wallace Monument in particular, but it has also done much for Scotland's political rhetoric.

All sides of the political spectrum in Scotland have made claim to Wallace's memory. The Scottish National Party has tried hardest to capture this ground. Despite concerns from the film's star and director Mel Gibson and apparently without permission, the SNP has used the film's imagery in its recruitment drives and proclaimed 'Winning with Wallace' to be a realistic aspiration.[7] The MP Andrew Welsh, who addressed the Wallace Rally on 26 August 1995, was hoping to share the platform with Mel Gibson who had been invited.[8] The then party leader, Alex Salmond, presented a copy of an advertisement for the film as his contribution to the representations of twentieth-century Scotland in the Museum of Scotland. The SNP were not alone in avowing Wallace's guardianship of Scotland and his fight against the English as being symbolic of Scotland's constitutional position in the late twentieth century. Others have joined in the attempt to cash in on the story, all promoting their commitment to Scotland.[9] The Secretary of State for Scotland at the time, Michael Forsyth used the events to proclaim 'Be a patriot, not a nationalist' in support of his Conservative administration.[10] After viewing the film in a special screening with Mel Gibson, Forsyth produced an extra £100,000 to be given to the Scottish Tourist Board (STB) to market the film abroad[11] with special focus on the market in France and Germany.[12] It was money well spent, and the STB estimated it had received over £11 million worth of free advertising from *Braveheart* and *Rob Roy* (1995), with eleven per cent of visitors to Scotland in 1995 rising to twenty-six per cent in 1996, claiming they had come as a response to viewing the heroics of Gibson as Wallace or Neeson as Roy.[13]

UNIONISM-NATIONALISM

This chapter explores how the nationalists have constructed and made political use of the Wallace myth. Others have also found their own niche in this many-sided myth, yet it would seem strange not to dedicate a little time to those who have been explicit in the use of nationalism to mobilise opinion around a political programme. Indeed, the construction of the Wallace myth by nationalist groupings has a longer history than the modern-day SNP. The National Association for the Vindication of Scottish Rights (NAVSR) (1852–56), the first of such movements, cherry-picked favourite elements of the historical past to demand the restoration of Scottish rights.[14] It was a movement which, in today's language, would be called cross-party, such was the heterogeneous composition of its leadership. The brothers James and John Grant used their literary skills to produce a myriad of pamphlets, petitions and newspaper contributions to make their case that Scotland's right as a nation, not a region of Britain, should be recognised in complete equality with England in matters of taxation, expenditure and parliamentary time.[15] The chairman was the romantic Tory the Earl of Eglinton and Winton and the membership included representatives from the town councils of Scotland, with provosts providing representation from Ardrossan to Stirling. There were many from the professional classes, but never a mass of people, despite the spread of affiliated branches.[16] It is a period renowned for its Jacobite sentimentalism and romantic notions of a lost chivalric age: Eglinton organised a medieval tournament on his lands in 1839 – an event the managers of EuroDisney or the Millennium Dome would have been proud to have staged.[17]

The NAVSR combined Scottish and British heroes, at its very first public meetings in Edinburgh and Glasgow to launch its claims: 'We glory in the triumph of a Marlborough, a Nelson and a Wellington, but might we not look with pride to the achievements of a Wallace and a Bruce?'[18] James Begg, writing on the issue of the forty-shilling freehold, declared that '[n]otwithstanding the dreams of missionaries, and our monuments to Knox and Wallace, Scotland must either reconquer her liberty, or run the risk of sinking into the basest of kingdoms'.[19] Its evocation of Wallace was not to further mere sentimental musings over a dram, but to make detailed judgements on past and future trends in Scotland's governance. The nationalism of the NAVSR, which was framed within explicit loyalty to the Union, focused on how Scottish rights had been established on a par with those of England in the Union of 1707. Now, it was argued, those rights were lost because Westminster was too large and unwieldy, insensitive and unaccountable to local people and local needs: 'the crushing policy of centralisation . . . has placed Scotland in a position little better than Yorkshire or any other English county'.[20] In one contemporary analysis it was claimed that 'It is not the civil service which is to blame, but the political branch of the administration.' This author argued that the civil service was recruited to serve political interests, not to achieve efficiency.[21] It was the kind of inference which gave weight to the nationalists' assertions that the political integrity of Britain had been compromised by undermining municipal government. In these debates, it was how Scotland achieved this equality – through Union – that the Wallace myth was used and even added to. Here the link is made between Wallace (d.1305) and Bruce (d.1329) and the joining of Scotland and England in 1707. Four centuries of discord were wiped away as the two medieval patriots were thanked for bringing Scotland and England together into peaceful eighteenth-century Union. This was most explicit in an attempt to build a monument to Wallace and Bruce in Edinburgh in 1859: 'It is the deliverance and its results, as distinguished from the Deliverers.' It was entitled *A National Memorial of the War of Independence under Wallace and Bruce and its Results in the Union of England and Scotland to be Erected in the Metropolis in Scotland.*

The rhetoric of this period, as was seen in the analysis of the chapbook literature, was far removed from the anti-English bile which marked Harry and its reprints in the Scots vernacular. Here the great patriots of Wallace and Bruce achieved Scotland's freedom, allowing the people to come as a free nation to the Union and, as the argument developed, how much greater that freedom had become and would continue to flourish, if only that equality was adhered to.

This was how Scottish nationalism could be pro-Unionist. Unionist-nationalism became the prefered constitutional solution, because it did not add to the remit of central government, be it at Westminster or a devolved body at Edinburgh, but instead made the locality, and local government, the guarantor of those freedoms. The solution of the NAVSR was not to add another layer of centralised government, which a Scottish parliament would do, but to strengthen the independence of local government in both town and country. It explains the involvement of Scotland's town councillors. It sustained the politicisation of national identity which was against independent nation-statehood: good legislation was only possible from local action and local appointments.[22]

The belief that the independence of the town councils was essential to Scottish national identity was one offered as the basis of Scottish citizenship rights: the good burgher was the good citizen. It was carried through the 1880s into the first two decades of the twentieth century with support for municipal trading and, on occasion, municipal socialism. The local politician was a force to be reckoned with and who embodied the spirit of respectability and civic duty:

> In the homely burghs of Scotland we may find the first spring of that public spirit, the voice of the people, which in the worst of times, when the Crown and the law were powerless and feudal aristocracy altogether selfish in its views, supported the patriot leaders, Wallace and Bruce, in their desperate struggle, and sent down that tide of native feeling which animated Burns and Scott, and which is not yet dead. . . . Whatever of thought, of enterprise, of public feeling, appears in our poor history took rise in our burghs and among the burgess class.[23]

The end of the NAVSR coincided with the events in Crimea. Momentum had clearly been lost, but the war provided the excuse for getting out with the patriotic flag still flying.[24] Some, such as Sawers, celebrated British victories in Russia as they wrote.[25] It helped tie Wallace to the best of warrior heroes in history. It was a path Walter

116

Scott had trod in earlier years: he had not been averse to offering the services of the thirteenth-century patriot for contemporary conflicts in Europe: 'A Wallace, Dundee, or Montrose, would be the man for Spain at this moment.' These were times he likened to the 'days of Wallace'.[26] Likewise, a century later, the First World War was described as futile, 'with success only possible if war is noble, as in the achievements of Wallace and his army'. Whatever the contemporary politics, the mid-nineteenth-century Wallaciana made plain that these military exploits were honoured in themselves and not for their English blood-letting, which so marked Harry's creation:

> The writer of these pages has a great respect for English people, and does much business with many of them; but he cannot see how a judicious history of our hero should give them any offence, for they have enjoyed all the benefits resulting from his achievements as much as we (the Scots) have done.[27]

Quoting approvingly a 'living English historian', Hutchison's political comment from 1859, surmised: 'The Englishman who now reads of the deeds of Wallace or of Bruce, or hears the stirring words of one of the noblest lyrics, feels that the call to 'lay the proud usurpers low', is one which stirs the blood as much as that of the Scotsman'.[28] Wallace was to be shared, Scotland and England were now blessed by a Union of equals, and now each had the right to have their respective prides raised by the warrior-patriot.

HOME RULE ALL ROUND

The remnants of the NAVSR wound up in the National Wallace Monument Movement. It first met in 1859, being in a position to lay the foundation stone two years later. Despite the events of 1869, when the monument was finally opened, there was a gap in the organisation of Scottish national identity until the Scottish Home Rule Association was formed in 1886. Of its active leadership, only John Romans bridged the thirty year gap. These nationalists were still Unionist, but the argument for federalism, mobilised through the Liberal Party, was a new departure. Their rationale was not different, however. It was still based on the evils of centralisation at Westminster, the inequalities of the Exchequer and the lack of parliamentary time for discussion of Scottish legislation.[29] Moir, for example mirrored the arguments of the NAVSR when he introduced his study of Harry in 1888:

> Had the result of Edward's wars in Scotland been to make him its lord, we might have had today a Scottish Home Rule Question as difficult to settle as the Irish one. The aggression of Edward only helped to consolidate Scotland and make the country not a geographical expression, but a nation. Dr Arnold of Rugby points out that the battles of Bannockburn and Orleans, in both of which the English were defeated, were really blessings for England. The one secured the independence of Scotland, the other put an end to the English pretensions to a continental sovereignty. The conquest of Ireland, on the other hand, was complete, with the result that the Irish have always been dissatisfied with their position, whereas the Scots can look back to the Wars of Independence with pride, and can feel that when the Union took place it was between equals, and not between a conquered and a conquering nation.[30]

Charles Waddie, William Mitchell, Dr G.B. Clark, MP for Caithness, and J.S. Blackie comprised the remainder of the leadership and all were active in penning pamphlets and submitting letters to the newspaper to further their cause. Failure to persuade Gladstone to place Scotland's claims alongside those of Ireland, despite his brief support during his first Midlothian campaign, an issue he then tried to avoid on subsequent visits, was a constant sore.[31] Nor could the SHRA persuade Rosebery that the creation of the Scottish Office was no substitute for a federal structure.[32] Despite his belief in Imperial Federation, Rosebery was remarkably lukewarm to such reform at home.[33] Both failures confined the SHRA to the margins of Scottish and British politics.[34] This did not stop an immensely active propaganda campaign in the regional press, politicising national identity, although still not of itself influencing party politics.[35] The

13. *The Story of William Wallace*, by Lewis Spence. (*Oxford University Press*)

PRO LIBERTATE

ENSIGNS ARMORIAL
OF
HUGH ROBERT WALLACE ESQUIRE OF BUSBIE AND CLONCAIRD
HEAD AND REPRESENTATIVE OF THE WALLACE FAMILY

14. The Wallace clan coat of arms with the motto *Pro Libertate*, the frontispiece of *The Book of Wallace* (Vol. 1) by Charles Rogers (1889), published by the Grampian Club, Edinburgh. (*National Library of Scotland*)

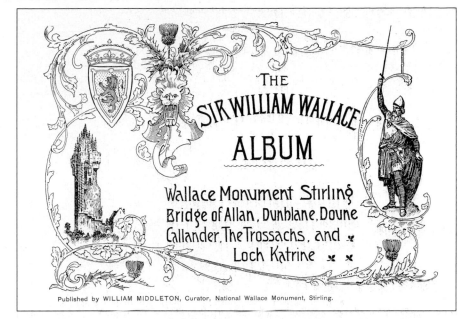

15. *The Sir William Wallace Album* (1904). (*National Library of Scotland*)

16. An advertisement for the National Wallace Monument. (*National Library of Scotland*)

17. A Wallace statue being restored by Graciella Ainsworth at Dryburgh. (*Peter Kemp*)

18. Clan Wallace postcard. The first Wallaces are thought to have been Britons who settled in the ancient kingdom of Strathclyde after being forced to move north in the tenth century. The inset picture shows present Wallace family members charging into battle during the filming of *Braveheart*. (*Lang Syne publishers*)

19. Like its famous namesake Wallace IPA, Maclay's India pale ale is strong and proud to be Scottish. (*Maclay Brewery*)

20. The Wallace statue in Aberdeen, unveiled in 1888, two years after the formation of the Scottish Home Rule Association. The statue was built with funds bequeathed by John Steill. (*Author's collection*)

ERECTED
to the
MEMORY
of that
CELEBRATED
SCOTTISH HERO
SIR WILLIAM
WALLACE
2nd Auguſt
1810

21. The monument at Wallacestone overlooking Falkirk, built in 1810, marks the site of Wallace's defeat in 1298. (*Author's collection*)

22. Freedom! Mel Gibson as Wallace. This statue by Tom Church was placed in the car park of the National Wallace Monument in 1998. A special cage has been constructed to protect it from vandalism. (*Author's collection*)

23. This lorry cab was seen in a car park in Falkirk on 20 August 2000, the second *Braveheart* Day, while yet another screening of *Braveheart* goes on in the cinema. (*Author's collection*)

composition of its membership was little different from the NAVSR, mixing old Liberal radicals with younger politicos and the odd disaffected aristocrat.[36] It was formed on the back of Gladstone's first Home Rule Bill for Ireland being presented to parliament, which gave the movement its early impetus.[37] The Irish situation was to became its nemesis, as Ireland, not the Scots, received cross-party discussion.[38] Writing in the newspapers in 1896, Charles Waddie recalled an earlier trip to Dublin, made in an effort to join the claims of the two Celtic countries into the All Round principle. While applauding the hospitality he received, Waddie was clearly marginalised by his hosts:

> it was painfully evident to me that they cared not two straws about anybody's interest but their own. It was Ireland, first, last and only. We have repeatedly invited the Irish Nationalists to join the Scottish, but they have always refused, and recently they in the most offensive manner declared if the Liberal Party took up Home Rule All Round they would vote against them.[39]

A decade after its formation, the SHRA was caught in the harm Irish home rule was causing to their own claims: 'Let our Liberal leaders drop "Ireland first" and patriotically and logically include their own country as well as Ireland. This will make the case a stronger one, and England (with Scotland, Ireland and Wales demanding Home Rule) will not long continue opposing their combined demand'.[40] The first phase of the Scottish Home Rule Association was becoming moribund by the late 1890s because of this political failure. However, one response was to develop the cultural roots of Scottishness, in the hope that it would arouse the voters from apathy towards the home rulers. Theodore Napier, from Melbourne, of the SHRA and later, member of the Scottish Patriotic Association, in complaining that the Scots were indifferent to their political subjugation, used Wallace to inspire them:

> They are more interested in a football or a golf match than in the political welfare and freedom of their country. Was it for

this our great hero-patriot Wallace struggled for so long and lost his life? Was it not for the object of delivering Scotland from English aggression and predominance? Do we not hail Bruce as the successful champion of our independence from English thralldom? And yet we have basely surrendered our political freedom to England. For a country that does not govern itself cannot be regarded as free.[41]

Napier was also secretary of the Wallace Robroyston Memorial.[42] The *Montrose Review* of 22 May 1896 carried a poem of Bannockburn which used Wallace's contribution as a never-ending inspiration:

> Shades o' the immortal Wallace,
> Bruce an' Burns tae duty call us,
> Shail we let oor foes enthrall us,
> Merit thy eternal scorn;
> Shall thy monuments revile us,
> Base degenerate cowards style us,
> Frae thy bluid-bocht gift exile us,
> Freedom gained at Bannockburn?[43]

In the same week the movement gained publication for the verse 'Patriot Scot', which likewise took Bruce as consummating the legacy of Wallace:

> Hoo noble Wallace in the strife,
> For independence lost his life,
> A martyr tae the headsman's knife,
> An' despot's ire,
> Whilk nocht but bribes and traiters rife,
> Cud e'er acquire?
>
> An' hoo the Bruce, wi royal micht,
> Avenged that deed as dark as nicht,
> An saved intact oor country's right,
> A nation's place,

An' left her bairns wi honour bricht
A free born race.[44]

It was Bannockburn, not Stirling Bridge, which acted as the focus
to valorise the life of Wallace. In 1896 the Scottish Home Rule
Association marked the 582nd anniversary of Bruce's great victory
with the now orthodox view that it was Bruce who avenged the
death of Wallace, and completed his work. They confirmed it in
verse spoken at Bannockburn field:

> Departed heroes! Whose great presence now
> We feel around us on this hallowed spot!
> No eloquence is needed to tell how
> Your noble deeds shall never be forgot!
> Scotland had fallen – lay bleeding on the ground,
> And basely trampled on by southron foes,
> And Wallace wight was dead, her martyred chief;
> And everywhere around
> Was dark and stormy when Bruce arose
> And with his valiant comrades brought relief.
> . . .
> And friendly voices speak across the Tweed,
> And we are brethren now, no longer foes;
> Each helps the other in the hour of need,
> And mutual love with every season grows.
> We are both loyal to one common crown,
> But claim to have our Parliament restored.
> Scotland shall never leave the task undone
> Till she get back her own,
> Her name and nationhood; nor cease to guard
> The sacred freedom which her heroes won.[45]

Rather than focus on Elderslie or Abbey Craig, the 600th
anniversary of the Battle of Stirling Bridge was marked by verse
published in a range of Scottish newspapers and over forty
newspapers in the USA, indicating the importance this date marked

at least in the minds of the newspaper editors: 'Where'er our eyes we turn/Twas here that glorious Wallace fought –/There, Bruce at Bannockburn'.[46] In 1899 Waddie staged a series of historical plays in an attempt to stimulate Scottish patriotism, including 'Wallace' and 'The Bruce'.[47] It was a decade which witnessed a marked resurrection of Bruce as the key patriot. John Romans, for example, mentions Bruce and the Declaration of Arbroath, not Wallace, when introducing his case for Home Rule for Scotland, wishing to 'celebrate the glorious day of freedom on 24 June', Bannockburn Day. Although, to be fair, he did then exhort the Scottish people to teach all children over the age of ten the words of 'Scots wha hae'.[48] In 1896 Theodore Napier contributed the following verse:

> Scotland awake – why sleep'st thou now
> Beneath the yoke which galls thy brow?
> Land of the brave, the fair, the free,
> Hark to the voice of Liberty!
>
> Land of the Bruce, awake, reply,
> Assert your rights, avenge or die!
> Break now your chain, be free, ye brave,
> Nor live degraded – England's Slave![49]

William Mitchell wrote a short history of Bannockburn for the *Stirling Observer* in 1893 which was then picked up in pamphlet form by the publishers of the Scottish Home Rule Association.[50] Napier wrote to the *Stirling Observer* on 17 August 1896, to remind the people of Stirling of the approaching 591st anniversary of Wallace's execution, clearly worried that amnesia had set in, but, if anything, it stimulated interest in Bruce rather than Wallace.[51] Elsewhere, these nationalists contributed to the Wallace literature themselves. J. Morrison Davidson, writing in 1893, linked Wallace to the demand for Home Rule, quoting the following, with approval:

'Nothing', says Goldwin Smith, 'contributed more than the distinct national character (entirely Wallace's work), and the distinct national religion of the Scots to save Britain from being entirely subjugated by the absolutism of Strafford and the Anglicanisation of Laud.'[52]

Other events could be brought into the equation as well. Davidson used Wallace in his analysis of the Boer War: 'William Wallace, the stainless knight of Elderslie, was the Scottish Kruger and Steyn, Botha, de la Rey and De Wit rolled into one. In contrast [to] an unreasoning anti-Boer' which was typical, he argued, of the English.[53] Others, such as Sir Archibald H. Dunbar, while contributing to the dating of Harry's *Wallace*, plumping for about 1460, could not resist the honour of being allowed to have his first edition dedicated to Queen Victoria.[54] Mitchell celebrated the inauguration of the cross at Kinghorn for Alexander III, which marked the most quoted point of origin for any explanation of Wallace's rise to prominence.[55] It was the kind of royalism which prioritised Bruce over Wallace, and it sat alongside a sanitised radical legitimation of Wallace by modern heroes like Burns and Garibaldi.[56]

When the Scottish Home Rule Association folded in 1900, the mantle was taken up by the Young Scots Society (YSS) which formed in that year. The society was very much a Liberal Party organisation, becoming particularly active on the issues of free trade, temperance, education and working-class poverty.[57] Only after 1909 did the YSS focus all its attentions on Scotland's governance and it did achieve some electoral success up to 1914.[58] It published greatly and produced leaflets in the thousands.[59] It was argued, among politicians of the Empire, that Home Rule in Britain was the question that most excited the dominions – with the considered interpretation that Scotland would be content with land reform and some vague promise of Home Rule all round following legislation for Ireland.[60] It was an intransigence which blocked any headway.

Others played the patriotic British card when seeking to show how Wallace's fight for independence could affect current events. Lewis Spence, soon to form the Scottish National Movement from the disaffected in the Scots National League in 1926, was influenced to compile his story of Wallace as the First World War was coming to a close:

... in older days men did not stop to discover whether their cause was right or wrong. It was enough for them to know that their country was at war. The land in which they lived was sacred to them, and to defend it was part of their religion. Their patriotism and their faith was as one.[61]

Spence built up his personal nationalism as one of most profound belief, a life's-purpose, and he projected this through the Wallace story: 'To him [Wallace] patriotism was a religion, deep, passionate, intense.'[62] The story was used as a resource to politicise and mobilise national identity: 'We cannot all be Wallaces, but we can all serve the land that gave us birth as our strength or abilities permit.'[63] Spence insisted that the hero's father Malcolm Wallace was a member of the lower landed gentry, a squire or laird in the land of Ellerslie or Elderslie.[64] He keeps Wallace's place within the rhetoric of Unionism-nationalism, even if politically Spence wished to bend the Union more than most, if not to break it. Yet he does it in the cause of freedom, as an international cry, which, he argued, continued after the hanging and quartering of the patriot:

> ... though Wallace was no more, the patriotic soul which animated him lived on and inspired the people of Scotland to still greater efforts in the cause of liberty. Through his life and work, Scotland was enabled to keep her self-respect and to make a Union with England on equal terms, instead of becoming a second Ireland. Edward's tyrannical wickedness was short-lived, for only nine years after Wallace's death . . . Scotland had become a nation once more by the brilliant victory at Bannockburn.

Despite these nationalist statements, the amorphous establishment which fixed opinion at Westminster displayed complacency that the Scots would continue to accept the Union, despite the neglect of their affairs.[65]

SCOTTISH PATRIOTIC ASSOCIATION

Objects. – The cultivation of the spirit of Patriotism: the defence of Scotland's national rights: the study of Scottish History, and the proper teaching of it in our schools, &c. All patriotic Scots are invited to join. Apply to the *Treasurer*, Mr. Wm. Bowes, Offices of the Association, 74 Bath Street, Glasgow.[66]

INDEPENDENCE

By the 1920s federal home rule was losing to the rhetoric of independence, but organisationally there were problems. The celebrations at Elderslie did continue, despite the many party schisms. In the Revd James Barr's address at the Wallace Memorial on 27 August 1921, Wallace was proclaimed as the only prominent Scot not to have changed sides during the Wars of Independence. Wallace's simplistic loyalty to the people of Scotland was put up to contrast with the sophisticated (and therefore untrustworthy and personally motivated) actions of Bruce. Unlike the pro-Unionism of the nineteenth-century nationalists, Barr received great cheers for his resurrection of the radical sentiment of betrayal, bribery and English gold:

> Above all, their patriotism sought to recover for Scotland her lost Parliament, her free institutions, her ancient independence. How she lost her Parliament all the world knows – by the most shameless bribery ever known in the most corrupt ages of human history'.[67]

Note, interestingly, the mixed-up chronology, which is full of implications that Wallace was trying to recover the 1707 loss. It is no surprise, then, that the verse of Robert Burns was recited to rouse the gathering:

Be Britain still to Britain true,
Among ourselves united!
For never but by British hands
Mauny British wrongs be righted!

. . .

Be Scotsmen still to Scotsmen true
Among ourselves united!
For never by Scottish hands
Mauny Scottish wrongs be righted![68]

Barr failed to guide his Bill on Home Rule through parliament in 1927 and it appeared to take much out of the Scots National League and the Scottish Home Rule Association during its second phase.[69] Cultural events did continue and the Scottish Historical Pageant at Craigmillar Castle near Edinburgh from 14 to 16 July 1927, had, in the interlude, some 'hardy Scots, remembering the traditions of Wallace and Bruce, [to] fit themselves to bear arms for their native land, should the need arise'. Some mention of the medieval patriots then, but the re-created historical episodes, involving 3,000 performers watched by 50,000 ticket holders, were predominantly from the sixteenth century.[70] They fitted the usual pattern, identified by Lynch, whereby the Middle Ages were downplayed in favour of the post-Reformation triumph of Protestantism.[71] The Wars of Independence were not the chosen focus here and politically there was a short lull in the Wallaciana.

The demise of the Edinburgh branch of the SHRA in 1929 was marked by its executive committee inviting George Mavers, MP for west Edinburgh, in a strictly social capacity, to receive and hand over gifts of commemoration for those who served the branch.[72] The National Party of Scotland (NPS) was to take up much of the slack and at the 624th celebration at Elderslie in that year, the NPS President Roland Muirhead regarded the 'fully 1,000 people' who attended as evidence 'of the gradual awakening of the spirit of Scottish nationalism'.[73] In 1931 R.B. Cunninghame Graham could feel the 'demand for home rule in the air all over the world' and 'since the war many states have risen into being, and if these states were worthy of independence, surely it was a strange thing if Scotland, the best educated of all, should be the one State without it.'[74] Like the NAVSR, however, he did not want Scotland to be just favoured with nationalism, but to receive it out of rights and do it as an independent nation: 'if angels come down from heaven today to govern Scotland, we would say, get your wings ready and fly back again. We can govern ourselves better than any outside power'.[75]

This was a time of central government control over a more streamlined local government, following its reform in the Local Government (Scotland) Act of 1929. Other bodies were formed to structure Scotland's governance and civil society at this time, which moved the debate from the locality towards that of national parliament. The National Trust for Scotland (1931), the Saltire Society (1936) and the Gilmour Report (1937), which precipitated the move of the Scottish Office from London to Edinburgh, are rightly identified as marking a change in perceptions of how the state should intervene in society.[76] As it developed, the Scottish Office adopted a more corporatist approach to government and the move north and the slow expansion of its staff and in the seniority of its leadership, revealed the ideological shift in the superiority of central over local government.[77]

Taking evidence from a selection of the Wallace commemorations at Elderslie offers a simple indicator of the nationalist politicisation of that memory. It leaves the world of abstract politics – of freedom, of community, socialism, of loyalty and self-sacrifice – and becomes focused on contemporary politicking. The Commemoration Day in 1933 was important for it was at a time which marked the final moves towards the creation of the Scottish National Party out of various tensions and nationalist structures. That particular Wallace Day was chaired by the veteran Roland Muirhead with Cunninghame Graham leading the speakers.[78] The latter framed his interpretation of the lasting value of Wallace's life history as one directly relevant to the pressures facing the Scottish economy:

[Wallace] saw the problems from many angles. Firstly he fought for an independent state. But he did not forget that no man can live upon ideals than upon bread alone. Wallace saw this in his short vagrancy. His first care was to make treaties with foreign states and to foster Scottish trade. We must imitate him and take in hand our bread and butter questions. Look at the Clyde, as silent and as shipless as the Orinoco. While Liberals, Socialists and Tories fight their mimic wars at Westminster, Scottish questions are postponed or neglected. We call on Scotsmen, and above all Scotswomen – the hand that rocks the cradle shapes the man – to join the National Party, and not allow the martyrdom of Wallace to be lost.[79]

The speech by R.M. Black proclaimed that Wallace was the highest personification of the virtues of our race: 'he was no imported ruler, no feudal baron preying upon the land, no hireling of any foreign overlord.' The Commemorative Programme for the day carried the words to 'Scots Wha Hae', Scotland's 'national anthem', and a picture of a Wallace demonstration held at Suva, Fiji, in the South Pacific. This expatriate romanticism was placed alongside the more mundane, a plea from the Scottish Co-operative Wholesale Society:

Pending the full recognition of Scotland's right to manage her own affairs, every Scotsman and Scotswoman can do something to promote the prosperity of their own country. They must recognise that the most pressing need of the present day is the development of Scottish industries. This object has been kept steadily in view by the Scottish Co-operative Wholesale Society ever since its inception 65 years ago.[80]

At the Bannockburn Day rally held by the SNP in Stirling's King's Park in 1935, Sir Alexander Malcolm MacEwen said that Stirling Bridge and Bannockburn are still names that thrill.[81] Now the history of Wallace and his links to Bruce are confined to single victorious battles. The complexity of their respective relationships to the community of the realm and to Scotland's nobility, or even Wallace's martyrdom, was lost. A decade later, the ongoing war did not stop the commemoration at Elderslie. The polymath and nationalist Douglas Young produced some of the most singular pronouncements of any of these occasions:

> William Wallace would never have believed that a day could come when Scotsmen would be hauled off like sheep to defend far-flung tracts of the London profiteer's empire, while the defence of the Scottish homeland was committed to the polyglot and heterogeneous influx of Poles, Czechs, Anglo-Saxons, Negroes and other species. Incidentally, conscription furth of Scotland is unconstitutional under the Scots-English Treaty of 1707, which instituted a lamentable affair called Great Britain.[82]

The racist element was a product of its time, but Young has linked Wallace to the mass movement of refugees around mainland Europe. The same analogy was made to the effects of state propaganda, not against Nazi Germany, but modern Scotland:

> The English took the guts out of Wallace in a literal way, by their butchery in Smithfield Market. They take the guts, and the wits, out of modern so-called Scots, more correctly North Britons, by continued intensive propaganda through the schools, the radio, cinema, Press, Kirks and numerous other ways.[83]

Young used the language of democracy: 'that Wallace was a constitutional officer of our kingdom of the Scots, namely Guardian, appointed under the authority of the Estates.'[84] In his electoral activity, fighting the Kirkcaldy by-election of 1944, he again displayed his opposition to the war, obtaining a respectable 41.3 per cent of the vote, but by losing only 800 votes in the 1945 general election his share in third place was down to 17 per cent.[85]

129

Election	Candidate	Party	Votes	%
1944	T.F. Hubbard	Labour	8,268	51.6
	D.C.C. Young	SNP	6,621	41.3
	H. Hilditch	Christian Socialist	1,136	7.1
1945	T.F. Hubbard	Labour	15,401	45.0
	C.E.G. Guest	Conservative	10,099	29.5
	D.C.C. Young	SNP	5,811	17.0
	J. McArthur	Communist	2,898	8.5

Young was twice imprisoned for his refusal to be conscripted.[86] In contrast, perhaps, Dr Robert McIntyre had made his appeal to the electors of Wishaw with the claim: 'I stand for the democratic freedom of the Scottish people to run their own affairs', chastising Labour and Unionist MPs for casting adrift Scotland's concerns. At the April 1945 by-election, McIntyre became the SNP's first MP, securing 51 per cent of the vote, although losing his seat twelve weeks later at the general election.[87] Such patriotism was still not evident in the Scottish nationalists of the 1950s. The anniversary of the SHRA and NPS former president R.B. Cunninghame Graham's birth (he died on 20 March 1936) was marked by the Young Scots National League in a gathering at the lake of Menteith on 24 May 1952, an event closed with 'Scots Wha Hae'.[88] In the celebration of Wallace Day on 22 August 1953, the procession to the Elderslie monument was presented with an 'exact replica' of the Wallace sword which was then carried in a procession comprising representatives from all branches of the Young Scots and Fianna Na H-Alba, an event followed by the 1953 Celtic Congress.[89] In the Scots Secretariat's pamphlet on Wallace produced in 1955, the war is not remembered for its *esprit de corps*:

> Even in the recent world war of 1939–45, the northern country found itself denuded of its young manhood, conscripted for war service, and its young womanhood likewise, while its territory itself was flooded by southerners and foreigners fleeing from the horrors of a war which English politicians did so much to promote.[90]

The pamphlet *How Scots opposed the peacetime call-up*, published by the Scots Secretariat, clarified the party's motives, justifying its lack of British patriotism.[91] It concluded with a 'Buy Scottish' campaign,[92] in contrast to John Bull and his bulldog in the 'Buy British' rhetoric.[93] Produced to commemorate the 650th anniversary of the patriot's death, it used the occasion to belittle the efforts of the 'English-controlled' political parties to satisfy the demand for home rule. The Conservative and Unionist Party was painted as having never made Home Rule part of its platform and was accused of following a policy of increased centralisation of government. Despite Keir Hardie's Scottish credentials, home rule was also lost among the 'witch-hunting gang of power-greedy wire-pullers who now dictate the policies of the Labour Party'. The name of the patriot was called to remedy this neglect: 'The story of William Wallace is an inspiration to the modern Scot in the struggle he is called upon to pursue'.[94] From the twentieth century to the thirteenth century, a connection was made.

A survey of the pamphlet and campaign literature of the SNP in the decades which followed suggest there was not much appeal to the memory of Wallace or to Bruce – its explanatory power for contemporary politics appeared to have been lost.[95] Social, economic and democratic claims could be wrapped in the Wallace myth in the 1920s, 1930s and 1940s respectively but faltered thereafter. Ian Hamilton for instance, argued for practical not emotional issues to come to the fore.[96] The 1950s were a decade of direct cultural protest: the theft of the stone of destiny, the fire-bombing of postboxes displaying EIIR (there never was an Elizabeth I in Scotland) and Wendy Wood's ink-filled egg-bombing of the offending royal shield on a lamp post on Edinburgh's North Bridge on the morning of King Olaf's visit in 1962.[97] Wood's left-wing credentials perhaps endeared her more than most to the medieval martyr, seeing 'Freedom as of the same content down the ages', linking the time of Wallace and Bruce to Czechoslovakia in the 1950s and 1960s.[98]

However, when the SNP launched an appeal for funds it chose to evoke the spirit of St Andrews and not Wallace in 1962.[99] The

'Ladybird' children's story of Bruce, from 1964, makes only two mentions of Wallace, his rebellion which Bruce joined and his defeat at Falkirk, from which point Edward had believed Scotland subdued.[100] Nor was Wallace trumpeted as the inspiration when the SNP made its modern, political breakthrough, with Winnie Ewing's by-election victory in 1968 in Hamilton, normally a Labour heartland, held until the 1970 general election. That governance took over from democratic deficit continued in the Kilbrandon Report of 1973 – a document strong on administration, but short on inspiration from a chivalric past. Indeed, in this respect it was no different from the 1980s' Constitutional Convention and its *Claim of Right* (1988), although the latter embodied the power of the people's will in some stirring rhetoric. In response, the Conservative Administration's 'Taking Stock' programme, *Scotland and the Union: A Partnership for Good*, defined Scotland's history as successful through Union.

The 1970 general election had seen gains in the popular vote, but the high point of SNP success came in the October 1974 election with eleven MPs being elected. The claim to Scotland's oil was the single most important campaigning gambit, but it was not enough to overwhelm the referendum on a Scottish parliament conducted in 1979. The popular vote was in favour of devolution for Scotland. However, George Cunnigham's clause requiring that 40 per cent of the whole electorate, not just of votes cast, be in favour, meant the nationalists' hopes were dashed. Splits then occurred, one of which, the '79 Group, held its first meeting on Saturday 18 August 1979 with around seventy people attending, co-chaired by Margo MacDonald and Andrew Currie.[101]

During the last quarter of the twentieth century practical politics made little of its emotive and rabble-rousing past, so marginalising Wallace. At the end of its last decade, by contrast, clear lines have been drawn on the ideological claims to Scotland's medieval patriots. The royal versus radical divide has again surfaced. Apart from its importance as a tourist attraction, Edinburgh Castle is a powerful medium which connects Scottish people to the myths of the Scottish past and draws them, directly and indirectly, into the politics of present-day Scotland. The symbolic importance of the castle for the Scottish people is illustrated by the concerns of a *Sunday Post* reader:

> I'm appalled Historic Scotland is allowing Sean Connery to hire Edinburgh Castle for what amounts to his own personal Hollywood-style Oscars party. He's only a public entertainer who has made vast sums of money from success in his chosen profession. While I don't begrudge Sean his success or wealth, it's entirely wrong that Edinburgh Castle, a part of Scotland's heritage, should be used for such a purpose. It's all the more regrettable since Sean Connery, in spite of previously living as a tax exile in Spain, is now a prominent supporter of the SNP. Though there will presumably be no overt SNP propaganda there to avoid it being included in election expenses, such a high profile event so soon before the Scottish parliamentary elections will obviously be of immense advantage to the SNP. It is outrageous Historic Scotland should even contemplate such a deal.[102]

At the end of the twentieth century it seems that the symbolic importance of 'capturing' the castle is still a very political issue. Any use for the castle, or its presentation, not fitting the 'official' communication with the past – of royal Scotland – was criticised as objectionable and biased. Of the castle's place in Scottish politics and society, the tourist is left with an interpretation long unchanged. Yet it is one increasingly hard to maintain as radical Wallace again takes over from royal Bruce. This chapter began with three contrasting quotes which displayed the language of the nationalist movement in its early years. In its current incarnation it is not royal or federal or unionist Scotland which dominates the rhetoric, it is instead the language of independence. My conclusion, and final example, comes from the leader of the SNP in the *Braveheart* years: 'So that we can say with Wallace – head and heart – the one word which encapsulates all our hopes – Freedom, Freedom, Freedom.'[103]

wallace.com

Death seed blind man's greed
Poets' starving children bleed
Nothing he's got he really needs
Twenty first century schizoid man[1]

TWENTY-FIRST-CENTURY SCHIZOID MAN

By now the reader should be no closer to finding the real
Wallace. If you have followed this text on its journey here to
chapter eight – its close – then you might just be hoping the author
will go on and tell you who this Wallace really was. You ask, but
you really know the answer anyway. Wallace fought and beat the
English, he was betrayed before suffering an unfair trial and a
barbaric execution. He was and is Scotland's political martyr. That's
all we need to know, and the historian can tell us where the evidence
is stronger and where it is not – but that doesn't alter the story, does
it? Historians just want to spoil the story, but they can't break it,
right?

Right. We can't break the story, because there is no story. There
are some corroborated facts, which can be put together into a
narrative, but that is quite inconsequential. The Wallace story is not
a singular but a plural. It is not a book, it is a phenomenon. The
Wallace myth is a collective. It is a gathering of many stories which
overlap and borrow content, style and substance from one another.
No wonder there is little point debunking the history of Wallace,
because our target forever changes. National identity may be a
category on a form, but it flows from a state of mind. The very idea
of the imagined community, that eloquent phrase coined by Benedict
Anderson, stresses national identity through recollection and under-

standing, among people who have never met. A sense of nationhood comes to like-minded inhabitants of a demarcated territory, usually one that has its own state, or makes the demand for one.[2] The Wallace story is part of Scotland's imagined community, but we have seen how different groups have used the story for their own ends. As the state of mind changes, so does the Wallace story. And we have seen examples of this in the pro-Union/anti-Union claims made in the patriot's name.

This fluidity within the many stories which make up the Wallace myth has reached new extremes in the twenty-first century. The *Braveheart* effect from 1995, coupled to the expansion of cheap and easy internet access and web publishing, has transformed the Wallace cult. If Wallace tried to make sense of his own life today, he would need all the help he could obtain from his therapist, such are the claims made on him and around him Through his networked myth, Wallace represents the twenty-first-century schizoid man. An icon of a hybrid culture: yet, as his story fragments, its centrality to Scottish national identity has rarely been more secure.

GLOBALISATION, TIME, HISTORY

The proliferation of new media should remind us that how we tell stories is as important as the story itself. From the sixteenth until the eighteenth century, reprints of a single text (by Harry) were the story. From the end of the eighteenth century, throughout the nineteenth and into the twentieth century it was still the written text which ruled the transmission of the Wallace myth, but it was added to by song, poetry and monument. The scope of the myth could expand and permeate the national conscience from a number of different directions. In the nineteenth century Jane Porter caused a sensation in America with her romanticised history of the patriot. The market for books remained a middle-class preserve for most of the century, but newspapers, magazines and the all-encompassing chapbook literature ensured the printed text could be read by everyone.[3]

Technological change has had an immense and well-documented impact on storytelling. Now the key skill has the rather bland title of 'information processing', whether filing tax returns on line, or forwarding a dubious Christmas e-mail to colleagues at work. The information city has taken over from the manufacturing city in the rank order of urban size.[4] One of the most useful aids to organising the revolutionary movements which split the USSR was the humble photocopier. The ability to cheaply and rapidly reproduce and then distribute clandestine literature was a key component in organising resistance against the state from within civil society. It channels communication in the construction of civil society. Where such structures have been lacking, argues Hall, social and economic growth is found wanting in the challenge created by the fall of state socialism.[5] Communication knits the associations of civil society and, of course, identity formation, too, flows through every available channel of communication.

What is important is how individuals, groups or leaders dominate the cultural frame of reference. From Charles Tilly's work on revolutions and uprisings in the nineteenth century to Alberto Melucci's studies of new social movements in the late twentieth century, the emphasis is on the constraints and the opportunities available to organisations and political leaders. It is this, it is argued, which explains at any given point why a riot or political movement is conducted in a certain way. The phrase offered by Melucci is 'resource mobilisation' – those resources available to be exploited.[6] The expansion of printing and publishing have been the key resources which have been mobilised to transmit the Wallace myth. The photocopier did much to free the reproduction of materials and now it is the turn of the internet. In many ways the reduction in the cost of accessing the World Wide Web and sending and receiving e-mails is analogous to the removal of the Stamp Tax in 1855: the barrier to access was dismantled. It became easier to pass on and to circulate information. Examples of just how the internet has transformed the reproduction of the Wallace myth will be turned to in a moment. However, this is more than just cheap reproduction we are talking about here; it is more than just presenting text, pictures, sound and video clips over the internet as direct replication of older forms of media (text, engraving, canvas, videotape). The internet has had a profound influence on how its content is read or viewed or listened to. The medium itself has changed how the story is consumed. It is not just that it is cheap and easy to post some text relating to Wallace on a website and count up the number of page impressions reproduced by those who point their browser to that web address. The internet has changed the relationship between author, text and reader which has shattered any sense of coherence with the narrative. In effect, the Wallace story has become organic; it is growing.

The concept of globalisation is behind many explanations of these changed relationships, but it has been utilised in so many different settings in recent years that confidence in its precision has wavered. At the core of its definition, globalisation is more than increased levels of economic and political interaction, it is the creation of a single 'international society'.[7] McDonaldisation and Disneyisation are terms coined to mirror this society, and the dominance of Microsoft within the personal computer market has elicited an unprecedented foreboding of Big Brother.[8] However, doubts persist about how complete this transition has been and even whether it is really new. That the world is increasingly interconnected in matters of trade, commerce and communication has been a feature since the sixteenth century, if not before. It is certainly not a phenomenon of our age alone, a point made by a number of authors in their critique of this concept and it is certainly not clear that an international society has replaced the political and cultural power of the nation-state.[9] In an analysis of the movements of people through the European Union, for example, the concept of globalisation has been criticised for analysing cross-national linkages without stressing the rigidities which persist in national boundaries.[10] Immigration policies have tightened within the European Union, despite moves to free up and harmonise employment legislation within its boundaries. Indeed, the nation and the nation-state has retained remarkable resilience in the face of political, military and economic transnational organisations, such as the United Nations, NATO, G7 as well the large multi-national business and financial speculators who wield immense power over credit flows and interest rates.[11]

Strong reservations are voiced against such global power. Helena Norberg-Hodge has criticised the effects of the move to a single form of agriculture in the global world, seeing it as destructive to the localities and an inherent danger to the ecosystem if diversity is denied.[12] The concept is flawed, she goes on to argue, because it is giving credence to a set of economic and social processes which are themselves flawed: to avoid agricultural catastrophe the localities will need to survive. Added to these specific criticisms, Hirst and Thompson have been among the most explicit opponents of the very concept of globalisation itself, suggesting that nothing but ongoing change is being witnessed. They conclude that the current fashion for this concept is unwarranted and superfluous.[13]

Still, theoretical weight seems to come down to acknowledge that the *pace* of change has quickened, even if the relative amount of change has not, and rather than find the homogenisation of culture dominate from the late twentieth century, new momentum has imbued peripheral cultures. What currency globalisation has gained has been boosted by the internet revolution which has impacted most on personal communication, with e-commerce catching up. From the telephone call to the internet, new technology has transformed culture. The *Trend Report* produced in 1997 by Jean-Guy Lacroix and Gaëtan Tremblay charted the effect developments in technology have had on the presentation of culture over the twentieth century. They argue that opportunities afforded by the internet have produced a level of consumption of culture and information to a degree never seen before. They argue that by exploiting the internet, in particular our ability to digitise text and images and to present it in a number of different guises, we have decimated the one-time coherence of national cultures. It has turned the essence of our culture into, to use their term, a mosaic, comprising many elements rather than dominated by a small number of core institutions or debates. 'More importantly', they argue, 'cultural products themselves are made into mosaics, the unity of which becomes increasingly fragile as consumer needs grow more particular and specific.'[14]

Coincidentally or not, *Mosaic* was the name give to the world's first popular Web browser. However, the point of this analogy is to state that although the internet – and the process of globalisation – contribute to the standardisation of economic and cultural processes, it also has an almost illogical counter effect. It affords the opportunity for the particular and the specific to be emphasised on a global scale. As Appadurai has argued, despite being its impelling force 'the globalisation of culture is not the same as its homogenisation'.[15] For every McDonald's franchise there is a *local* seller of cider or cheese or whisky who is using what is distinctive about their product to establish its niche market.[16]

This is how we can begin to interpret the Wallace myth through the prism of the internet. It is more than the Hollywoodisation of the life of this Scottish patriot. That was a start, but much more has followed. Through this prism, the Wallace myth has secured a niche market for Scottish culture. Sometimes the story from the film is reinforced, sometimes it is claimed back for Scotland, but the debate is part of the organic growth in the Wallace myth. This is why, despite doubts about how new or complete the globalisation process can be said to be, there is an important new level of interaction between those who present and those who consume the Wallace myth through the internet. It has blurred the divide between core and peripheral cultures, allowing individuals to move easily between the two. We should expect people to be hybrids, moving between cultures, sometimes with friction, sometimes seamlessly. What we have now are 'global cultures in the plural'.[17]

Our ability to exist across cultures is facilitated by the break between time and location. Time can be 'compressed'. Radio commentary on Scottish football matches is no longer constrained by local transmitters on the medium wave frequency, now it can be listened to live, via the internet, around the world.[18] Online hotel reservations across time zones, multiple copied e-mails sent from a handset while travelling on a train, are commonplace. The regimentation of time, work and discipline, with which E.P. Thompson categorised the industrialising process in nineteenth-century Britain, is not now applicable.[19] The Wallace myth can easily be projected around the world. The break between author, text and reader is complete. Everyone can be the author *and* the reader, and the myth has grown through an interaction between them. For Wallace I diagnose schizophrenia, for the myth I see a new potential. I have called it wallace.com.

WALLACE.COM

The coincidence of this ongoing technological change, the Oscar-winning success of *Braveheart* (1995) and the 700th anniversary of Wallace's exploits (1997) was opportune, but continues to impress. The internet has taken over as the dominant media in the Wallace myth: purporting to offer both historical record ('the truth') and interactive discussion. The coming together of fan(atic)s around the common love of *Braveheart* is at the root of much of this. The MacBraveHeart site has a viewings list, detailing the number of screenings of the film, attended in the cinema or seen on home video.[20] It offers some frighteningly broad categories: more than eighty people claim to have seen the film between 30 and 500 times (although only one person goes beyond 100 and of course there is some round-up and exaggeration going on here). Around seventy people fit the category of 15–29 viewings, and over thirty claim to have sat through 11–15 viewings, with similar numbers for the 8–10 and 2–7 bands. Top of the list is Betty Austin:

> My name is Betty Austin and I've seen *Braveheart* 500 times. I love it. I want it. I want some more of it. It's the first movie I've ever seen that an actor has actually become the character in the movie. There are parts where it seems he actually isn't Mel anymore and actually is William Wallace. I am 46 years old, and it's the best movie I've ever seen in my entire life!!!!! I want to get some statues, and visit Scotland and . . . I could go on and on. I love it!!!![21]

Ms Austin is not alone. There are many more explanations of how these feats of perseverance were achieved, and reasons why. Such obsession is not unusual for popular Hollywood films. The *Star Wars* series of films has twice provoked such a craze twenty years apart. The story told by Sir Alec Guinness, who played Obi Wan Kenobi in the early films, is apposite: when attempting to persuade a young American fan who had seen the films over one hundred times, never to watch *Star Wars* again, he was met with tears from the child and accusations of meanness from an incredulous and irate parent. The fantasy had become sacred and not to be challenged.[22] Science fiction fans have also supported *Star Trek* and other such creations. The Trekkies have long focused their activities around a series of conventions where actors and others associated with the show have been invited to address and meet their fans. *Braveheart* has now been the focus to two major conventions, organised through the MacBraveHeart website established by John and Linda Anderson.[23]

We have no connection with any political organisation, and do not edit or censor the e-mail submissions we receive before posting them (without comment in most cases). We feel the meaning and the spirit of *Braveheart* is best expressed through the world-wide community whose voice we try to represent here on the MacBraveHeart web pages. We are indebted to all those who have taken the time and trouble to put their thoughts and feelings in writing and send them to us.[24]

The first Braveheart Convention was held from 12 to 14 September 1997, opening the day after the referendum vote in favour of a Scottish Parliament with tax-varying powers. The star attractions of the event were Randall Wallace, who wrote the screenplay for *Braveheart*, and Seoras Wallace, head of the Wallace Clan and re-creator of historical battles for screen and festival. The organisers of the first convention were delighted to have 'someone to thank' for *Braveheart*, and this was one of the organising goals of the convention.[25]

The second gathering, 'Braveheart 2000', took place in Stirling, Falkirk and Airth Castle from 18 to 20 August 2000.[26] The festivities included 'Stirling Day' with a 'Braveheart Banquet' in the King's Chambers in Stirling Castle; 'Wallace Day' with the planned re-enactment of the storming of Airth Castle, and 'Braveheart Day', with exhibition and talks offered, including a fifth anniversary screening of the film in the company of some of its stars.[27] These events were arranged by e-mail and online booking. Immediately prior to this second convention, the website had attracted 220,348 visitors since its inception, albeit the claim was made back to 1314 (but why not 1297!?). The convention experienced intense and persistent rain which fell throughout that weekend – unsurprisingly this was not conducive to re-creating outdoor battle scenes, but the event attracted the interest of the media and comment from both the organisers and academics.

Broadcast on Scottish Television's cultural magazine programme *Seven Days*, John Anderson revelled in the 'confidence in Scotland' which the film created. He highlighted the support he had received from English fans, many of whom had come to the convention and many of whom had declared their wish 'to be Scottish'. He recounted an anecdote from his first viewing of the film, waiting a week for a ticket and seeing a woman punch the air and shout 'yes' upon the film's conclusion, prompting the audience to give a standing ovation. His interview was interspersed with comment from Professor Bill Scott who likened the film to a kitsch cartoon, which was badly made, and grossly anti-English through their characterisation as upper-class vicious fascists and/or pampered pansies, while the Scots were presented as boisterous and democratic individuals able to achieve success through teamwork.[28]

The structure given to the Wallace story here is clearly based around *Braveheart*, as was the critique. Anderson picks up on the pride and political confidence which the film inspired, following the narrative of peripheral culture now self-assured (now real) in distinction to a core culture.[29] The Hollywood core culture took Scotland by the hand to face-up to an English core culture. Scott's critique was on the film's perpetuation of key Scottish narratives which are themselves myth-histories: that the Scots are a more democratic nation than the English and are basically an anti-

English nation. There are good academic traditions which undermine the openness of Scottish society while acknowledging the continuing influence of these beliefs in Scottish society.[30] Opinion polls and other data disprove such simple assertions as that following the Scottish football team, as a member of the Tartan Army, is the single clearest indicator of Scottish national identity.[31] Yet simple 'them' and 'us' narrations are still being perpetuated here, and it is no surprise that the film frames the debate. This is added to by the new-found high-profile film career which has opened up for the Wallace Clan. Seoras Wallace and his colleagues have been able to make a living from what was a hobby of battle re-enactments since their work with Mel Gibson on *Braveheart*, through work on *Rob Roy* (1995) and Ridley Scott's epic *Gladiator* (2000). In the rhetoric of Seoras Wallace: 'Ridley said that our reputation in Hollywood was second to none because they couldn't buy our experience.'[32] Part of the legitimacy of the Wallace Clan Trust comes from the support it has received from Randall Wallace. They worked together when filming *Braveheart* and engaged in statements of mutual admiration at the first Braveheart Convention in 1997. The Wallace Clan Trust pages on the MacBraveHeart website quote Randall Wallace, declaring: 'The spirit of Braveheart is the spirit of the Clan Wallace'.

How mutually reinforcing this narrative has become. Randall Wallace's book produced the screenplay, then the film, the Wallace Clan Trust were hired for the battle scenes, the film was followed by two Braveheart Conventions, more film roles for the Wallace Clan Trust and continuing statements of mutual admiration are offered on how essential each of them is to the new *Braveheart* geist. Is this, then, the fulcrum of the Wallace story today?

The difficulty is not necessarily that one might not think *Braveheart* is the greatest film ever made, despite its Oscar winning success. Or one might not think that Randall Wallace's novel is a superb piece of literature, despite the healthy sales it has achieved. The danger is, paradoxically, that the myth is being taken for granted. People are aware of it, but cannot do anything about it from the historical sources, so it is left in place. What makes this complacency worse is that the need for corroboration is not forgotten. However, now there is a new discourse of corroboration, one that places it in fiction. The absent sources and mythical inventions about Wallace's life that each century has propagated, are taken out of the loop. It is too messy to say this or that cannot be proved. Instead, the acceptance of historical doubt fuels the fiction, to the extent that the fiction now appears as the primary source. After all, it is text on paper, not digitised hypertext. The paper supports the website in the way the manuscript supported the monograph in years gone by.

Here are three examples of the main acts of fiction, each of which has featured in the many websites dedicated to William Wallace. They come from Randall Wallace, James Mackay and Nigel Tranter:

Historians agree on only a few facts about Wallace's life, and yet they cannot dispute that his life was epic. There were times when I tried myself to be a fair historian, but life is not all about balance, it's about passion, and this story raised my passions. I had to see through the eyes of a poet.[33]

In trying to explain the enigma that was William Wallace I have carefully re-examined the poetic chronicle of Wyntoun and the saga compiled by Blind Harry the Minstrel. Unless we are to believe that these authors, without any motive, asserted deliberate falsehoods, capable at the time of instant refutation, there did exist in their day numerous 'gestis and deedis', the popular accounts, both oral and written, concerning Wallace's exploits. It seems that Harry also had access to a Latin manuscript compiled by Wallace's chaplain, Master John Blair, and those portions of his poem possessing a wealth of circumstantial detail appear to have been derived from this long-lost source.[34]

Here is the epic story of a young man of lofty stature but not very lofty birth who, driven to desperation and tears by the savagery and indignities perpetrated upon his fellow countrymen and women, as the policy of Edward Plantagenet, Hammer of the Scots, took upon himself to challenge almost single-handed the might of the greatest military machine in Christendom; and who by indomitable courage, shrewd strategy, brilliant tactics, sublime faith and a kind of holy impatience, raised a stricken and leaderless nation to self-respect again and, in the absence of its king, became its acknowledged head as well as its saviour; and then was shamefully betrayed.[35]

Mackay had set out to write biography, not fiction, but his use of the historical sources has followed similar techniques. It is not necessarily the debate over historical accuracy which is the key issue when placing the impact of these texts on web publishing. Historians will always point out when they are made. However, it is the role of his work in the phenomenon of myth-creation that is problematic. It is not so much whether the men who fought under Wallace's command painted their faces blue and bared their bottoms to the enemy which is important, although gaffes such as Wallace's affair with a Princess of Wales who had not been born yet,[36] are worrying. Historical error is one thing, but it is the substitution of historical corroboration with fictional corroboration which is of concern.

Tammy MacLaren Saari's brief history of the Wallace story produced for *Clannada na Gadelica* in 1998 used Mackay as one of the two cited sources.[37] The Highlander Web Magazine used Mackay ('from which most of this information is gathered') in comparison with *Braveheart*.[38] This was not just to add to the popular genuflection to all things Wallace, but 'These pages have been constructed and written with the truth at heart'.[39] Matt Ewart's article in the *Herald* newspaper aimed 'to outline the historical truth of Wallace as we know it, then look at the developing myth'.[40] The film has been sold as the 'only fact-based story from the High Middle Ages to have won a Best Picture Oscar' and 'in spite of its inaccuracies, the film manages to convey an impressive sense of 13th-century Britain'.[41] To be fair, a number of the websites have based their work on firmer foundations, such as *Highlander Web Magazine*'s use of Andrew Fisher at simplenet.com,[42] and scotsmart.com's use of Fisher and Hamilton of Gilbertfield,[43] and Matt Ewart's piece for the *Herald*, including an advert for Fisher's book at its close on the braveheart.co.uk pages.[44] But the bibliographies rarely go beyond that, with no mention, for example, of McDiarmid's standard introduction to Harry's *Wallace*, let alone the chronicles.[45] Others have not made their sources plain and the stories feed on each other. Take the example of a review of the Wallace phenomenon produced in 1999 for the website *Scottish Radiance*:

> There are many books about William Wallace and interpretations of his life. Since it happened so long ago and no substantial written records exist, no one knows for certain what happened. It is good to look at all viewpoints since no one knows the truth. In all the books I have read about William Wallace, Nigel Tranter's 'The Wallace' shows the most what the man must have been like. From its opening pages we meet William Wallace, a man, like us, with human emotions of pain, weakness, joy and courage. . . . If you want to know more about what William Wallace, a person, might have been like then this book is a 'must' for you. It is because . . . it happened so long ago and no substantial written records exist, no one knows for certain what happened, that we should turn to a book like Tranter's which shows the most what the man must have been like.[46]

A review of Mackay's *William Wallace: Braveheart* by Tobi Liedes-Bell for the internet book review site, *Under the Covers*, was published in April 1997, but remained unchanged throughout the subsequent controversies over Mackay's works:[47]

> The film BRAVEHEART catapulted William Wallace into the status of world wide hero. Admittedly, both author, Randall Wallace, and the film's director/actor, Mel Gibson, used creative license for the book and film, but there is still some fact in their relatings.

When I first picked up WILLIAM WALLACE BRAVEHEART, I was bogged down with who-beget-whom, but once past that, the book took off. So much so, that I began to doubt its accuracy. Therefore, I did what any skeptical reader does in this case – checked the Internet. Apparently, James Mackay's book is one of the most thorough books on William Wallace on the market. His research centers around the epic poem of William Wallace by Blind Henry, as well as surviving documents and historical and archaeological references.[48]

The ease of html allows links to other websites to be readily made. The McCoist site – dedicated to Scottish history – makes uses of the highlanderweb.co.uk site 'to explain the significance of these two great patriots [Wallace and Bruce]'.[49] It creates the web between them – and how appropriate that is for Robert Bruce, who watched the spider's perseverance in the fabricated story by Walter Scott. Schizophrenic Wallace is now tied to an interlocking web-based story where the myths come around and around: a truth that comes from repetition or fictional corroboration. It has also turned Wallace – as a cultural product – into a mosaic. As his story starts to be standardised for a web-based generation of consumers, so the Wallace reputation fragments. Here are two diverse examples: a collection of domain names and something for the sweet tooth of Scotland:

(a) The braveheart.com Website Directory

battle-dyke.braveheart.com
david.braveheart.com
dunblane.braveheart.com
eggo.braveheart.com
forever.braveheart.com
g444.braveheart.com
thegame.braveheart.com
viking.braveheart.com
william.wallace.braveheart.com

braveheart.com is shared by MailBank clients for their personal e-mail and matching website addresses.

Subdomains
Personalized e-mail address for US$9.95 per year
Matching website for US$19.95 per year
US$19.95 onetime setup & administration charge.
Select from 12,000+ Shared Domains[50]

(b) Chunkier than William Wallace's thighs, smoother than Robert the Bruce's patter, big enough to satisfy the most Rampant Lion. *Independence* is 60 glorious grammes of pure Scottish milk chocolate, wrapped in the proudest colours. If ever there was a chocolate bar which a nation could unite behind, then this is the one.

'Oh bar of Scotland, wan will we see yir like again. . .'. *Independence* is sure to raise a few eyebrows (and a few Saltires). In the words of Braveheart himself: they may take our country, but they'll never take our chocolate! It's bound to be a firesome seller. So show your true colours and put *Independence* on your shelves today.[51]

Here it is more fun than an attack on what is really known about Wallace. These are adverts for products based on name association, others are more emblematic. Dr Celt's Celtic Treasure has produced a 4 inch tall pewter figurine on a mahogany base depicting Sir William Wallace: 'One of Scotland's greatest warriors' and 'featured in the movie *Braveheart*'.[52] Clan Crafts offer 'specialist hand painted lead figures' including: William Wallace, Robert the Bruce, Bonnie Prince Charlie and Highland Clansmen. A display of William Wallace with Bruce was offered at £240. Individual figures were available as well, though a Wallace was £50 more than a Bruce.[53] Interest has focused around the clan name, with requests for information on the Wallaces in West Virginia during the Civil War, the Wallaces of Tennessee and other attempts to find the genealogical history of the clan name.[54]

Others, however, mix advertisement with historical myth-making in a more serious way. The Randall Wallace factor – if it can be so called – has reinforced belief in the existence of the Wallace sword.[55] As it carries no mark it is thought difficult to date, rather than a forgery. It is reported that it was rehilted in 1505. 'The sword, which is a traditional two handed broad sword, is approximately 66 inches in length with the blade itself being around 52 inches long. The quality of the metal used for the blade suggests that it may have been forged in Scotland, unlike other swords of the period which were often Flemish or German in origin'. Such details easily cloud the truth. The sword is now housed in the National Wallace Monument; its size is used as evidence that Wallace was a giant of a man, otherwise how could he have wielded a sword so large?[56] From the world-interactive.com website, a replica of the Wallace sword can be purchased:

> The Wallace Sword is named for the legendary Scottish hero who battled the English for control of his native land at the end of the 13th century. The double-handed sword, almost four and a half feet long, has a leather-covered ricasso to provide the leverage necessary to wield the weapon at close quarters. Now available in both solid brass (3600B-AM) and nickel (3600-AM) finished hilts, the Wallace Sword is a must for those who trace their ancestry to the Highlands. Blade: 40" Overall: 54" We recommend our back scabbard to the clansmen wishing to carry the Wallace Sword with pride.[57]

In Edinburgh's South Bride a shop sells the 'William Wallace Sword' for £120 – not a patch on the £277,000 paid for the 'real' *Braveheart* sword used by Mel Gibson in the film when sold at auction to raise money for AIDS research.[58] In all these examples it is the particular which is globalised. The niche market is no longer a narrow market. The interest has allowed the commodification of the Wallace myth to grow beyond the National Wallace Monument and its 1930s Tea Garden.

Finally, on viewing the Brave Art Exhibition at the Stirling Smith Art Gallery and Museum I was confronted by a picture of Mel

Gibson as Wallace, accompanied by Gary Cooper and Sgt George Morton.[59] It tells of a soldier who fought for his country during the First World War. As a result of being injured, his return home to Scotland after the war was delayed. His family thought he was dead; his wife married another man. He had fought and survived only to return to this. The artist James W. Hardie is asking us to choose the real hero from the three. That sergeant was my paternal grandfather – I leave the judgement to others.

FINAL REMARKS FROM THE SCAFFOLD
(. . . BY WAY OF CONCLUSION)

With the *Braveheart* video game and the opportunities for role playing at the Clan Shop, at Celtic weddings or at weekend battle re-enactments, enthusiasts no longer need to rely on their imagination – like Carnegie or Macaulay – to be inspired by Wallace. They can *be* Wallace, at least for a while. With the internet they can publish their contribution to the myth, free of editors or referees. Combining *Braveheart* with newly accessible means of text and image reproduction has taken the story from the historians to the people – and almost completely so. Yes, this is analogous to the chapbooks of the late eighteenth and the nineteenth centuries, but it has become easier and quicker, with the change in technology, to create the opportunity to make a world wide impact. Time, space and boundary are here transcended.

New opportunities, certainly, but also new dangers. Permeating so many of these websites is the simplistic message of anti-Englishness which is out of place in Scottish society and politics. In chapter two the medieval historian Fiona Watson raised doubts about back-projecting today's political issues to the thirteenth and fourteenth centuries.[60] If only the film and its fanatics did this it would be criticism enough, but this phenomenon then compounds the error by over-simplifying today's politics. Two people, having sat through a screening of *Braveheart*, decided to attack a police officer in Stirling because of his English accent but, fortunately, they were harshly treated by the law and ridiculed in the press. We have seen in the previous chapter that all shades of political opinion have tried to make use of the memory of Wallace and that his most obvious allies, the Scottish National Party, frequently renounce signs of anti-Englishness. Levels of national allegiance show that Scots prioritise their Scottish identity, but maintain a dual allegiance to a sense of Britishness. These opinions were reflected in the administrative structure and composition of the first intake to the Scottish Parliament (opened officially by the Queen in 1999). The Parliament has reconvened, but the Union is not yet dead.

Whereas Randall Wallace may be trying to reflect levels of anti-Englishness during a medieval war, the melodramatic approach has tried to simplify what were quite complex regional and national loyalties into a unified 'national' identity. We are dealing with a period which was five centuries before the acknowledged 'age of nationalism'.[61] The expressions of national allegiance were of course present, but their coherence and meaning is too easily conflated by what is meant by nationhood and independence (in their crudest of forms) now: can we really compare the community of the realm with the quangos of civil society?

No justification for perpetuating the myth can be offered here. As a nation it cannot be right that historical error is deliberately perpetuated. There is justification for careful historical study of the sources. We need to know the truth as far as it can be established and within the limitations of the intellectual decision-making each of us engages in when constructing the narrative. At the same time, there is no reason for the people of Scotland to become obsessive about the falsity of its history. Fighting over history is what national identity is all about. This is how nations are formed. There is no need to be obsessive about every myth, casting it out lest it corrupts Scotland's claims in the face of other core cultures. As long as people know it is not really true – but might be – then myth-history will work to sustain the nation. When supposed authenticity is constructed from fiction or is obviously inaccurate, then there is a problem.

Clearly, this work will not be the last word on the Wallace myth and nor could it hope to be. The historical time-frame is too great for any one historian to understand more than superficially when outside one's own specialism. However, that does not stop a plea that Wallace, just perhaps, has done enough already. Lay his ghost to rest. Fourteenth-century politics is not the same as the politics of today. Wallace was no Nostradamus, offering to predict the future. It is not helpful to get lost looking for a real history; it is not helpful to live the myth. Being xenophobic and bloodthirsty is not the way forward. Accept what is known of this short-lived historical actor; accept that myths have been important to national identity since the fifteenth century. Much debunking has been done here and in the citations found in the notes, and more can readily be done. Today's hybrid culture is too complex for one medieval hero to provide the explanation. The man is dead, god save the myth. That myth reflects the Scottish nation, but it is not the only identity. Here, too, we speak in the plural. The identities of the Scots are dual, multiple, hybrid and they are as real as in the next nation.

Notes

Chapter One

1. Wallace, R. *Braveheart*, 273.
2. McCrone, D. *The Sociology of Nationalism* 3–10; R. Brubaker, *Nationalism Reframed*; Mellor, R.E.H. *Nation, State and Territory*, 3–31.
3. Mitchell, J. *Strategies for Self-government*, 74; Finlay, R.J. *A Partnership for Good?*, 70–2.
4. *Scotland Yet! An Address Delivered by the Revd James Barr, B.D., at the Wallace Monument, at Elderslie, on 27 August, 1921; and now reprinted from the 'Forward' of 3 September, 1921*, 15.
5. McCrone, D. *Understanding Scotland*; McCrone, D. *Sociology of Nationalism*; Morris, R.J. 'Scotland, 1830–1914: The making of a nation within a nation', in W.H. Fraser and R.J. Morris (eds), *People and Society in Scotland, Volume II, 1830–1914*; Paterson, L. *The Autonomy of Modern Scotland*; Paterson, L. 'Civil Society and Democratic Renewal', in S. Baron, J. Field and T. Schüller (eds), *Social Capital*; Hearn, J. *Claiming Scotland* 19–21, 59–65, 117–19; Morton, G. *Unionist-Nationalism*; Morton, G. and Morris, R.J. 'Civil Society, Governance and Nation: Scotland, 1832–1914', in W. Knox and R.A. Houston (eds), *The New Penguin History of Scotland*.
6. Keane, J. (ed.), *Civil Society and the State*; K. Kumar, 'Civil Society: an inquiry into the usefulness of an historical term', *British Journal of Sociology*, Vol. 44, No. 3, September (1993), 383.
7. Morris, R.J. 'Civil Society and the nature of urbanism: Britain, 1750–1850', *Urban History*, Vol. 25, No. 3 (1998); Bryant, C.G.A. 'Social self-organisation, civility and sociology: a comment on Kumar's "Civil Society"', *British Journal of Sociology*, Vol. 44, No. 3 (1993).
8. Nairn, T. *The Break-up of Britain*, 126–95.
9. Nairn, T. 'Internationalism and the second coming', *Daedalus*, Vol. 122, No. 3 (1993); Nairn, T. *Faces of Nationalism*, 73–88; Mitchell, J. 'Conservatism in Twentieth-Century Scotland: Society, Ideology and the Union' in M. Lynch (ed.), *Scotland, 1850–1979*, 26–34; Mitchell, *Strategies for Self-government*, 38–9.
10. Morton, G. 'What if? The significance of Scotland's missing nationalism in the nineteenth century', in D. Broun, R. Finlay, M. Lynch (eds), *Image and Identity*.

11. The histories of the Scottish national movement can be found in: Mitchell, *Strategies for Self-government*; R.J. Finlay, *Independent and Free*; Finlay, *A Partnership for Good*.

12. The wider appeal of such sentiment is discussed in T.C. Smout, *A Century of the Scottish People*, 236–7.

13. This change in the social composition of those who live in the Scottish countryside has been examined in K. MacNee, *Living in Rural Scotland*. This is replicated in England through the so-called 'Laura Ashley factor' (*The Times*, 30 January 1997) and has been studied in H. Newby, *The Countryside in Question*. A summary of these issues is presented in A. Morris and G. Morton, *Locality, Community and Nation*, 31–3.

14. McCrone, D., Morris, A. and Kiely, R. *Scotland – the Brand*; Morris and Morton, *Locality, Community and Nation*, 128.

15. Billig, M. *Banal Nationalism*.

16. Morton, G. 'What if?', in Broun, Finlay, Lynch (eds), *Image and Identity*, 169.

17. Although authors schooled around A.D. Smith would downplay any rejections of an ethnic identity in favour of a civic identity, A.D. Smith, *The Ethnic Origin of Nations*. The best discussions on this debate are found in McCrone, *Sociology of Nationalism* and Hearn, *Claiming Scotland*.

18. Reported in *The Scotsman*, 18 December 1999.

19. Foster, R. 'Storylines: narratives and nationality in nineteenth-century Ireland', in G. Cubitt (ed.), *Imagining Nations*, 38.

20. Anderson, B. *Imagined Communities*, 33.

21. Brennan, Timothy quoted in H.K. Bhabha, *Nation and Narration*.

22. Gellner, E. *Nations and Nationalism*, 33–4. The best historical study of the rise of the regional newspaper press remains D. Read, *The English Provinces*.

23. Hall, S. 'The question of cultural identity', in S. Hall, D. Held and A. McGrew (eds), *Modernity and its Futures*, 299.

24. Ibid., 273–5.

25. Giles, J. and Middleton, T. 'Introduction', in J. Giles and T. Middleton (eds), *Writing Englishness 1900–1950*, 1–12. The type of politics which is shaped by a 'state of mind' has been superbly studied for Ireland: O. Macdonagh, *States of Mind*.

26. Cornell, S. 'That's the Story of our Life: Ethnicity and Narrative, Rupture and Power', in P.R. Spickard and W.J. Burroughs (eds), *We are a People*; Cornell, S. *Ethnicity and race*.

27. Although there are also many similarities in their respective antiquarian heritages, a useful angle on this revision is found in C. O'Halloran, 'Ownership of the past: antiquarian debate and ethnic identity in Scotland and Ireland', in S.J. Connolly, R.A. Houston and R.J. Morris (eds), *Conflict, Identity and Economic Development*.

28. The main polemic against Scottish capture by the language of inferiorism comes from the essays by C. Beveridge and R. Turnbull, *The Eclipse of Scottish Culture*, and A. Calder, *Revolving Culture*. The haunting language of parochialism is explored in C. Craig, *Out of History*, 11–30.

29. Both Prebble and Tranter have produced many best-selling histories and historical novels. The latter's academic histories have enjoyed healthy sales: M. Lynch, *Scotland: A New History*; T.M. Devine, *The Scottish Nation, 1700–2000*.

30. Craig, *Out of History*, 12.

31. McCrone, D. *Understanding Scotland*, 188; McCrone, Morris, Kiely, *Scotland – the Brand*, 61–72; C. Craig, 'Myths against History, Tartanry and Kailyard in nineteenth-century Scottish literature', in C. McArthur (ed.), *Scotch Reels*; I. Campbell, *Kailyard*; A. Carter, 'Kailyard: the literature of decline in nineteenth-century Scotland', *Scottish Journal of Sociology*, Vol. 1, No. 1 (1976).

32. Craig, *Out of History*, 29.

33. This point, and the quote from Nesbitt, are taken from the superb analysis by Colin McArthur, 'The Exquisite Corpse of Rab(elais) C(opernicus) Nesbitt', in M. Wayne (ed.), *Dissident Voices*, 108–9, 118.

34. This thankfulness has been examined in C. McArthur, '*Braveheart* and the Scottish Aesthetic Dementia', in T. Barta (ed.), *Screening the Past*, 177–8.

35. The unionist vs. nationalist interpretations of Scottish history can be followed in the arguments of P.H. Scott 'The Distortions of Unionism', *Scotlands*, Vol. 5, No. 1 (1998); R. Mitchison (ed.), *Why Scottish History Matters*; the debates on Scottish history found in two recent special editions of *The Scottish Historical Review*, in 1994 and 1997. For a balanced review of this debate when focused on the Union of 1707 the work of C.A. Whatley is unsurpassed: 'Bought and Sold for English Gold?' *Studies in Scottish Economic and Social History*, No. 4: *Glasgow* (1994) and *Scottish Society 1707–1830*.

36. McCrone, *Understanding Scotland*, 190–5. From the satirical poem *The Hunting of the Snark: an Agony in Eight Fits* (1872).

37. Smout, T.C. 'Perspectives on the Scottish identity', *Scottish Affairs*, No. 6, Winter (1994), 104.

38. Craig, *Out of History*, 65.

39. Turner L. and Ash, J. *The Golden Hordes*, quoted in Brown and Hall, 'Introduction: the paradox of the peripherality', in F. Brown and D. Hall (eds), *Case Studies of Tourism in Peripheral Areas*, 7.

40. Gellner, *Nations and Nationalism*; E. Gellner, *Nationalism*; McCrone, *The Sociology of Nationalism*, 67–72, 83; D. Conversi, 'Ernest Gellner as critic of social thought: nationalism, closed systems and the Central European tradition', *Nations and Nationalism*, Vol. 5, No. 4 (1999), 565; M. Guibernau,

Nationalisms: The Nation-State and Nationalism in the Twentieth Century, 141.

41. McCrone, *Sociology of Nationalism*, 83.

42. A critical debate on the intellectual history of the concept of 'primordialism' is found in J.E. Eller and R.M. Coughlan, 'The poverty of primordialism: the demystification of ethnic attachments', *Ethnic and Racial Studies*, Vol. 16, No. 2 (1993), 183–202. A good introduction to some classic interpretations of primordialism, and more recent literature on ethnicity, is contained in the selections edited by J. Hutchinson and A.D. Smith, *Ethnicity*.

43. Llobera, J. *The God of Modernity*, 86, quoted in McCrone, *The Sociology of Nationalism*, 12.

44. Hobsbawm, E.J. and Ranger, T. (eds), *The Invention of Tradition*.

45. Gellner restated his position just before he died in 'Reply: Do nations have navels?' part of the 'Warwick Debate' with A.D. Smith, published in *Nations and Nationalism*, Vol. 2, No. 3 (1996), 357–70; A.D. Smith, 'Memory and modernity: reflections on Ernest Gellner's theory of nationalism', *Nations and Nationalism*, Vol. 2, No. 3 (1996), 371–88. The ethnic/civic conceptions of nationalism are worked out in many case studies, but one of the best early studies is L. Greenfeld, *Nationalism: Five roads to modernity*, chapter one. Accessible summaries of the debate, including attempts, most explicitly by McCrone, to reject the division, are found in McCrone, *Sociology of Nationalism*. 8–10; Morris and Morton, *Locality, Community and Nation*, 77–81; Hearn, *Claiming Scotland*, 3–8.

46. Dîaz-Andreu, M. 'The Past in the Present: the search for roots in cultural nationalism. The Spanish case', in J.G. Beramendi, R. Máiz, X.M. Núñez (eds), *Nationalism in Europe: Past and Present*, Vol. I, 199, 203–4.

47. Hastings, A. 'Special peoples', *Nations and Nationalism*, Vol. 5, No. 3 (1999), 381–2.

48. Grosby, S. 'The chosen people of ancient Israel and the Occident: why does nationality exist and survive?', *Nations and Nationalism*, Vol. 5, No. 3 (1999), 357–80.

49. Kearney, H. *The British Isles*, 37–8; Evans, N. 'Introduction: Identity and Integration in the British Isles' in N. Evans (ed.), *National Identity in the British Isles*, 15–16; Grant, A. and Stringer, K. 'Introduction: the enigma of British history', in A. Grant and K. Stringer (eds), *Uniting the Kingdom?* 3–11.

50. Williams, A.T.P. 'Religion', in E. Barker (ed.), *The Character of England*, 56.

51. Stapleton, J. *Englishness and the Study of Politics*.

52. Lowenthal, D. *The Past is a Foreign Country*.

53. McCrone, 'Scotland – the Brand: Heritage, Identity and Ethnicity' in R. Jackson and S. Wood (eds), *Images of Scotland*, in *The Journal of Scottish Education* Occasional Paper, No. 1, 43.

Notes

54. Smith, A.D. *The Ethnic Origin of Nations*, 2–12; Smith, A.D. 'The myth of the "Modern Nation" and the myths of nation', *Ethnic and Racial Studies*, Vol. 11, No. 1 (1988) 12; Armstrong, J.A. *Nations before Nationalism*, 3; Langlands, R. 'Britishness or Englishness: The historical problem of national identity in Britain', *Nations and Nationalism*, Vol. 5, No. 1 (1999), 54–6.

55. Smith, A.D. *Nations and Nationalism in a Global Era*, 157.

56. Ibid, 158.

57. Ibid.

58. Sellar, W.C. and Yeatman, R.J. *1066 and All That*.

59. 'Britannia Flyer'.

60. Ascherson, N. *Games With Shadows*, 154.

61. Alton Templin, J. 'The ideology of a chosen people: Afrikaner nationalism and the Ossewa Trek, 1938', *Nations and Nationalism*, Vol. 5, No. 3 (1999), 410–11, 415–16.

62. Scholes, P.A. *God Save the Queen!* 41.

63. Ibid., 163.

64. Ibid., 142.

65. Eriksen, T.H. 'Formal and informal nationalism', *Ethnic and Racial Studies*, Vol. 16, No. 3 (1993), 1–25.

66. Morton, 'What if?', in Broun, Finlay, Lynch (eds), *Image and Identity*, 167.

67. McCrone, *Understanding Scotland*, 164–73, 212; Paterson, *The Autonomy of Modern Scotland*; M. Keating, 'Response' to 'Ethno-nationalist movements in Europe: a debate', *Nations and Nationalism*, Vol. 4, No. 4 (1998), 575.

68. A sensitive examination of the lay and academic definitions of culture and identity, and the relationship between the two, comes from A.P. Cohen, 'Culture as Identity: An Anthropologist's View', *New Literary History*, Vol. 24 (1993), 195–209.

69. What is 'real' and what is 'discourse' in the definition of a nation is discussed in McCrone, *Sociology of Nationalism*, 3–4.

70. Barrow, G.W.S. *Robert Bruce and the Community of the Realm of Scotland*, 130.

71. Published by Robert Lekpreuik.

72. Lindsay, M. *History of Scottish Literature*, 22–3.

73. Rendall, J. 'Tacitus engendered: "Gothic feminism" and British histories, *c.* 1750–1800', in G. Cubitt (ed.), *Imagining Nations* 60; C.W.J. Withers, 'The Historical Creation of the Scottish Highlands', in I. Donnachie and C. Whatley (eds), *The Manufacture of Scottish History*, 145.

74. Hearn, *Claiming Scotland*, 155–74.

75. Craig, *Out of History*, 29.

76. Barrow, *Robert Bruce*, 130.

77. Seal, G. *The Outlaw Legend*, 2.

78. Keen, M. *The Outlaws of Medieval Legend*, 74.
79. Ibid., 64.

Chapter Two

1. *The Scotsman*, 19 February 1999. The headline of the article was 'Scots learn their history through Hollywood' below a still from *Braveheart* depicting Mel Gibson as William Wallace. The article quotes David Ross, historical adviser to the William Wallace Society, complaining that the 'Scots don't know their history'. All the answers to this quiz can be found in this chapter. The same edition of the newspaper carried an editorial entitled: 'Missing out on the story of Scotland', quoting a complaint from the foremost historical novelist Nigel Tranter about the lack of knowledge of Scottish history among Scots. The editorial concludes on the link between national history and the likely success of the new Scottish parliament: 'It is as absurd as it is shameful that the people of Scotland should be contemplating remaking their parliament with little or no common knowledge of the nation's past. Future generations must not be denied their heritage in this dismal manner.'

2. Cowan, E. 'The Wallace Factor in Scottish History', in R. Jackson and S. Wood (eds), *Images of Scotland*, in *The Journal of Scottish Education*, Occasional Paper, No. 1, 7; Nicholson, R. *Scotland: The Later Middle Ages*, 55; Barrow, *Robert Bruce*, 128.

3. Mackay, J. *William Wallace: Brave Heart*, 13–17. These claims were repeated in *The Scotsman*, 12 April 1995. Doubts on the veracity of Mackay's researches on Wallace have, however, been raised, in G. Morton, 'Review: Sir William Wallace and other tall stories (unlikely mostly)', *Scottish Affairs*, No. 14, Spring (1996), 103–15. Doubts on this and his later work have been much reported: *The Scotsman*, 22 February 1999, 5 October 1999; *Scottish Daily Mail*, 23 February 1999; *New York Times*, 21 November 1999. Edward Cowan has cast equally forthright reservations on Mackay, commenting that he 'unwittingly demonstrat[es] the utter futility of utilising Harry as a strictly historical source', asserting that the book is 'a waste of trees', in 'The Wallace Factor in Scottish History', in Jackson and Wood (eds), *Images of Scotland*, 17.

4. Spence, J.L.T.C. *The Story of William Wallace*, 7.

5. Nicholson, *Scotland: The Later Middle Ages*, 52.

6. Ibid.

7. Barrow, *Bruce*, 129; Nicholson, *Scotland: The Later Middle Ages*, 52.

8. Cowan, E.J. 'Identity, Freedom and the Declaration of Arbroath', in Broun, Finlay and Lynch (eds), *Image and Identity*, 60; Barrow, *Robert Bruce*, 116; Verse contained in the Lanercost chronicle, later in this chapter, focuses on

Wallace's knighthood, although the chronicle's editor, Herbert Maxwell, can find no record of this, *The Chronicle of Lanercost, 1272–1346*, 168.

9.   Recounted by Bower, quoted in Nicholson, *Scotland: The Later Middle Ages*, 58.
10. Dalrymple of Hailes, D. *Annals of Scotland*, 318.
11. Ibid., 319.
12. *Documents Illustrative of Sir William Wallace, his life and times*, J. Stevenson (ed.), xv.
13. See J.G. Bellamy, *The Law of Treason in England in the Later Middle Ages*.
14. Bellamy cited in Nicholson, *Scotland: The Later Middle Ages*, 67–8.
15. The problems of government propaganda and the back-projection of contemporary political understandings into the machinations of the Wars of Independence, particularly in the treatment of William Wallace, is explored in F. Watson, 'The Enigmatic Lion: Scotland, Kinship and National Identity in the Wars of Independence', in Broun, Finlay and Lynch (eds), *Image and Identity*, 23–4.
16. Cowan, 'Declaration of Arbroath', in Broun, Finlay and Lynch (eds), *Image and Identity*, 58.
17. My thanks to Steve Boardman for advice on the early Scottish chronicles during our often lengthy Scotrail journeys from Fife to Edinburgh.
18. The work was added to by Walter Bower in the 1440s, with eleven additional books, known as the *Scotichronicon, Johannis de Fordun Chronica gentis Scotorum*, W.F. Skene (ed.), xii–xiii.
19. Ibid., ix.
20. Maxwell, H.E. *The Early Chronicles Relating to Scotland*, 228–9.
21. Ibid., 234.
22. Cowan, 'The Wallace Factor in History', in Jackson and Wood (eds), *Images of Scotland*, 7; Cowan, 'Declaration of Arbroath', in Broun, Finlay and Lynch (eds), *Image and Identity*, 59.
23. Maxwell, *Early Chronicles*, 247.
24. Bannerman, J. 'MacDuff of Fife', in A. Grant and K.J. Stringer (eds), *Medieval Scotland: Crown, Lordship and Community*, 35, 38. The MacDuff family suffered great losses, which are recorded in the chronicles: *Scotichronicon*, by Walter Bower, (eds) N.F. Shead, W.B. Stevenson and D.E.R. Watt with A. Borthwick, R.E. Latham, J.R.S. Phillips and M.S. Smith, Vol. 6, 97, lines 46–7; *The Orygynale Cronykil of Scotland by Andrew of Wyntoun*, Vol. II, ed. David Laing 347; *A History of Greater Britain as well England as Scotland compiled from the ancient authorities by John Major*, 200.
25. Young, A. *Robert the Bruce's Rivals*, 1–2.
26. Ibid., 2.
27. MacQueen, J. 'The literature of fifteenth-century Scotland', in J.M. Brown (ed.), *Scottish Society in the Fifteenth Century*, 196.

28. *Scotichronicon*, by Walter Bower, ed., D.E.R. Watt, Vol. 9, 83, lines 313–15.

29. Ibid., p. 83, lines 321–5, 330–3.

30. *Scotichronicon*, by Walter Bower, eds, N.F. Shead, W.B. Stevenson and D.E.R. Watt, with A. Borthwick, R.E. Latham, J.R.S Phillips and M.S. Smith, 63, lines 50–4, 73, line 63.

31. Ibid., 83, lines 3–8.

32. Ibid., 83, lines 11–23.

33. Ibid., 83, line 24; 83–5, lines 35–45.

34. Ibid., 93, lines 1–7, 16–19.

35. Ibid., 95, 97, lines 9–42.

36. Young, *Robert the Bruce's Rivals*, 3.

37. Reid, N.H. 'Alexander III: The Historiography of a Myth', in N.H. Reid (ed.), *Scotland in the Reign of Alexander III 1249–1286*, 191, 193.

38. *The Orygynale Cronykil of Scotland by Andrew of Wyntoun*, ed. David Laing, 339–45.

39. Ibid., 348.

40. Cowan, 'The Wallace Factor', in Jackson and Wood, *Imagining Scotland*, 7.

41. Major, J. *A History of Greater Britain*, 195, fn 1, 196.

42. Ibid., 199. Although Mair would otherwise support the nobility as the mainstays of the constitution, argues E.J. Cowan in 'The political ideas of a covenanting leader: Archibald Campbell, marquis of Argyll 1607–1661' in R.A. Mason (ed.), *Scots and Britons*, 244–5.

43. Major, J. *A History of Greater Britain*, 200.

44. Ibid., 203.

45. Ibid., 204–6. It was the kind of argument to be later dismissed by J.D. Carrick, 'we do not see that a great lie told in the classical language of ancient Rome should be entitled to a larger portion of public faith than a lesser one told in the modern patois of Scotland', *Life of Sir William Wallace*, preface.

46. A point made in A. King, 'Englishmen, Scots and Marchers: National and Local Identities in Thomas Gray's *Scalacronica*', *Northern History* vol. xxxvi, No. 2 (2000), 231.

47. Reid, 'Alexander III', in Reid (ed.), *Scotland in the Reign of Alexander III*, 183.

48. *Chronicle of Lanercost*, 163. The *Guisborough Chronicles* also state that Wallace was put to this bloody task by James the Stewart and Bishop Wallace, a point made in G. Barrow and A. Rogan, 'James Fifth Stewart of Scotland, 1260(?)–1309', in K.J. Stringer (ed.), *Essays on the Nobility of Medieval Scotland*, 177.

49. *Chronicle of Lanercost*, 164. Fergusson has pointed out the story of the skin being turned into horse-girths is likely to originate from the *Scalacronica* which states that 'It was said that the Scots caused him to be flayed, and in

token of hatred made thongs of his skin'. Fergusson gives greater weight to Hemingsburgh: 'the Scots flayed him, and divided his skin among themselves in moderate-sized pieces, certainly not as relics, but for hatred of him', J. Fergusson, *William Wallace: Guardian of Scotland*, 68–9.

50. *Chronicle of Lanercost*, 164.
51. Ibid., 179.
52. Reid is doubtful that the chronicle was actually completed at the priory, but is convinced that it is of northern English origin, 'Alexander III', in Reid (ed.), *Scotland in the Reign of Alexander III*, 183.
53. Seal, G. *The Outlaw Legend*, 1–18.
54. *Chronicle of Lanercost*, 165.
55. Ibid., 166.
56. Ibid., 167–8, 176.
57. Watson, F.J. *Under the Hammer*, 51.
58. Reid, 'Alexander III', in Reid (ed.), *Scotland in the Reign of Alexander III*, 183–4.
59. Duncan, A.A.M. 'The Process of Norham, 1291', in P. Cross and S. Lloyd (eds), *Thirteenth-century England*, No. 5, 207–8; M. Prestwich, *The Three Edwards*, 44.
60. Watson, *Under the Hammer*, 11–20, untangles the web well.
61. Prestwich, *War, Politics and Finance under Edward I*, 35.
62. Ibid., 52.
63. Prestwich, *The Three Edwards*, 49.
64. Ibid., 49–50.
65. Watson, *Under the Hammer*, 52–4, who argues that Yorkshire was an area suffering because of the Scottish threat, but not yet devastated like the English border counties.
66. Ibid., 50.
67. Prestwich, M. *The Three Edwards*, 50.
68. Grant, A. *Independence and Nationhood*, 24.
69. Ibid., 24–5.
70. Watson, 'The Enigmatic Lion', in Broun, Finlay and Lynch (eds), *Image and Identity*, 24.
71. McDiarmid, M.P. 'The Date of the *Wallace*', *Scottish Historical Review*, Vol. xxiv (1955), 29, with 1478 as the most likely date of publication; McDiarmid, M.P. *Hary's Wallace*, Vol. I, xvi. Sir Archibald Dunbar's guess was 'about 1460', A.H. Dunbar, *Scottish Kings*, 215. The manuscript version is in eleven books, the printed versions tend to contain twelve, *The Acts and Deeds of Sir William Wallace*, 1570, W. Craig (ed.), iii.
72. Terry, C.S. *A Catalogue of the Publications of Scottish Historical and Kindred Clubs and Societies*.

73. Ash, M. *The Strange Death of Scottish History*. Arguments against this decline can be found in K. Iwazumi, 'The Union of 1707 in Scottish Historiography, *c.* 1800–1914', (unpublished MPhil thesis, University of St Andrews, 1996), 37–59; C. Kidd, '*The Strange Death of Scottish History* revisited: Constructions of the Past in Scotland, *c.* 1790–1914', *The Scottish Historical Review*; Morton, 'What if?', in Broun, Finlay and Lynch (eds), *Image and Identity*, 168–9.

74. *Documents Illustrative of Sir William Wallace, his life and times*, ed. J. Stevenson.

75. Ibid., x–xi.

76. Barrow, *Robert Bruce*, 15, 107.

77. Translation of the Latin offered by the Museum of Scotland in its accompanying notes to this display.

78. Watson, *Under the Hammer*, 50.

79. http://www.nms.ac.uk/mos/

80. Barrow, *Robert Bruce*, 128, fn 2. The 1976 edition states that the Lübeck letter was displayed at the Glasgow Exhibition of 1911 but was destroyed during the Second World War, 129, fn. 3.

81. 'An original letter dictated by William Wallace . . . has been found by *Scotland on Sunday*. The confirmation of its existence is a huge embarrassment to the newly-opened Museum of Scotland which claimed it could not include Wallace in its 'Story of Scotland' exhibition because there was no authenticated physical object associated with him anywhere in the world', *Scotland on Sunday*, 6 December 1998.

82. *Scotland on Sunday*, 21 February 1999, reports on the Museum of Scotland's new display on Wallace, including the Lübeck letter.

83. Craig, *Out of History*, 12.

84. *Scotland on Sunday*, 18 February 2001.

85. Renan, E. *Qu'est-ce qu'une nation?*, trans. I.M. Snyder; an extract can be found in S. Woolf (ed.), *Nationalism in Europe*, 50.

86. *Scotland on Sunday*, 'Seven Magazine', 9 May 1999, 2–4, 23.

87. A good introduction to this question is found in S. Wood and F. Payne, *The Knowledge and Understanding of Scottish History of S4 Pupils in Scottish Schools*.

88. See, respectively, E.J. Cowan, R.J. Finlay, W. Paul, *Scotland Since 1688: struggle for a nation*, and the magazine *Scotland's Story* published throughout 2000.

89. Ashby McGowan argued that Wallace and his closest associates came from Ayton in the Scottish Borders, rather than the west of Scotland, and that Wallace's father was Alan, not Malcolm Wallace (*The Scotsman*, 25 September 2000). Details can be found in A. McGowan, 'Searching for William the Welshman', *The Double Treasure*, No. 22 (1999). My thanks go to Duncan McAra for passing on this article.

Notes

Chapter Three

1. Letter from Andrew Carnegie to his uncle George Lauder, 30 May 1852, quoted in J.F. Wall, *Andrew Carnegie*, 101.
2. *Scotichronicon by Walter Bower*, ed. Watt, vol. 9, 83.
3. *Chronicle of Lanercost*, 163.
4. Grant, *Independence and Nationhood*, 24–5; Watson, 'The Enigmatic Lion', in Broun, Finlay and Lynch (eds), *Image and Identity*, 24.
5. Reid, 'Alexander III', in. Reid (ed.), *Scotland in the Reign of Alexander*.
6. *Autobiography of Andrew Carnegie*, 18.
7. Lindsay, M. *History of Scottish Literature*, 20.
8. Brown, J.T.T. 'The Wallace and The Bruce Restudied', in *Bonner Beiträge zur Anglistik*, 7–8; MacQueen, 'The literature of fifteenth-century Scotland', in Brown (ed.), *Scottish Society in the Fifteenth Century*, 195.
9. Lindsay, *History of Scottish Literature*, 19.
10. Major, J. *A History of Greater Britain*, 205. Cowan extends this quote to include Mair's doubts on the reliability of Harry, which was still used to promote the greatness of Wallace, in 'The Wallace Factor', in Jackson and Wood (eds), *Imagining Scotland*, 11.
11. MacQueen, 'The literature of fifteenth-century Scotland', Brown (ed.), *Scottish Society in the Fifteenth Century*, 202.
12. McDiarmid, 'The Date of the *Wallace*', 29–31.
13. McDiarmid, *Hary's Wallace*, Vol. I, xxvi.
14. Schofield, W.H. *Mythical Bards and the Life of Sir William Wallace*, 6–7; McDiarmid, *Hary's Wallace*, Vol. I, xxvi.
15. Brunsden, 'Scotland's Social, Political and Cultural Scene', in Cowan and Gifford (eds), *The Polar Twins*, 77, 107.
16. Brown, 'The Wallace and The Bruce Restudied', 80–1. Refutation comes from Neilson, G. 'On Blind Harry's *Wallace*', *Essays and Studies* (by members of the English Association), Vol. I, 86. Almost a century earlier, Sibbald had declared there was no ground for suspecting this in *Chronicle of Scottish Poetry from the thirteenth century to the Union of the Crowns, to which is added a glossary*, Vol. I, 82.
17. Ibid.
18. Ibid., 7, 99; see also McDiarmid, *Hary's Wallace*, Vol. I, xxvi–xxvii.
19. McDiarmid, *Hary's Wallace*, Vol. I, xxvi.
20. Brown, 'The Wallace and The Bruce Restudied', p. 3.
21. Schofield, *Mythical Bards*, 6–7.
22. Veitch, J. *The Feeling for Nature in Scottish Poetry*, Vol. I, 174.
23. Hill Burton, J. *The History of Scotland*, Vol. II, p. 183.
24. Veitch, *The Feeling for Nature in Scottish Poetry*, Vol. I, 174.

25. Burton, *History of Scotland*, Vol. II, 183.
26. Holt, J.C. *Robin Hood*, 111–13, 137–41; Seal, *The Outlaw Legend*, 23.
27. Keen, *The Outlaws of Medieval Legend*, 73.
28. Henderson, T.F. *Scottish Vernacular Literature: a succinct history*.
29. This was discussed in chapter two, p. 21–4.
30. Maxwell, H.E. *The Early Chronicles Relating to Scotland*, 247; Young, *Robert the Bruce's Rivals*, 1–2.
31. Macdougall, N.A.T. 'The sources: a reappraisal of the legend', in J.M. Brown (ed.), *Scottish Society in the Fifteenth Century*, 18.
32. Macdougall, 'The sources', in Brown (ed.), *Scottish Society*, 111, fn. 106. The parish of Craigie in Ayrshire is the site of the Barnweill monument to Wallace, see chapter six.
33. Miller, J.P. 'Editions of Blind Harry's "The Wallace"' (1912, read 13 December 1913), prepared for the Glasgow Bibliographical Society [NLS: LC.3351(16)]; J.F. Miller, 'Some additions to the Bibliography of Blind Harry's *Wallace*' (Read 19 March 1917), *Records of the Glasgow Bibliographical Society*, Vol. VI, 19; W. Geddie (ed.), *A Bibliography of Middle Scots Poets: with an introduction on the history of their reputations*, 133–45; *The Actis and Deidis of Schir William Wallace*, 1570, ed. W. Craigie; McDiarmid, *Hary's Wallace*, 2 Vols.
34. A more recent survey identified eight editions in the seventeenth century and 'several' in the eighteenth century, Lindsay, *History of Scottish Literature*, 23.
35. Miller, 'Some additions', *Records of the Glasgow Bibliographical Society*, 14–15.
36. McKinlay, R. 'Barbour's Bruce', *Records of the Glasgow Bibliographical Society*, Vol. VI, 35–6.
37. MacQueen, 'The literature of fifteenth-century Scotland', in Brown (ed.), *Scottish Society in the Fifteenth Century*, 200.
38. *The Complaynt of Scotland* (1549), *With an appendix of contemporary English tracts*, J.A. Murray (ed.) (London, Early English Text Society, 1872), 63, lines 16–17. My thanks go to Adam Fox for passing on a copy of this text.
39. Anderson, *Imagined Communities*, 33–4.
40. Brunsden, G.M. 'Aspects of Scotland's Social, Political and Cultural Scene in the late seventeenth and early eighteenth Centuries, as Mirrored in the Wallace and Bruce Traditions', in E.J. Cowan and D. Gifford (eds), *The Polar Twins*, 106, fn. 5. The number of copies of the *Wallace* can be gauged from the estates of Scottish publishers in the seventeenth century compiled in *The Bannatyne Miscellany*, 163.
41. Craigie, W.A. 'Barbour and Blind Harry as Literature', *The Scottish Review*, Vol. XXII, July (1893), 175.
42. The belief in its inaccessibility was perpetuated by Patrick Yule. Although there were many editions of Blind Harry published, he argues that it was

apparently never read by the peasantry because of the difficulty of the language. A Former Subscriber for a Wallace Monument [General Patrick Yule], *Traditions, etc., respecting Sir William Wallace*, 21.

43. The Preface by Henry Charteris to his edition of Henry's *Wallace*, printed in Edinburgh, 1594, in *The Bannatyne Miscellany* No. 19, 163.

44. Brunsden, 'Social, Political and Cultural Scene', in Cowan and Gifford (eds), *The Polar Twins*, 78–9.

45. *The Actis and Deidis of the Illustere And Vailzeand Campioun Schir William Wallace, Knight of Ellerslie by Henry the Minstrel, commonly known as Blind Harry*, J. Moir (ed.) (Edinburgh, Scottish Text Society), 1889, xix; Lindsay, *History of Scottish Literature*, 22–3; Brunsden again downplays the differences in the respective texts, in 'Social, Political and Cultural Scene', in Cowan and Gifford (eds), *The Polar Twins*, 78. The copy of this ms. held in the British Museum is said to be unique and to have once been the property of Queen Elizabeth, see: Geddie (ed.), *A Bibliography of Middle Scots Poets*, 134. This period of patriotic Protestantism is discussed in M. Lynch, 'A Nation Born Again? Scottish Identity in the Sixteenth and Seventeenth Centuries', in Broun, Lynch, Finlay (eds), *Image and Identity*, 87, 94.

46. Brundsen highlights the subtitle of Hamilton's *Wallace* which makes great claims for its easy language, 'Social, Political and Cultural Scene', in Cowan and Gifford (eds), *The Polar Twins*, 76, 106, fn. 10, see Hamilton of Gilbertfield, *A New Edition of the Life and Heroick Actions of the Renoun'd Sir William Wallace*. It still argued a century later that Harry's glossary was very incomplete 'and without Jamieson's dictionary we can make little progress in it; even with it to aid, there are many words and some lines the sense of which is obscure to us . . . and we are inclined to think it is only the modernising *Life of Wallace* written by William Hamilton of Gilbertfield, early in the last century, which has been read by the peasantry, in recent times at least . . .', Yule, *Traditions, etc.*, 22; P.F. Tytler gave credit to Jamieson's text as the basis for his *Lives of the Scottish Worthies*, Vol. I, 282–3.

47. Lindsay, *History of Scottish Literature*, 23.

48. Ibid., 23.

49. *Actis and Deidis*, ed. Moir, xx–xxi.

50. Lindsay, *History of Scottish Literature*, 23.

51. Edwards, O.D. *Macaulay*, 7.

52. Forrest, M. 'The Wallace Monument and the Scottish National Identity', unpublished BA (Hons) dissertation, University of Stirling, 1993, 42.

53. *Autobiography of Andrew Carnegie*, 16. The story is repeated and accompanied with a description of the wider influence of his Uncle Lauder on Carnegie's understanding of Scotland, in B.J. Hendrick, *The Life of Andrew Carnegie*, Vol. 1, 22–8.

54. Lindsay, *History of Scottish Literature*, 169.
55. Miller, 'Editions of Blind Harry's "Wallace" '.
56. King, E. 'Introduction', *Blind Harry's 'Wallace', William Hamilton of Gilbertfield*, xi.
57. *Lives of the Scottish Poets in Three Volumes*, ed. J. Robertson, Vol. I, 55.
58. Ibid., 56–7.
59. Henderson, *Scottish Vernacular Literature*, 64; Neilson, 'Blind Harry's *Wallace*', 85; Moir provides a glossary of Harry's language which is derived from Latin and French, *Actis and Deidis*, Moir (ed.), while Brown, 'The Wallace and The Bruce Restudied', 13–4 provides a shorter list.
60. The title page, among many, is listed in Geddie (ed.), *Middle Scots Poetry*, 142.
61. Quoted in Henderson, *Scottish Vernacular Literature*, 66.
62. Schofield, *Mythical Bards*, 127.
63. Brown, 'The Wallace and The Bruce Restudied', 30–4.
64. McDiarmid, *Hary's Wallace*, i, xxxvii.
65. Craik, G.L. *A Compendious History of English Literature and the English Language from the Norman Conquest*, Vol. I, 387; Brown, 'The Wallace and The Bruce Restudied', 18.
66. These tales have inspired a BBC Radio Scotland series and a book by Magnus Magnusson, *Scotland: the Story of a Nation*.
67. *Lives of Scottish Poets*, ed. Robertson, 58.
68. Watson, J.S. *Sir William Wallace, the Scottish Hero*, iii.
69. Fyfe, W.T. *Wallace, the Hero of Scotland*, 10–11, 157.
70. Henderson, *Scottish Vernacular Literature*, 73; Schofied, *Mythical Bards*, 7ff.
71. Henderson, *Scottish Vernacular Literature*, 73.
72. Neilson, 'Blind Harry's *Wallace*', 85.
73. Veitch, *Feeling for Nature*, Vol. I, 173, 177; Tytler, *Lives of Scottish Worthies*, Vol. I, 132–3.
74. *Actis and Deidis*, Moir (ed.), ix–x; J. Moir, *Sir William Wallace: a critical study of his biographer Blind Harry*, 18. It is of passing interest to note that the copy of this text, now in the possession of the Special Collections Department of Edinburgh University Library, was once part of the library of Lewis Grassic Gibbon (James Leslie Mitchell).
75. Craigie, 'Barbour and Harry as Literature', 200–1.
76. McDiarmid, *Hary's Wallace*, Vol. I, xxvii, lviii.
77. Brown, 'The Wallace and The Bruce Restudied', 20–1.
78. Neilson, 'Blind Harry's "Wallace"', 93–8; G. Neilson, *John Barbour: Poet and Translator*, 1.
79. Neilson, 'Blind Harry's "Wallace" ', 95–6.
80. *Calendar of Documents*, ed. Bain, Vol. iii, xxxvi.
81. Ibid., xxxvi–xxxvii.

82. Moir, *Sir William Wallace*, v–vi, 11.
83. Maxwell, *Early Chronicles Relating to Scotland*, 235–6.
84. Lindsay, *History of Scottish Literature*, 12.
85. Craik, *A Compendious History of English Literature*, 387.
86. Mackenzie, A.M. (ed.), *Scottish Pageant*, 146.
87. Dalrymple of Hailes, D. *Annals of Scotland*, 298–9, 312.
88. Cowan, 'The Wallace Factor in Scottish History', in Jackson and Wood (eds), *Images of Scotland*, 17; Mackay has claimed the value of Harry as historical source, despite awareness of its many shortcomings, J. Mackay, *William Wallace: Brave Heart*, 9–15.
89. Ibid., 15.
90. Jones, D. *A Wee Guide to William Wallace*, iv, 5, 80.
91. McNie, A. *Clan Wallace*.
92. Carruth, J.A. *Heroic Wallace and Bruce*.
93. King, E. *Introducing William Wallace: the life and legacy of Scotland's liberator*.
94. Gray, D.J. *William Wallace: the King's Enemy*, A. Fisher, *William Wallace*, 139.
95. Finlay, J. *Wallace, or the Vale of Ellerslie, with other poems*, xi.
96. Tytler, *Lives of Scottish Worthies*, Vol. I, 132.
97. Brunton makes this claim in *A New Work in Answer to the Pamphlet, 'Wallace on the Forth'*, 27.
98. Renan, E. *Qu'est-ce qu'une nation?*

Chapter Four

1. Letter of Sir Walter Scott to Mathew Weld Harstonange thanking him for the Latin poem *Valliados* (1633) May 6 1817, *The Letters of Sir Walter Scott*, ed. H.J.C. Grierson (London, Constable, 1932–7), Vol. IV, 442.
2. Brunsden, 'Social, Political and Cultural Scene', in Cowan and Gifford (eds), *The Polar Twins*, 78–9.
3. *Lives of Scottish Poets*, ed. Robertson, 55.
4. Goldstein, R.J. *The Matter of Scotland: Historical Narrative in Medieval Scotland*, 220.
5. Brown, S.J. '"Echoes of Midlothian" Scottish Liberalism and the South African War, 1899–1902', *Scottish Historical Review*, Vol. LXXI, 1, 2: Nos 191/2, 158.
6. *In Memory of Sir William Wallace: Address by Lord Rosebery* (Stirling, Eneas Mackay, 1897), reprinted in *Wallace, Burns, Stevenson: Appreciations by Lord Rosebery* (Stirling, Eneas Mackay, 1905).
7. This is the key passage from Fordun, see: Cowan, 'The Wallace Factor in Scottish History', in Jackson and Wood (eds), *Images of Scotland*, 7.

8. *Appreciations by Lord Rosebery*, 12–16.

9. Hume Brown, P. *History of Scotland to the Present Time*, Vol. I, 117–22, 123–37.

10. *The Life and Heroic Achievement of Sir William Wallace, the Scottish Patriot; and the life of Robert Bruce, King of Scotland: from the original verse* (Jedburgh, 1845), iii.

11. Pears, I. 'The Gentleman and the Hero: Wellington and Napoleon in the Nineteenth Century', in R. Porter, *Myths of the English*, 216–22.

12. McKay, K. *Mel Gibson* (London, Sidgwick & Jackson, 1988), 11; Morton, G. 'Review: Sir William Wallace and other tall stories (unlikely mostly)', *Scottish Affairs*, No. 14, Spring (1996), 103–15. Doubts on the great size of Wallace are raised in C. Knightley, *Folk Heroes of Britain*, 158.

13. Book 9, lines 1918–34, *Wallace; or the life and acts of Sir William Wallace, of Ellerslie.*

14. *The Tragedy of the Valiant Knight Sir William Wallace*, 9.

15. Keith, A. *Several Incidents in the Life of Sir William Wallace*, 3–6, 9–10.

16. Watson, J.S. *Sir William Wallace, the Scottish Hero*, 2–3.

17. Murison, A.F. *Sir William Wallace*, 152.

18. Ibid., 152–3.

19. *Scotland Yet!*, 3.

20. Wallace Commemoration Day, Saturday 26 August 1933.

21. Ross, D.R. *The Story of William Wallace*, 6–7.

22. 700th Anniversary Guide to Events: Easter to Autumn, 1997.

23. Schama, S. *History of Britain*, BBC Television, 18 October 2000.

24. Fergusson, J. *William Wallace: Guardian of Scotland*, 20.

25. *Wallace, the Hero of Scotland; or Battle of Dumbarton*, 5–6.

26. L.G.M.G., *Authentic Life of Sir William Wallace, with chapter on Traditional Wallace. Compiled from the best authorities*, 20.

27. Alexander, G. *Sir William Wallace: the Hero of Scotland. An Historical Romance*, 13.

28. *History of Sir William Wallace: The renowned Scottish Champion*, 4.

29. Porter, J. *The Scottish Chiefs*, 21–38.

30. *Wallace, the Hero of Scotland, a drama, in three Acts*, 8–10.

31. Donaldson, P. *The Life of Sir William Wallace*, 128.

32. Macrae, D. *The Story of William Wallace, Scotland's National Hero*, 9.

33. *Wallace's Women*, a play in two acts by Margaret McSeveney and Elizabeth Roberts, 31 October–2 November 1997, Stirling Smith Art Gallery and Museum.

34. Donaldson, *The Life of Sir William Wallace*, 84.

35. Sawers, P.R. *Footsteps of Sir William Wallace. Battle of Stirling: Or, Wallace on the Forth.*

36. Brunton, A. *A New Work in Answer to the Pamphlet, 'Wallace on the Forth'*, 3, 4.
37. Brunton, *A New Work in Answer*, 16.
38. Fergusson, *William Wallace*, 54.
39. Page, R. 'The Archaeology of Stirling Bridge', One Day Wallace Conference, 17 May 1997, Stirling Smith Art Gallery and Museum.
40. Schama, *History of Britain*.
41. J.C., *Life of Sir William Wallace*, 105.
42. *William Wallace: National Hero of Scotland*, Special Commemorative Publication to Mark the 650th Anniversary of his Martyrdom, 11.
43. Macrae, *Story of William Wallace*, 15.
44. Anon, *The Life of Sir William Wallace, the Scots Patriot*, 3–4.
45. Ibid., 24, 93.
46. J.C., *Life of Sir William Wallace*, 122.
47. *William Wallace*, Special Commemorative Publication to Mark the 650th Anniversary of his Martyrdom, 13.
48. Ibid. 15.
49. Sibbald, J. *Chronicle of Scottish Poetry from the thirteenth century to the Union of the Crowns*, Vol. 1, 82ff.
50. *The Metrical History of Sir William Wallace, Knight of Ellerslie by Henry*, Vol. III.
51. Porter, *The Scottish Chiefs*, 370.
52. Ibid., 370–2.
53. Fergusson, *William Wallace*, 217–18.
54. *The Scotsman*, October 2000.
55. McDiarmid, *Hary's Wallace*, Vol. I, xciv.
56. *Wallace, or, the Vale of Ellerslie with Other Poems*, 9–10.
57. Paterson, J. *Wallace and His Times*, xx.
58. My thanks to Linas Eriksonas for this point and for hinting at his own fascinating researches into heroic Wallace at the University of Aberdeen.
59. The quote refers to the 1890s, Ash, 'William Wallace and Robert the Bruce', in Samuel and Thompson (eds), *Myths We Live By*, 92.
60. Traquair, P. *Freedom's Sword*, 124.
61. Fergusson, *William Wallace*, ix.
62. Murison, *Sir William Wallace*, 56.
63. Craigie, W.A. 'Barbour and Harry as Literature', *The Scottish Review*, 176.
64. Taylor, J. *Pictorial History of Scotland*, 95.
65. Craik, *A Compendious History*, 389.
66. *Calendar of Documents Relating to Scotland*, ed. J. Bain (Edinburgh, 1887), ii, p. xxix, xliv.
67. *Documents Illustrative of Sir William Wallace, his life and times*, Maitland Club 54, ed. J. Stevenson (Edinburgh, 1841), xi.

68. Henderson, *Scottish Vernacular Literature*, 74.
69. Brown's critique; Hill Burton, *History of Scotland*, Vol. II, 183.
70. Craigie, 'Barbour and Harry as Literature', 174, 201.
71. Brunton, A. *A New Edition of the Life and Heroic Actions of Sir William Wallace, Knight of Elderslie: in three parts* (Glasgow, 1881), part III.
72. Moir, *Sir William Wallace*, preface, 11.
73. Paterson, *Wallace, the Hero of Scotland*, xii–xiii.
74. Fisher, *William Wallace*, 6–7.
75. Jones, *A Wee Guide to William Wallace*, 5.
76. McDonald, T. 'Why has Scottish culture flourished in North America?' unpublished MSc dissertation, University of Edinburgh, 2000.
77. Cookson, J.E. 'The Napoleonic Wars, Military Scotland and Tory Highlandism in the Early Nineteenth Century', *The Scottish Historical Review*, Vol. LXXVIII, 1: No. 205 (1999), 63–9.
78. Morton, G. and Morris, R.J. 'Civil Society, Governance and Nation: Scotland, 1832–1914', in W. Knox and R.A. Houston (eds), *The New Penguin History of Scotland*, 362.
79. Morton, *Unionist-Nationalism*, 79–81.
80. Donaldson, G. *The Scots Overseas*, 180.
81. Ibid.
82. *Prospectus of the Scottish Home Rule Association*, 3.
83. De Tocqueville, A. *Democracy in America*, trans. G. Lawrence, ed. J.P. Mayer.
84. See, for this debate, Greenfeld, *Nationalism*, and Smith, *Ethnic Origin of Nations*.
85. MacPherson, J.A. 'Beyond the Memories: Drawing Strength from the Diaspora', in J.M. Fladmark (ed.), *Sharing the Earth*.
86. Pederson, R. 'Scots Gaelic as a tourism asset', in Fladmark (ed.), *Sharing the Earth*.
87. Child, F.C. *English and Scottish Ballads*, Vol. VI, 231–2.
88. Child, F.C. *English and Scottish Ballads*, 'Gude Wallace', lines 51–74, 234–5.
89. Ibid., 'Sir William Wallace, lines 1–20, 39–40, 65–8, pp. 237–42.
90. *Early Popular Poetry in Scotland and the Northern Border*, D. Laing (ed.) in 1822/26, Rearranged and revised with additions and glossary by W. Carrew-Hazlitt, 2 Vols, Vol. II, 6. Laing could not date the poem, but believed it belonged to the fifteenth or sixteenth century.
91. Holt, *Robin Hood*; Keen, *The Outlaws of Medieval Legend*; Seal, *The Outlaw Legend*.
92. *To His Grace, James, Duke of Perth, &c. Lieutenant General of His Majesty's army, under the command of His Royal Highness Charles, Prince of Wales, &c.* (n.p., *c.* 1745?) [NLS]: Mf.SP.159(14)].
93. *Four new songs, and a prophecy: I. A song for joy of our ancient race of Stewarts. II. The Battle of Preston, that was fought by his Royal Highness*

Prince Charles, the 21st of September 1745. III. On an honorable achievement of Sir William Wallace, near Falkirk. IV. A song, call'd, The rebellious crew. V. A prophecy by Mr Beakenhead, Song III (Edinburgh?, 1750?) [NLS: Ry.1.2.85(21); F.C. Child, *English and Scottish Ballads*, vi, 232.

94. From Harry's *The Wallace*, Book VI, line 1400. *The Metrical History of Sir William Wallace, Knight of Ellerslie*, frontispiece to volume III.

95. 'The Sword of Wallace' found within *Wallace, or, the Vale of Ellerslie*. [NLS: H.32.h.33].

96. *The Shade of Wallace: A poem* (Glasgow, D. Mackenzie, 1807), 11.

97. Holford, M. *Wallace; or, the Fight of Falkirk; a Metrical Romance* (London, 1809), Canto 1, CH XXXII, 24–25; Letter of Sir Walter Scott to J. Baillie, February 20, 1810, *The Letters of Sir Walter Scott*, H.J.C. Grierson (ed.), Vol. ii, 302.

98. *The Tragedy of the Valiant Knight Sir William Wallace*, 2.

99. *Sub-committee appointed by a General Committee of Subscribers at Edinburgh, for carrying into execution the design for erecting a National Monument in Scotland in Commemoration of the Triumphs of the Late War by Sea and Land*, (Edinburgh, 1822). Morton, *Unionist-Nationalism*, 184–7.

100. *Wallace and Bruce, a poem* (n.p., 1825?), 96 [NLS: 5.5194(21)].

101. Davidson, J.M. *Leaves from the Book of Scots, The Story of William Wallace, Robert the Bruce, Fletcher of Saltoun and Other Patriots*, 9.

102. *Political Squibs, Edinburgh 1820–21* [Edinburgh Public Library, YJN1213.820, A106X].

103. Baur, C. 'Lament to the Seventy-niners after R. Burns', quoted in Mitchell, *Strategies for Self-government*, 228.

Chapter Five

1. British Tourist Authority (BTA), *Media Briefs* (1999).

2. The television character Rab C. Nesbitt, written by Ian Pattison, quoted in McArthur, 'Exquisite Corpse of Rab(elais) C(orpernicus) Nesbitt', in Wayne (ed.), *Dissident Voices*, 122.

3. A plan was made for such a marker in April 1954, to 'be made in Scotland of an Aberdeen grey granite slab, surmounted by a bronze plaque and enameled bronze shields bearing the National emblems, and protected by a wrought iron grill', see: *An appeal to Scots and Friends at Home and Abroad for a London Memorial to Sir William Wallace, Scots Patriot* (1954) [NLS: HP3.85.1009].

4. Ross, D.R. *On the Trail of William Wallace*; Ross, D.R. *On the Trail of Robert the Bruce*.

5. Scottish Tourist Board, personal communication. My thanks are due to Angela Morris for guiding me through the place of Scottish history in the modern heritage industry. I am indebted for much of this work to the path-breaking McCrone, Morris and Kiely, *Scotland – the Brand*.

6. British Tourist Authority (BTA Research Centre, 1999).

7. Nenadic, S. 'Museums, Gender and Cultural Identity in Scotland', *Gender and History*, Vol. 6, No. 3 (1994), 426; G. Rosie, 'Museumry and the Heritage Industry', in I. Donnachie and C. Whatley (eds), *The Manufacture of Scottish History*, 167–70.

8. BTA *Media Briefings* (1999). Suggestions that the former Royal Yacht has lost its lustre as a tourist attraction were widely reported during autumn 2000.

9. *Metro*, 4 May 2000.

10. Morris and Morton, *Locality, Community and Nation*, 27–8, 30; P. Allanson and M. Whitby, *The Rural Economy and the British Countryside*; A. Rogers, 'A Planned Countryside', in G. Mingay (ed.), *The Rural Idyll*.

11. Hewison, R. *The Heritage Industry: Britain in a Climate of Decline*; Wright, P. *On Living in an Old Country: the National Past in Contemporary Britain*; Samuel, R. *Theatres of Memory*, Vol. 1: *Past and Present in Contemporary Culture*.

12. Quoted in T. Nairn, *The Enchanted Glass: Britain and its Monarchy*, 94–5.

13. Pocock, J.G.A. 'The Limits and Divisions of British History: in search of an unknown subject', *American Historical Review*, Vol. 87, No. 2 (1982), 311–36; Pocock, J.G.A. 'Conclusion: Contingency, identity, sovereignty' in A. Grant and K. Stringer (eds), *Uniting the Kingdom? The making of British History*; Pocock, J.G.A. 'The New British History in Atlantic Perspective: An Antipodean Commentary', *American Historical Review*, Vol. 104, No. 2 (1999), 490–500; Landsman, N.C. 'Nation, Migration, and the Province in the First British Empire: Scotland and the Americas, 1600–1800', *American Historical Review*, Vol. 104, No. 2 (1999), 463–75; Armitage, D. 'Greater Britain: A useful category of historical analysis?' *American Historical Review*, Vol. 104, No. 2 (1999), 427–45.

14. Ascherson, N. *Games With Shadows*, 153.

15. Storry, M. and Childs, P. 'Introduction', in M. Storry and P. Childs (eds), *British Cultural Identities*, 10.

16. The phrase comes from McCrone, *Understanding Scotland*.

17. Ascherson, *Games with Shadows*, 153.

18. Crang, M. 'On the heritage trail: maps of and journeys to olde Englande', *Environment and Planning D: Society and Space*, Vol. 13 (1994), 341.

19. Lowenthal, D. *The Past is a Foreign Country*, 211.

20. For an extended discussion of these themes, consult McCrone, Morris, Kiely, *Scotland – the Brand*, 1–48. The familial relationship between tourism and heritage is found on p. 12.

21. Samuel, *Theatres of Memory*, 15.
22. Johnson, N.C. 'Framing the past: time, space and the politics of heritage tourism in Ireland', *Political Geography*, Vol. 18, No. 2 (1999), 190.
23. Wright, *On Living in an Old Country*; Hewison, *Heritage Industry*.
24. McCrone, Morris, Kiely, *Scotland – the Brand*.
25. An argument developed in Morris and Morton, *Locality, Community and Nation*, 119–31.
26. Urry, J. *The Tourist Gaze: Leisure and Travel in Contemporary Societies*.
27. Samuel, *Theatres of Memory*, 11.
28. Scottish Tourist Board, personal communication.
29. Gladstone, J. and Morris, A. 'Farm accommodation and agricultural heritage in Orkney' in F. Brown and D. Hall (eds), *Case Studies of Tourism in Peripheral Areas*, 119.
30. *Subscription Schedule for the National Monument of Sir William Wallace on the Abbey Craig, Near Stirling* (n.p., n.d.).
31. Stirling of Keir, W. 'The Designs for the Wallace Monument: a letter to the Lord-Advocate of Scotland, convenor of the committee of the Wallace Monument', *Stirling Journal*, 28 January 1859 (printed at the Journal and Advertiser Office, Stirling, 1859), 8.
32. *National Wallace Monument Stirling: Minute Book kept by William Burns*. Minutes of the meeting held at Glasgow, 1 May 1856.
33. Ibid.
34. 'Scheme of the Acting Committee', National Monument to Sir William Wallace on the Abbey Craig near Stirling (n.p. 1856).
35. Wallace Monument. *Official Papers and Newspaper Extracts relating to the Wallace Monument Movement kept by Wm. Burns.*
36. *The Scotsman*, 25 June 1856.
37. Ibid.
38. Buchanan, R. *Wallace: A Tragedy in Five Acts*; Hutchison, *Life of Sir William Wallace; or Scotland Five Hundred Years Ago*.
39. See postcard produced by the Stirling Smith Art Gallery and Museum showing these letters of support preserved and framed in fragments of Wallace's oak.
40. Fraser, *Scottish Popular Politics*, 80.
41. *The Scotsman*, 7 July 1869.
42. *The Builder*, 28 January 1860.
43. A fuller description is found in Morton, *Unionist-Nationalism*, 177–81.
44. *The Scotsman*, 13 September 1869; *Some Records of the Origin and Progress of the National Wallace Monument Movement, initiated at Glasgow in March 1856* (Printed for private circulation, 1880), 25–6.
45. *The Scotsman*, 13 September 1869.

46. Forrest, M. 'The Wallace Monument and the Scottish National Identity', unpublished BA (Hons) dissertation, University of Stirling, 1993, 32–4.

47. Alcohol was not sold at the monument, Forrest, 'The Wallace Monument', 37.

48. *The Stirling Antiquary*, Vol. 1 (n.d.), 52.

49. Meeting of the Custodian's Committee [National Wallace Monument], 14 Dec. 1936.

50. *Glasgow Evening News*, 9 November 1936; *Record and Mail*, 10 November 1936.

51. A useful discussion on the patriotic belief in the authenticity of the Wallace sword and that it may indicate Wallace was a large man, is found in Magnusson, *Scotland: the Story of a Nation*, 126–8.

52. Morton, 'The heritage of William Wallace', 246–7. It can be compared with visiting figures to Walter Scott's home, Abbotsford, produced by Durie, for the period 1838–98:

1838	2387	1878	7890
1848	1364	1883	6534
1858	5013	1888	6559
1868	6229	1893	6214
1873	6892	1898	7004

A. Durie, 'Tourism in Victorian Scotland: the case of Abbotsford', *Scottish Economic and Social History*, Vol. 12 (1992), 45.

53. *Meeting of the Custodians' Committee* [National Wallace Monument], Stirling, 12 February 1906, 131.

54. *The Scotsman*, 22 May 1993. Stirling District Council co-ordinated the restoration with financial help from the Scottish Tourist Board, Forth Valley Enterprise and the European Community.

55. See, for example, A. Keith, *Several Incidents in the Life of Sir William Wallace*, 3–6, 9–10.

56. See the advertising packaged with the *Braveheart* video cassette upon its first release.

57. *Stirling News*, 13 August 1992 quoted in McCrone, Morris, Kiely, *Scotland – the Brand*, 191.

58. *Scotland Where To Go and What To See*, the Scottish Tourist Board's main overseas guide for 1999.

59. *William Wallace, Special Commemorative Publication to Mark the 650th Anniversary of his Martyrdom* (Glasgow, Scottish Secretariat, 1955), frontispiece.

60. Cant, R.G. 'David Steuart Erskine, eleventh Earl of Buchan: Founder of the Society of Antiquaries of Scotland', in A.S. Bell (ed.), *The Scottish Antiquarian Tradition*.

61. 'Colossal Statue of Sir William Wallace', *Gentleman's Magazine*, Vol. lxxxvii (1817), 621.

62. Ainsworth, G. 'Repairing Wallace Monuments', One Day Wallace Conference, 17 May 1997, Stirling Smith Art Gallery and Museum.

63. *Glasgow Herald*, 14 September 1991.

64. 'Wallace Statue Appeal by the Saltire Society, Edinburgh', designed and published by Clydesdale District Council (*c.* 1992).

65. Ainsworth, 'Repairing Wallace Monuments'.

66. *The Scotsman*, 31 August 1993.

67. *Look at Ayr*, 5.

68. *Metro*, 30 October 2000, 7.

69. Hutchison, *Life of Sir William Wallace*, frontispiece.

70. Spence, *The Story of William Wallace*, 94.

71. Ross, D. *In Wallace's Footsteps*, 14.

72. Barrow, *Robert Bruce*.

73. Ross, *Wallace's Footsteps*, 20.

74. The casket containing the heart was examined by Historic Scotland's experts in a two and a half hour operation. It was later returned to Dunfermline. *The Scotsman*, 30 August 1996.

75. Ibid., 23.

76. Ross, *Trail of William Wallace*, 77.

77. *Description of Wallace State, Aberdeen; Lord Provost's Greeting* (December 1951) [NLS: Pt.sm.1.(7)].

78. Ibid.

79. *Glasgow Herald*, 22 August 1900.

80. *Conditions Relative to Proposed Public Competition for the Wallace and Bruce Memorial*, Captain Reid's Bequest, City of Edinburgh (1882).

81. Turnbull, M.T.R.B. *Monuments and Statues of Edinburgh*, 77–8.

82. 'Index to the Inventory of Monuments maintained by the District', Edinburgh District Council, Department of Architecture.

83. Robertson, D., Wood, M. and Mearns, F.C. *Edinburgh 1329–1929*, li.

84. Robertson, Wood, Mearns, *Edinburgh 1329–1929*, l, liii.

85. *Six Hundredth Anniversary of the Granting of the Bruce Charter* (City and Royal Burgh of Edinburgh, 1929).

86. Ibid.

87. Detail on the search for a true likeness of Wallace is found in Morton, 'The Heritage of William Wallace', 232–3.

88. Yule, *Traditions, etc.*, 6–8.

89. Rogers, C. *The Book of Wallace in Two Volumes*, Vol. II, 229.

90. Ross, *Wallace's Footsteps*, 13.

91. L.G.M.G., *Authentic Life*, 261–3; Yule, *Traditions, etc.*, 6–19; Rogers, *Book of Wallace*, Vol. I, 304–5.

92. Donaldson G. and Morpeth, R.S. *A Dictionary of Scottish History*, 223.

93. Ross, *Wallace's Footsteps*, 6; D.R. Ross, *On the Trail of William Wallace*, 32.
94. Ross, *Wallace's Footsteps*, 8.
95. Rogers, *Book of Wallace*, Vol. II, 94; *Copy of Earl of Buchan's Letter to General Washington*, (1811).
96. Carrick, *Life of Sir William Wallace*, 96–7.
97. The chair was presented in 1820 by the antiquarian Joseph Train, *The Letters of Sir Walter Scott*, vii, 176.
98. *Shearer's Illustrated Souvenir of the National Wallace Monument, Stirling* (Stirling, 1896).
99. Revd Bain, J. and Paterson, J. *The Surroundings of the Wallace Monument as seen from the top*, 20; *The Sir William Wallace Album*.
100. *Illustrated Souvenir of the National Wallace Monument, Stirling*.
101. *Guide to the National Wallace Monument* (n.d.), SPL, Box 19, LC/SAL, 6/64, 16; The custodians bought the Tea Pavilion from their tenant, R.W. Salmond, in 1937 for £60, *Correspondence of the Custodians of the National Wallace Monument, 1936–1938*, 29 January 1837, 2 April 1937, Stirling Council Archive [SCA], SB10/1/1–SB10/4/1.
102. *Guide to the National Wallace Monument*, 16.
103. Correspondence of Custodians, 1936–38, letter from R.W. Salmond to D.B. Morris, Town Clerk of Stirling, dated 29 January 1937. The purchase was confirmed in the Custodians' Committee Meeting in Stirling on 2 April 1937.
104. http://www.impressions.uk.com/castles/castle_8.html
105. The shop is well placed in Edinburgh's Royal Mile, not far from the Scottish Parliament. Although now it is closed due to rent rises caused by the Parliament!
106. Wallis Simpson married King Edward VIII on 3 June 1937, *Scotland on Sunday*, October 24 1999.
107. *The Scotsman*, 8 June 2000.
108. C. McArthur, 'Scotland and the Braveheart Effect', *Journal of the Study of British Cultures*, Vol. 5, No. 1 (1998), 32.
109. *Caledonia*, June 2000, 40–2
110. *The Scotsman*, 6 November 2000.
111. Gilchrist, J. 'The Curse of Mel', *The Scotsman*, 1 June 2000.
112. *The Scotsman*, 24 May 2000.
113. *Scotland on Sunday*, 18 February 2000.
114. A representative speaking on behalf on Ian Cree, 'Braveheart and the Work of the Wallace Clan Trust', One Day Wallace Conference, 17 May 1997, Stirling Smith Art Gallery and Museum.
115. *Stirling Initiative Update*, May 1997, 1, 3.
116. Ibid., 3.
117. Johnson, 'Framing the past', 190.

Chapter Six

1. Bone, J. *Edinburgh Revisited*, 158–9. My thanks to Bob Morris for alerting me to this extract.
2. Smith, *Nations and Nationalism in a Global Era*, 128–41.
3. Ash, 'William Wallace and Robert the Bruce' in Samuel and Thompson (eds), *The Myths We Live By*, 84.
4. Johnston, T. *The History of the Working Classes in Scotland*, 16.
5. Mackenzie, A.M. *Robert Bruce: King of Scots*, 96. Although not a view shared in the chronicles.
6. Fry, M. 'The Whig interpretation of Scottish History', in I. Donnachie and C. Whatley (eds), *The Manufacture of Scottish History*.
7. Kidd, C. 'Sentiment, race and revival: Scottish identities in the aftermath of Enlightenment', in L. Brockliss and D. Eastwood (eds), *A Union of Multiple Identities*.
8. King, B. *The New English Literatures: cultural nationalism in a changing world*, 42.
9. *Wallace, Burns, Stevenson: Appreciations by Lord Rosebery*, 17–18.
10. *Wallace, Braveheart*, 204.
11. Mackenzie, *Robert Bruce*, 117.
12. Cowan and Gifford, *The Polar Twins*.
13. Mackenzie, *Robert Bruce*, 5.
14. Hearn, *Claiming Scotland*, 102.
15. Cowan, 'Identity, Freedom and the Declaration of Arbroath', in Broun, Finlay, Lynch (eds), *Image and Identity*.
16. Ibid., 58.
17. Ibid., 41.
18. Young, *Robert the Bruce's Rivals*.
19. Watson, 'The Enigmatic Lion', in Broun, Finlay, Lynch (eds), *Image and Identity*, 28–30.
20. Stones, E.L.G. 'The Submission of Robert Bruce to Edward I, *c.* 1301–2', *The Scottish Historical Review*, Vol. XXXIV, No. 118, October (1955), 125–6.
21. Johnston, *History of the Working Classes in Scotland*, 23–4.
22. The suggestion that Bruce was there has been comprehensively dismissed in A.M. Mackenzie, *Robert Bruce: King of Scots*,146–50.
23. Craigie, W.A. 'Barbour and Harry as Literature', *The Scottish Review*, Vol. XXII (1893), 199.
24. Brunton, A. *A New Edition of the Life and Heroic Actions of Sir William Wallace, Knight of Elderslie*, 96.
25. McKerlie, P.H. *Sir William Wallace: the Hero of Scotland*, 18.
26. Mackenzie, *Robert Bruce*, 157.

27. Murison, A.F. *Sir William Wallace*, 150.
28. Ross, *The Story of William Wallace*, 25.
29. 'Bannockburn Flyer', Public Affairs Division of the National Trust for Scotland (1999).
30. Edensor, T. 'National Identity and the politics of memory: remembering Bruce and Wallace in symbolic space', *Environment and Planning D: Space and Society*, Vol. 15, No. 2 (1997), 178.
31. McCrone, Morris, Kiely, *Scotland – the Brand*, 188.
32. Ibid., 104.
33. McCrone, Morris, Kiely, *Scotland – the Brand*, 188; Edensor, 'National Identity', 177.
34. Smout, *Century of the Scottish People*, 237.
35. Ibid., p. 146; Fraser, *Scottish Popular Politics*, 146.
36. McArthur, C. 'Culloden: A pre-emptive strike', *Scottish Affairs*, No. 9 (1994).
37. Although the Scottish Home Rule Association had been holding demonstrations there from at least the 1890s. W. Mitchell, *Bannockburn: A Short Sketch of Scottish History*, 3.
38. *The Scotsman*, 27 November 1993.
39. Ross, *Wallace's Footsteps; Trail of Wallace*, as seen in chapter five.
40. McArthur, '*Braveheart* and the Scottish Aesthetic Dementia', 176–7.
41. Pendreight, B. 'History in the faking', *The Scotsman*, 12 June 1995.
42. Ash, 'William Wallace and Robert Bruce', in Samuel and Thompson (eds), *Myths We Live By*, 83.
43. Samuel, *Theatres of Memory*, 259.
44. Quoted in Johnston, *History of the Working Classes in Scotland*, 32.
45. *Ayrshire Post*, 22 May 1896.
46. 'Internet Info', http://www.snp.org.uk (11 August 1995).
47. Calder, A. *Revolving Cultures*, 77.
48. Fraser, W.H. 'The Scottish Context of Chartism', in T. Brotherstone (ed.), *Covenant, Charter and Party*.
49. Fraser, W.H. *Scottish Popular Politics*.
50. John Maclean.
51. Donaldson, *The Scots Overseas*, 118.
52. These latter two points are made in R.J. Finlay, 'Controlling the Past: Scottish Historiography and Scottish Identity in the nineteenth and twentieth centuries', *Scottish Affairs*, No. 9, Autumn (1994), 138.
53. Wood, W. *Yours Sincerely for Scotland*, 72–5.
54. Quoted in Finlay, *Independent and Free*, 37.
55. Spence, *Story of William Wallace*, 92.
56. *The Scottish socialists: A gallery of contemporary portraits*, 22–3. My thanks to Linas Eriksonas for this citation.

57. *A Clear Voice. Douglas Young Poet and Polymath*, 98–9.
58. Quoted in J.D. Young, *The Very Bastards of Creation*, 58–9.
59. Ellis P.B. and MacA'Ghobhainn, S. *The Scottish Insurrection of 1820*, do most to argue the nationalist angle, but few sustain this view for long. The balanced discussion comes from Clark and Dickson, 'The birth of class?' in T.M. Devine and R. Mitchison (eds), *People and Society in Scotland*, Vol. I. Further discussion can be found in Morton, *Unionist-Nationalism*, 191–2.
60. 'Order of the Procession' (Edinburgh, Grand Procession and National Jubilee, n.d., *c.* 1832). [NLS: RB.1.54(5)].
61. *The Only True and Correct Copy. Order of the Procession* (August 1832). [NLS: RB.1.54(17)]; *The Scotsman*, 11 August 1832.
62. *Chairing of the Lord Advocate and the Honorable Mr. Abercrombie* (*c.* 1832). [NLS: RB.1.54(8)].
63. Morton and Morris, 'Civil Society, Governance and Nation' in Knox and Houston (eds), *The New Penguin History of Scotland* 390–3.
64. McKinlay, A. and Morris, R.J. (eds), *The ILP on Clydeside 1893–1932*.
65. Knox, W. 'The Red Clydesiders and the Scottish Political Tradition' in Brotherstone (ed.), *Covenant, Charter and Party*.
66. Macdonald, C.M.M. *The Radical Thread*.
67. Thompson, W. *The Good Old Cause*.
68. Leneman, L. *A Guid Cause*, 116–17.
69. Raeburn, A. *The Militant Suffragettes*, 124–5.
70. Leneman, *A Guid Cause*, 266–7.
71. Leneman, L. *Martyrs in Our Midst: Dundee, Perth and the Forcible Feeding of Suffragettes*, 15.
72. Raeburn, *Militant Suffragettes*, 124.
73. Ibid., 164.
74. Letter of Sir Walter Scott to Lord Montagu, 13 November, *The Letters of Sir Walter Scott*, ed. H.J.C. Grierson, Vol. VI, 15.
75. Quoted in Mitchell, *Strategies for Self-government*, 78.
76. Calder, *Revolving Cultures*, 141–2.
77. Wallace Commemoration Day, Saturday, 26 August 1933, held at Wallace Monument, Elderslie.

Chapter Seven

1. A Scotchman, *Scottish Rights and Grievances: A Letter to the Right Honorable Duncan McLaren, Lord Provost to the City of Edinburgh*, 11.
2. *Border Advertiser*, 8 April 1896.
3. Young, D.C.C. *William Wallace and this War*, speech at the Elderslie Commemoration (Scottish Secretariat, Glasgow, 1943), 6.

4. The idea introduced by Samuel to explain the interaction between historical records and folk memory, *Theatre of Dreams*.

5. http://www.braveheart.co.uk/macbrave

6. http://www.highlanderweb.co.uk/wallace/index.html

7. *The Scotsman*, 1 September 1995.

8. http://www.snp.org.uk (11 August 1995).

9. Morton, *Unionist-Nationalism*, 198–9.

10. *The Scotsman*, 31 October 1996.

11. *The Scotsman*, 12 September 1995.

12. Edensor, T. 'Reading Braveheart: Representing and Contesting Scottish Identity', *Scottish Affairs*, Vol. 21, 144.

13. Petrie, D. *Screening Scotland*, 220 for the 1995 figure; the latter is cited in C. McArthur, 'Scotland and the *Braveheart* Effect', *Journal for the Study of British Cultures*, Vol. 5, No. 1, 36 (1998).

14. For an extended analysis of this movement, G. Morton, 'Scottish Rights and 'centralisation' in the mid-nineteenth century, *Nations and Nationalism*, Vol. 2, No. 2 (1996), and Morton, *Unionist-Nationalism*, 133–54.

15. See *Memorial of the Council of the National Association, to the Right Honorable the Lords Commissioners of Her Majesty's Treasury*, 27 September 1854.

16. See a list of the provosts attending the Eglinton Banquet, along with many other notables, in *Banquet in Honour of the Right Honorable the Earl of Eglinton & Winton*. The Convention of Royal Burghs and twenty-four Town Councils signed an appeal to the Queen, *May it Please your Majesty. The Petition of the undersigned, your Majesty's loyal subjects, inhabiting that part of your Majesty's United Kingdom called Scotland* (c. 1854).

17. Anstruther, I. *The Knight and the Umbrella*.

18. *Justice to Scotland*, 8.

19. Begg, J. *Scotland's Dream of Electoral Justice*, 4–5.

20. Red Lion, *Scotland and 'The Times'*.

21. 'One Behind the Scenes', *Red-Tapism*.

22. A Scotchman, *Scottish Rights and Grievances*, 12–13.

23. Johnston, T. *The History of the Working Classes in Scotland*, 122, quoting from *Ancient Laws and Customs of the Burghs of Scotland*, Preface, xlix.

24. Without forgoing their claims as Scotsmen, stated William Burns in 1855, 'Association for the Vindication of Scottish Rights'.

25. Sawers, P.R. *Footsteps of Sir William Wallace*.

26. Letter of Sir Walter Scott to T. Scott, July 20 1808 and letter of Sir Walter Scott to J. Baillie, 18 September 1808, *The Letters of Sir Walter Scott*, ed. H.J.C. Grierson, Vol. II, 75, 92–3.

27. Brunton, A. *A New Work in Answer to the Pamphlet, 'Wallace on the Forth'*, 4.

28. Hutchison, *Life of Sir William Wallace; or Scotland Five Hundred Years Ago*, viii. A verbatim copy of this statement was made in C.G. Glass, *Stray Leaves from Scotch and English History, with the Life of Sir William Wallace, Scotland's Patriot, Hero and Political Martyr*, 8–9.

29. The continuities and discontinuities between the National Association for the Vindication of Scottish Rights and first Scottish Home Rule Association are discussed in. G. Morton, 'The First Home Rule Movement in Scotland, 1886 to 1918' in H. Dickinson and M. Lynch (eds), *Sovereignty and Devolution*.

30. Moir, J. *Sir William Wallace: a critical study of his biographer Blind Harry*, 60–1.

31. *Midlothian Campaign*, 44.

32. Brown, S.J. '"Echoes of Midlothian" Scottish Liberalism and the South African War, 1899–1902', *Scottish Historical Review*, LXXI, 1, 2: 191/2 (1992), 58. Indeed, Rosebery complained that he was fed up being always censured by the SHRA; see further comment in W. Mitchell, *Lord Rosebery and Home Rule for Scotland: A Challenge*, 5–6.

33. Akroyd, R.J. *Lord Rosebery and Scottish Nationalism*, 280.

34. Fry, M. *Patronage and Principle*, 105–7; I.G.C. Hutchison, *A Political History of Scotland 1832–1924*, 172–3.

35. This is argued in Morton, 'First Home Rule Movement' in Dickinson and Lynch (eds), *Sovereignty and Devolution*.

36. Finlay, *A Partnership for Good*, 45.

37. *Prospects of the Scottish Home Rule Association* (Edinburgh, Scottish Home Rule Association, 1892), 1.

38. This was explored in *Scottish versus Irish Grievances*.

39. *Methodist Times*, 28 May 1896.

40. *Scottish Highlander*, 21 May 1896.

41. *Scottish Highlander*, 11 June 1896.

42. Pike, W.T. (ed.), 'Contemporary Biographies', in *Edinburgh and the Lothians*, 128.

43. Verse five of seven, the *Montrose Review*, 22 May 1896.

44. Verses three and four of nine, appeared in various newspapers in May 1896.

45. First and last verse of seven, *Scottish Highlander*, 23 July 1896.

46. Scottish Home Rule Association, 10 September 1897.

47. Mitchell, *Strategies for Self-government*, 26.

48. Romans, J. *Home Rule for Scotland*, 6, 28.

49. Theodore Napier writing in the *Scottish Highlander*, 21 May 1896.

50. Mitchell, W. *Bannockburn: A Short Sketch of Scottish History*.

51. Napier, T. 'Honouring Sir William Wallace', *Stirling Observer*, c. 19 August 1896.

52. Davidson, J.M. *Scotia Rediva: Home Rule for Scotland with the Lives of Sir William Wallace, George Buchanan, Fletcher of Saltoun, and Thomas Spence*, 112.

53. Quoted in Fraser, *Scottish Popular Politics*, 145.
54. Dunbar, A.H. *Scottish Kings*, frontispiece, 215.
55. Mitchell, W. *Home Rule for Scotland and Imperial Federation*, 11.
56. Macrae, D. *The Story of William Wallace, Scotland's National hero*, 3.
57. Finlay, R.J. 'Continuity and Change: Scottish Politics, 1900–45', in T.M. Devine and R.J. Finlay (eds), *Scotland in the Twentieth Century*, 66–7; Finlay, *Partnership for Good?*, 52–3; Mitchell, *Strategies for Self-government*, 72.
58. Hutchison, *Political History*, 241.
59. Finlay, *Partnership for Good?*, 59.
60. *The Round Table*. Vol. 5, December (1911–12), 12, 15.
61. Spence, *Story of William Wallace*, 3.
62. Ibid., 4.
63. Ibid.
64. Ibid., 7.
65. *The Round Table*, Vol. 11 (1920–1), 234.
66. An advert for the Scottish Patriotic Association at the end of their published *Story of Wallace*.
67. *Scotland Yet!*, 12.
68. Ibid., 16.
69. Finlay, *Independent and Free*, 55–9.
70. *Scottish Historical Pageant to be held at Craigmillar Castle*, 99, 156.
71. Lynch, 'A Nation Born Again?', in Broun, Lynch, Finlay (eds), *Image and Identity*, 82–3.
72. *The Scotsman*, 19 August 1929.
73. *The Scotsman*, 26 August 1929.
74. *The Scotsman*, 24 August 1931.
75. Ibid.
76. Harvie, C. *Scotland and Nationalism*, 28–9.
77. McCrone, D. 'The Unstable Union: Scotland since the 1920s', in M. Lynch (ed.), *Scotland, 1850–1979*, 44–5; Levitt, I. 'Scottish Sentiment, Administrative Devolution and Westminster, 1885–1964', in Lynch (ed.), *Scotland, 1850–1979*, 35–7.
78. Wallace Commemoration Day Official Souvenir Programme.
79. Ibid.
80. Ibid.
81. NLS: P.la.7030 (1967–1993).
82. Young, *William Wallace and this War*, 3.
83. Ibid., 8.
84. Ibid., 1.
85. Craig, F.W.S. *British Parliamentary Elections 1885–1918*, Kirkcaldy District of Burghs [575].

86. Young, D.C.C. *A Clear Voice*, 17.

87. For more detail, consult Mitchell, *Strategies for Self-government*, 191.

88. NLS: P.med.3505 (1928–66).

89. *Scottish Newsletter*, No. 20, September 1953.

90. *William Wallace: National Hero of Scotland*, Special Commemorative Publication to Mark the 650th Anniversary of his Martyrdom, 3.

91. Lamont, A. *How Scots opposed the peace time call-up*.

92. NLS: P.la.7030 (1967–1993).

93. Taylor, M. 'John Bull and the Iconography of public opinion in England, *c.* 1712–1929', *Past and Present*, Vol. 134 (1992).

94. *William Wallace: National hero of Scotland*, 1–2.

95. A good selection can be found deposited in the National Library of Scotland: P.med.3505 (1928–66); P.la.7030 (1967–93); P.el.680 (Others).

96. Mitchell, *Strategies for Self-government*, 272.

97. A good pictorial account of the events of this period is found in A. Clements, K. Farquarson and K. Wark, *Restless Nation*, 28; Wood, *Yours Sincerely for Scotland*, 121–2.

98. Wood, *Yours Sincerely for Scotland*, 259.

99. 'Miscellaneous pamphlets and leaflets', Scottish National Party [NLS: P.med.3505 (1928–66)].

100. Du Garde Peach, L. *Robert Bruce: An Adventure from History*, 6, 16.

101. *The Scotsman*, 20 August 1979.

102. Stuart, R. from Arbroath, *The Sunday Post*, 28 March 1999.

103. Salmond, A. 'Winning with Wallace', Address to the 61st Annual National Conference of the Scottish National Party, 22 September 1995 (Perth City Halls).

Chapter Eight

1. '21st Century Schizoid Man' from *In the Court of the Crimson King*, An Observation by King Crimson, written and performed by R. Fripp, I. McDonald, G. Lake, M. Giles and P. Sinfield (1969).

2. Anderson, *Imagined Communities*.

3. See S. Nenadic, 'Middle-Rank Consumers and Domestic Culture in Edinburgh and Glasgow, 1720–1840', *Past and Present*, No. 145 (1994).

4. Harvey, D. *Money, Time, Space, and the City*; Sudjic, D. *The 100 Mile City*; Moss, M. 'Telecommunications, world cities and urban policy', *Urban Studies*, Vol. 24 (1987); Fujita, K. 'A World City and Flexible Specialisation', *International Journal of Urban and Regional Research*, Vol. 15, No. 2, June (1991); Coupland, A. 'Docklands: dream or disaster', in A. Thornley (ed.), *The Crisis of London*.

5. Hall, J.A. 'After the fall: an analysis of post-communism', *British Journal of Sociology*, Vol. 45, No. 4, December (1994), 525, 538.
6. Tilly, C., Tilly L. and Tilly, R. *The Rebellious Century 1830–1930* Melucci, A. *Nomads of the Present.*
7. Boli, J. and Thomas, G.M. 'World Culture in the World Polity: A Century of International Non-Governmental Organization', in *American Sociological Review*, Vol. 62, April (1997), 171.
8. Ritzer, G. *The McDonaldization of Society*, revised edition; Bryman, A. 'The Disneyization of Society', *Sociological Review*, Vol. 47, No. 1 (1999); Tramposh, W. 'Mickeying with the Muses: Disney World and Regional Identity', in Fladmark (ed.), *Sharing the Earth.*
9. Wallerstein, I. *The Modern World System*; Mann, M. 'Nation-states in Europe and other countries: Diversifying, developing, not dying', in G. Balakrishnan (ed.), *Mapping the Nation*, 298.
10. Morris, L. 'Globalization, migration and the nation-state: the path to post-national Europe?', *British Journal of Sociology*, Vol. 48, No. 2, June (1997), 192, 206–7.
11. Mann. 'Nation-states', in Balakrishnan (ed.); *Mapping the Nation*, 298.
12. Norberg-Hodge, H. 'Break up the Monoculture', *The Nation*, 15–22 July (1996), 21.
13. Hirst, P. and Thompson, G. *Globalization in Question.*
14. Lacroix, J.-G. and Tremblay, G. 'The Emergence of Cultural Industries into the Foreground of Industrialization and Commodification: Elements of Context', trans. R. Ashby, in *Current Sociology*, Vol. 45, No. 4, October (1997), 36.
15. Appadurai, A. 'Disjuncture and Difference in the Global Cultural Economy', *Theory, Culture and Society*, Vol. 7, Nos 2–3, June (1990), 307.
16. At time of writing, the potential for exploiting e-commerce by peripheral societies is the theme of television advertisements by IBM computers.
17. Fethersone, M. 'Global Culture: an introduction', *Theory, Culture and Society*, 7, 2–3, June (1990), 10.
18. 'Work smarter not harder' is the catch-phrase of current advertisements by BT to promote their internet-related services to business customers.
19. Thompson, E.P. 'Time, work-discipline, and industrial capitalism', *Past and Present*, No. 38 (1967).
20. http://www.macbraveheart.freeserve.co.uk/html/messages/bhtimes.htm
21. http://www.macbraveheart.freeserve.co.uk/html/messages/bhtim-01.htm
22. My thanks to Trevor Griffiths for reminding me of this story.
23. http://www.macbraveheart.freeserve.co.uk/
24. http://www.macbraveheart.freeserve.co.uk/about.htm
25. Ibid.

26. http://www.braveheart.co.uk
27. Ibid.
28. *Seven Days*, broadcast by Scottish Television, 20 August 2000.
29. The relationship between core and peripheral narratives was discussed in chapter one, 7–12.
30. Social mobility and egalitarianism in Scotland is examined in McCrone, *Understanding Scotland*, 88–120, while the main focus of the debate has been on the social openness of Scottish education: A. McPherson, 'An Angle on the Geist: Persistence and Change in the Scottish Educational Tradition', in W. Humes and H. Paterson (eds), *Scottish Culture and Scottish Education, 1800–1980*; R.D. Anderson, *Education and Opportunity in Victorian Scotland*; H. Corr, 'Where is the Lass o' Pairts: Gender, Identity and Education in Victorian Scotland', in Broun, Finlay, Lynch (eds), *Image and Identity*. All these works offer a response to the renowned G.E. Davie, *The Democratic Intellect*. Davie later followed up some of his early statements in *The Crisis of the Democratic Intellect*.
31. This research by Joseph Bradley into football and national identity has been reported in the press: *Metro*, 26 September 2000; *The Scotsman*, 26 September 2000. The journal *Scottish Affairs* provides summaries of monthly opinion poll data on Scottish identity and on voting intentions.
32. *Daily Record* 16 May 2000; http://www.macbraveheart.freeserve.co.uk/html/organisations/wallace_clan_trust/index.htm
33. Wallace, *Braveheart*, ix–x.
34. Mackay, *William Wallace*, 11.
35. Tranter, N. *The Wallace*, dust-jacket.
36. Pendreight, 'History in the faking'.
37. http://www.clannada.org/docs/wallace.htm
38. http://www.highlanderweb.co.uk/wallace/index2.html. An advert for Mackay's book followed the history. Highlanderweb's text is replicated and linked to by http://ctc.simplenet.com/braveheart/
39. http://www.highlanderweb.co.uk/wallace/index2.html
40. *The Herald*, 15 November 1997, reproduced at http://www.braveheart.co.uk/macbrave/history/wallace/ewart.htm
41. http://historymedren.about.com/homework/historymedren/library/movies/blmvbrave.htm?iam=dpile&terms=Wallace+William+History
42. http://ctc.simplenet.com/braveheart/
43. http://www.scotsmart.com/info/histfigures/wallace.html
44. http://www.braveheart.co.uk/macbrave/history/wallace/ewart.htm
45. McDiarmid, *Hary's Wallace*.
46. http://www.scottishradiance.com/wallrev.htm
47. See chapter two, n. 3.

48. http://www.silcom.com/~manatee/mackay_wallace.html
49. http://mccoist.hypermart.net/wallace.html
50. http://www.braveheart.com/
51. http://www.duncans-of-scotland.com/independence.html
52. http://www.drcelt.com/celtictreasure/sirwilwal.html
53. http://www.braveheart.co.uk/clann/
54. http://www.macbraveheart.freeserve.co.uk/html/clans/wallace/://www. macbraveheart.freeserve.co.uk/html/clans/wallace/:/
55. http://www.highlanderweb.co.uk/wallace/sword.htm. The link between the size of Wallace and the size of his sword is discussed in Magnusson, *Scotland: the Story of a Nation*, 126–8.
56. http://www.highlanderweb.co.uk/wallace/sword.htm
57. http://world-interactive.com/armory/Indexes/scottish_sword_index.htm
58. *Daily Record*, 14 November 2000; *The Scotsman*, 8 March 2001.
59. Full details are found in the programme for Brave Art, an exhibition of contemporary art celebrating the 699th Anniversary of the Battle of Stirling Bridge, 11 September – 8 December 1996, Stirling Smith Art Gallery and Museum.
60. Watson, 'The Enigmatic Lion', in Broun, Finlay and Lynch (eds), *Image and Identity*, 24.
61. Acknowledged, that is, in the modernist theories of nationalism. This debate has been examined in chapter one and can be followed in the Warwick debate between A.D. Smith and Ernest Gellner, published in *Nations and Nationalism*, Vol. 2, No. 3 (1996), 357–70.

Bibliography

WORLD WIDE WALLACE

http://ctc.simplenet.com/braveheart/
http://historymedren.about.com/homework/historymedren/library/movies/
    blmvbrave.htm?iam=dpile&terms=Wallace+William+History
http://mccoist.hypermart.net/wallace.html
http://world-interactive.com/armory/Indexes/scottish_sword_index.htm
http://www.biggar-net.co.uk/wallace700/
http://www.braveheart.co.uk
http://www.clannada.org/docs/wallace.htm
http://www.drcelt.com/celtictreasure/sirwilwal.html
http://www.duncans-of-scotland.com/independence.html
http://www.freedom-scotland.demon.co.uk/
http://www.highlanderweb.co.uk/wallace/index.htm
http://www.impressions.uk.com/castles/castle_8.html
http://www.macbraveheart.freeserve.co.uk/about.htm
http://www.nms.ac.uk/mos/
http://www.scotsmart.com/info/histfigures/wallace.html
http://www.scottishradiance.com/wallrev.htm
http://www.silcom.com/~manatee/mackay_wallace.html
http://www.rchams.gov.uk
http://www.snp.org.uk.

NEWSPAPERS AND PERIODICALS

Ayrshire Post
Border Advertiser
Caledonia
Glasgow Evening News
Methodist Times
Metro
Montrose Review

New York Times
Record and Mail
Daily Record
Seven Magazine
Scotland on Sunday
Scottish Daily Mail
Scottish Highlander

Bibliography

Scottish Newsletter
The Scotsman
Stirling Antiquary

Sunday Post
The Times

WALLACIANA AND PRINTED PRIMARY SOURCES

'21st Century Schizoid Man' from *In the Court of the Crimson King, An Observation by King Crimson*, written and performed by R. Fripp, I. McDonald, G. Lake, M. Giles and P. Sinfield (E.G. Records Ltd, Polydor, 1969).

700th Anniversary Guide to Events: Easter to Autumn, 1997.

Alexander, G. *Sir William Wallace: the Hero of Scotland. An Historical Romance* (London, 1903).

An appeal to Scots and Friends at Home and Abroad for a London Memorial to Sir William Wallace, Scots Patriot (1954) [National Library of Scotland [NLS]: HP3.85.1009].

Anon, *The Life of Sir William Wallace, the Scots Patriot* (Edinburgh, Oliver & Boyd, 1810).

The Actis and Deidis of Schir William Wallace, 1570, W. Craigie (ed.) (Edinburgh, Scottish Text Society, 1938).

The Actis and Deidis of the Illustere And Vailzeand Campioun Schir William Wallace, Knight of Ellerslie by Henry the Minstrel, commonly known as Blind Harry, ed. J. Moir (Edinburgh, Scottish Text Society, 1889).

'Bannockburn Flyer', Public Affairs Division of the National Trust for Scotland (1999).

Banquet in Honour of the Right Honourable the Earl of Eglinton & Winton, K.T., President of the National Association for the Vindication of Scottish Rights, held in the City Hall, Glasgow, 4 October 1854.

Bain, J. and Paterson, J. *The Surroundings of the Wallace Monument as seen from the top* (5th edn, 1920).

The Bannatyne Miscellany, Containing Papers and Tracts Chiefly Relating to the History and Literature of Scotland, T. Thomson (ed.), Bannatyne Club No. 19, 1823 (reprinted from the 1855 edn, New York, Ams Press, 1973).

Begg, J. *Scotland's Dream of Electoral Justice or the Forty Shilling Freehold Questions Explained. With Answers to Objections* (Edinburgh, James Nichol, 1857).

Bone, J. *Edinburgh Revisited* (London, Sidgwick & Jackson, 1911).

'Britannia Flyer', Britannia, Ocean Drive, Leith, Edinburgh (1999).

British Tourist Authority (BTA Research Centre, 1999) *Media Briefs*.

Brown, J.T.T. 'The Wallace and The Bruce Restudied', in *Bonner Beiträge zur Anglistik* (Bonn, 1900).

Bibliography

Brunton, A. *A New Edition of the Life and Heroic Actions of Sir William Wallace, Knight of Elderslie: in three parts* (Glasgow, Stirling, Dunfermline, Newburgh, Edinburgh, Inverkeithing, Porteous Brothers, R.S. Shearer, W. Clark & Son; J. Wood, J. Stillie, W. Pringle, 1881).

——. *A New Work in Answer to the Pamphlet, 'Wallace on the Forth', proving the stratagem at Stirling Bridge and that the Bridge was at Kildean, etc. Also the history of the famous Battle of Stirling Bridge, to which is added two letters written by Sir William Wallace himself, and Wallace's charter to Scrymgeour of Dundee* (Dunfermline, W. Clark, 1841, Stirling, R.S. Shearer, 1861).

Buchan, *Copy of Earl of Buchan's Letter to General Washington, President of the United States of America, sent enclosed in the box of Wallace's oak, June 28th, 1791; contained in The Earl of Buchan's Address to the Americas at Edinburgh on Washington's Birth-day, February 22nd* (1811).

Buchanan, R. *Wallace: A Tragedy in Five Acts* (Glasgow, Griffen & Co, 1856).

Burns, W. 'Association for the Vindication of Scottish Rights' (n.p. c. 1853).

Calendar of Documents Relating to Scotland, J. Bain (ed.) (Edinburgh, 1887), Vol. II.

Carrick, J.D. *Life of Sir William Wallace, Knight of Ellerslie and Guardian of Scotland*, 2nd edition (Glasgow, Griffen & Co, 1827).

——. *Life of Sir William Wallace*, 3rd edition (London, Griffen & Co., 1849).

Carroll, L. *The Hunting of the Snark: an Agony in Eight Fits* (1872).

Carruth, J.A. *Heroic Wallace and Bruce* (Norwich, Jarrold Colour Publications, 1986).

Chairing of the Lord Advocate and the Honourable Mr Abercrombie (c. 1832). [NLS: RB.1.54(8)].

'Colossal Statue of Sir William Wallace', *Gentleman's Magazine*, Vol. lxxxvii (1817).

The Complaynt of Scotland (1549), *With an appendix of contemporary English tracts*, J.A. Murray (ed.) (London, Early English Text Society, 1872).

Conditions Relative to Proposed Public Competition for the Wallace and Bruce Memorial, Captain Reid's Bequest, City of Edinburgh (1882).

Correspondence of the Custodians of the National Wallace Monument, 1936–1938, 29 January 1937, 2 April 1937 [Stirling Council Archive [SCA], SB10/1/1, SB10/4/1].

Davidson, J.M. *Scotia Rediva: Home Rule for Scotland with the Lives of Sir William Wallace, George Buchanan, Fletcher of Saltoun, and Thomas Spence* (London, William Reeves, 1888, 1893).

Dalrymple of Hailes, D. *Annals of Scotland: From the accession of Malcome III to the Accession of the House of Stewart*, 3rd edn (1776–79) (Edinburgh, A. Constable, 1819).

Description of Wallace Statue, Aberdeen; Lord Provost's Greeting (December 1951) [NLS: Pt.sm.1.(7)].

189

Donaldson, P. *The Life of Sir William Wallace, the Governor General of Scotland and Hero of the Scottish Chiefs. Containing his parentage, adventures, heroic achievements, imprisonment and death; drawn from authentic materials of Scottish History* (Hartford, Silus Andrus, 1825).

Du Garde Peach, L. *Robert Bruce: An Adventure from History*, Ladybird Series 561 (Loughborough, Wills and Hepworth, 1964).

Fergusson, J. *William Wallace: Guardian of Scotland* (London, Alexander Maclehose & Co., 1938).

Finlay, J. *Wallace, or the Vale of Ellerslie, with other poems*, 2nd edn (Glasgow, R. Chapman, 1804).

Four new songs, and a prophecy: I. A song for joy of our ancient race of Stewarts. II. The Battle of Preston, that was fought by his Royal Highness Prince Charles, the 21st of September 1745. III. On an honourable atchievement of Sir William Wallace, near Falkirk. IV. A song, call'd, The rebellious crew. V. A prophecy by Mr Beakenhead, Song III (Edinburgh?, *c.* 1750) [NLS: Ry.1.2.85(21)].

Fyfe, W.T. *Wallace, the Hero of Scotland* (Edinburgh, Anderson, 1920).

L.G.M.G., *Authentic Life of Sir William Wallace; with chapter on Traditional Wallace. Compiled from the best authorities* (Dundee, George Montgomery, 1877).

Gilchrist, J. 'The Curse of Mel', *The Scotsman*, 1 June 2000.

Glass, C.G. *Stray Leaves from Scotch and English History, with the Life of Sir William Wallace, Scotland's Patriot, hero, and Political Martyr* (Montreal, A. & A. Stevenson, *c.* 1873).

Gray, D.J. *William Wallace: the King's Enemy* (London, Robert Hale, 1991).

Guide to the National Wallace Monument (n.d.), [Stirling Public Library [SPL] Box 19, LC/SAL, 6/64, 16].

Guide to the National Wallace Monument. Situated on the Abbey Craig near Stirling containing the Great Sword of Sir William Wallace. The Finest View in Scotland (Stirling?, R.W. Salmond, *c.* 1964).

Hamilton of Gilbertfield, W. *A New Edition of the Life and Heroick Actions of the Renoun'd Sir William Wallace, General and Governour of Scotland. Wherein the Old obsolete Words are rendered more Intelligible; and adapted to the understanding of such who have not the leisure to study the Meaning, and Import of such, Phrases without the help of a Glossary* (Glasgow, William Duncan, 1722).

To His Grace, James, Duke of Perth, &c. Lieutenant General of His Majesty's army, under the command of His Royal Highness Charles, Prince of Wales, &c. (n.p., *c.* 1745?.) [NLS: Mf.SP.159(14)].

History of Sir William Wallace: The renowned Scottish Champion (Glasgow, Printed for the Booksellers, *c.* 1840).

Holford, M. *Wallace; or, the Fight of Falkirk; a Metrical Romance* (London, Cadell & Davies, 1809).

Bibliography

Hutchison, *Life of Sir William Wallace; or Scotland Five Hundred Years Ago* (Glasgow, Thomas Murray & Son, 1858).

Illustrated Souvenir of the National Wallace Monument, Stirling (Stirling, R.S. Shearer & Son, 1896).

'Index to the Inventory of Monuments maintained by the District', *Edinburgh District Council, Department of Architecture*.

Jones, D. *A Wee Guide to William Wallace* (Edinburgh, Goblinshead, 1997).

Justice to Scotland. Report of the Great Public Meeting of the National Association for the Vindication of Scottish Rights, held in the City Hall, Glasgow, December 15 1853.

Keith, A. *Several Incidents in the Life of Sir William Wallace, with an account of Lanark, the theatre of his exploits, and a description of the romantic scenery in the neighbourhood* (Lanark, 1844).

King, E. *Introducing William Wallace: the life and legacy of Scotland's liberator* (Fort William, Firtree Publishing, 1997).

——. 'Introduction', *Blind Harry's Wallace, William Hamilton of Gilbertfield* (Edinburgh, Luath Press, 1998).

The Chronicle of Lanercost, 1272–1346, trans. H. Maxwell (Glasgow, Maclehose, 1913).

The Life and Heroic Achievement of Sir William Wallace, the Scottish Patriot; and the life of Robert Bruce, King of Scotland: from the original verse (Jedburgh, 1845).

Lives of the Scottish Poets in Three Volumes, J. Robertson (ed.) (Edinburgh, The Society of Ancient Scots, 1821).

Look at Ayr (Doncaster, Bessacarr Prints, 1985).

Mackay, J. *William Wallace: Brave Heart* (Edinburgh, Mainstream, 1995).

Mackenzie, A.M. (ed.), *Scottish Pageant*, 2nd edn (Edinburgh, Oliver & Boyd for the Saltire Society, 1952).

——. *Robert Bruce: King of Scots* (London, Maclehose, 1936).

John Maclean, In the Rapids of Revolution. Essays, articles and letters 1902–23, ed. with introduction by N. Milton (London, Allison & Busby, 1978).

Macrae, D. *The Story of William Wallace, Scotland's National Hero* (Scottish Patriotic Association, 1905).

Mair, J. *A History of Greater Britain as well England as Scotland compiled from the ancient authorities by John Major* (1521), A. Constable (ed. and trans.) (Edinburgh, Publications of the Scottish History Society, Vol. X, 1892).

May it Please your Majesty. The Petition of the undersigned, your Majesty's loyal subjects, inhabiting that part of your Majesty's United Kingdom called Scotland (c. 1854).

McDiarmid, M.P. 'The Date of the *Wallace*', *Scottish Historical Review*, Vol. xxiv (1955).

McDiarmid, M.P. *Hary's Wallace (Vita Nobilissimi Defensoris Scotie Wilelmi Wallace Milits)* (Edinburgh, Scottish Text Society, 1968), Vol. I.

McGowan, A. 'Searching for William the Welshman', *The Double Treasure*, No. 22 (1999).

McKerlie, P.H. *Sir William Wallace: the Hero of Scotland. Contains Fresh Information about the Traitorous Opposition he had to encounter in his struggle for Scottish Independence* (Glasgow, Morrison Brothers, 1900).

McKinlay, R. 'Barbour's Bruce', *Records of the Glasgow Bibliographical Society*, Vol. VI (Glasgow, 1920).

McNie, A. *Clan Wallace* (Jedburgh, Cascade Publishing, 1986).

Meeting of the Custodians' Committee [National Wallace Monument], Stirling 12 February 1906.

Meeting of the Custodians' Committee [National Wallace Monument], 14 December 1936.

Memorial of the Council of the National Association, to the Right Honourable the Lords Commissioners of her Majesty's Treasury, 27 September 1854.

The Metrical History of Sir William Wallace, Knight of Ellerslie, by Henry, commonly called Blind Harry: carefully transcribed from the ms. copy of that work in the Advocates' Library, under the eye of the Earl of Buchan. And now printed for the first time, according to the ancient and true orthography. With Notes and Dissertations. In Three Volumes (Perth, Morrison & Son, 1790). Vol. III.

Midlothian Campaign. Political Speeches delivered in November and December 1879 and March and April 1880 by the Right Hon. W.E. Gladstone, MP (Edinburgh, 1880).

Miller, J.F. Editions of Blind Harry's '*Wallace*' (1912, read 13 December 1913), Prepared for the Glasgow Bibliographical Society [NLS: LC.3351(16)].

——. 'Some additions to the Bibliography of Blind Harry's *Wallace*' (Read 19 March 1917), *Records of the Glasgow Bibliographical Society*, Vol. VI (Glasgow, 1920).

Mitchell, W. *Home Rule for Scotland and Imperial Federation* (Edinburgh, Scottish Home Rule Association, 1892).

——. *Lord Rosebery and Home Rule for Scotland: A Challenge* (Scottish Home Rule Association, *c.* 1894).

——. *Bannockburn: A Short Sketch of Scottish History* (Scottish Home Rule Association, *c.* 1894).

Moir, J. *Sir William Wallace: a critical study of his biographer Blind Harry* (Aberdeen, 1888).

Murison, A.F. *Sir William Wallace* (Edinburgh, Oliphant, Anderson & Ferrier, 1898).

Napier, T. 'Honouring Sir William Wallace', *Stirling Observer*, *c.* 19 August 1896.

National Wallace Monument. Official Papers and Newspaper Extracts relating to the Wallace Monument Movement kept by Wm. Burns.

Bibliography

National Wallace Monument Stirling: Minute Book kept by William Burns. Minutes of the meeting held at Glasgow 1 May 1856.

The Only True and Correct Copy. Order of the Procession (August 1832). [NLS: RB.1.54(17)].

'Order of the Procession' (Edinburgh, Grand Procession and National Jubilee, n.d., *c.* 1832). [NLS: RB.1.54(5)].

Paterson, J. *Wallace and His Times* (Edinburgh, William Paterson, 1858).

——. *Wallace, the Hero of Scotland*, 3rd edn (Edinburgh, William P. Nimmo, 1881).

Political Squibs, Edinburgh 1820–21 [Edinburgh Public Library [EPL] YJN1213.820, A106X].

Porter, J. *The Scottish Chiefs and the Heroism of Sir William Wallace* (Wakefield, *c.* 1880).

Prospects of the Scottish Home Rule Association (Edinburgh, Scottish Home Rule Association, 1892).

Red Lion, *Scotland and 'The Times'. To the editors of the 'Edinburgh Evening Post' and the 'Scottish Record'* (1853).

Red-Tapism, 2nd edn (London, Ridgeway, 1855).

Rogers, C. *The Book of Wallace in Two Volumes*, (Edinburgh, Grampian Club, 1889).

Romans, J. *Home Rule for Scotland* (Edinburgh, Scottish Home Rule Association, *c.* 1894).

Rosebery, Lord *In Memory of Sir William Wallace: Address by Lord Rosebery* (Stirling, Eneas Mackay, 1897).

——. *Wallace, Burns, Stevenson: Appreciations by Lord Rosebery* (Stirling, Eneas Mackay, 1905).

Ross, D.R. *In Wallace's Footsteps: A Guide to Places Associated with the Life of William Wallace* (Glasgow, The Society of William Wallace, n.d.).

——. *The Story of William Wallace* (New Lanark, Waverley Books, 1998).

——. *On the Trail of Robert the Bruce* (Edinburgh, Luath Press, 1999).

——. *On the Trail of William Wallace* (Luath Press, 1999).

Salmond, A. 'Winning with Wallace', Address to the 61st Annual National Conference of the Scottish National Party, 22 September 1995 (Perth City Halls).

Sawers, P.R. *Footsteps of Sir William Wallace. Battle of Stirling: Or, Wallace on the Forth* (Glasgow, Thomas Murray & Son, 1856).

'Scheme of the Acting Committee', National Monument to Sir William Wallace on the Abbey Craig near Stirling (n.p. 1856).

A Scotchman, *Scottish Rights and Grievancies: A Letter to the Right Honourable Duncan McLaren, Lord Provost to the City of Edinburgh* (Edinburgh, *c.* 1854).

Scotichronicon by Walter Bower N.F. Shead, W.B. Stevenson and D.E.R. Watt (eds), with A. Borthwick, R.E. Latham, J.R.S Phillips and M.S. Smith (Aberdeen University Press, 1991), Vol. 6.

Scotichronicon, by Walter Bower, D.E.R. Watt (ed.) (Aberdeen University Press, 1998), Vol. 9.

Scotichronicon, Johannis de Fordun Chronica gentis Scotorum, Vol. 1, W.F. Skene (ed.) (Edinburgh, Edmonston and Douglas, 1871).

Scotland Where To Go and What To See (Scottish Tourist Board, overseas guide, 1999).

Scotland Yet! An Address Delivered by the Revd James Barr, B.D., at the Wallace Monument, at Elderslie, on 27 August 1921; and now reprinted from the 'Forward' of September 3, 1921 (Glasgow, Scottish Home Rule Association, 1921).

Scottish Historical Pageant to be held at Craigmillar Castle (13–16 July 1927, in aid of the Queen Victoria Jubilee Institute for Nurses (Scottish Branch), Official Souvenir Programme).

Scottish versus Irish Grievances (Edinburgh, Scottish Home Rule Association, c. 1890).

Seven Days, broadcast by Scottish Television, 20 August 2000.

Shade of Wallace, The: A poem (Glasgow, D. Mackenzie, 1807).

Shearer's Illustrated Souvenir of the National Wallace Monument, Stirling (Stirling, 1896).

Six Hundredth Anniversary of the Granting of the Bruce Charter (City and Royal Burgh of Edinburgh, 1929).

Some Records of the Origin and Progress of the National Wallace Monument Movement, initiated at Glasgow in March 1856 (Printed for private circulation, 1880).

Spence, J.L.T.C. *The Story of William Wallace* (Oxford University Press, 1919).

Stevenson, J. (ed.) *Documents Illustrative of Sir William Wallace, his life and times*, Maitland Club 54, (Edinburgh, 1841).

Stirling Initiative Update, May 1997.

Stirling, William of Keir, 'The Designs for the Wallace Monument: a letter to the Lord-Advocate of Scotland, convenor of the committee of the Wallace Monument', *Stirling Journal*, 28 January 1859 (printed at the Journal and Advertiser Office, Stirling, 1859).

Story of Wallace (Scottish Patriotic Association, n.d.).

Sub-committee appointed by a General Committee of Subscribers at Edinburgh, for carrying into execution the design for erecting a National Monument in Scotland in Commemoration of the Triumphs of the Late War by Sea and Land (Edinburgh, 1822).

Subscription Schedule for the National Monument of Sir William Wallace on the Abbey Craig, Near Stirling (n.p., n.d.).

'The Sword of Wallace' found within *Wallace, or, the Vale of Ellerslie*. [NLS: H.32.h.33].

Taylor, J. *Pictorial History of Scotland*, (London, 1859).

Bibliography

The Tragedy of the Valiant Knight Sir William Wallace to which is prefixed a brief Historical Account of the Knight, and his Exploits for the Delivery of Scotland, and added a more particular Account of the way which he was betrayed into the hands of the English (Glasgow, Hutchison & Co, 1815?).

Tranter, N. *The Wallace* (London, Hodder & Stoughton, 1975).

Tytler, P.F. *Lives of the Scottish Worthies* (London, John Murray, 1831), Vol. I.

Wallace and Bruce, a poem (n.p., *c.* 1825) [NLS: 5.5194(21)].

Wallace Commemoration Day, Saturday, 26 August, 1933, Held at Wallace Monument, Elderslie. Official Souvenir Programme.

'Wallace Statue Appeal by the Saltire Society, Edinburgh', designed and published by Clydesdale District Council, (*c.* 1992).

Wallace, or, the Vale of Ellerslie with Other Poems (Glasgow, Chapman & Lang, 1802).

Wallace, the Hero of Scotland, a drama, in three Acts: Adapted to Hodgeson's Theatrical Characters and Scenes in the Same (London, Hodgeson & Co, 1822).

Wallace, the Hero of Scotland; or Battle of Dumbarton, An Historical Romance in which the love of liberty and Conjugal Affections are exemplified in the characters of Sir William Wallace and Lady Wallace, with the unparalleled Bravery of the former against a band of Ruffians in the rescue of the Earl of Mar, and his revenge on the governor of Lanark for the Murder of Lady Wallace (London, Thomas Redruffe, 1825?).

Wallace; or the life and acts of Sir William Wallace, of Ellerslie. By Henry the Minstrel. Published from a manuscript dated MCCCLXXXVIII, J. Jamieson, (ed.) (new edn, Glasgow, 1820, 1869).

Wallace, R. *Braveheart*, (London, Signet, 1995).

Wallace's Women, a play in two acts by Margaret McSeveney and Elizabeth Roberts, Stirling Smith Art Gallery and Museum.

Watson, J.S. *Sir William Wallace, the Scottish Hero: A narrative of his Life and Actions, chiefly as recorded in the Metrical History of Henry the Minstrel on the authority of John Blair, Wallace's Chaplain, and Thomas Gray, Priest of Liberton* (London, Saunders, Otley & Co, 1861).

William Wallace: National Hero of Scotland, Special Commemorative Publication to Mark the 650th Anniversary of his Martyrdom (Glasgow, Scottish Secretariat, 1955).

William Wallace Album, Sir, Wallace Monument Stirling, Bridge of Allan, Dunblane, Doune, Callander, The Trossachs, and Loch Katrine (Stirling, 1904?).

Wyntoun, Andrew of, *The Orygynale Cronykil of Scotland* Vol. II, David Laing (ed.) (Edinburgh, Edmonston and Douglas, 1872).

Young, D.C.C. *William Wallace and this War*, speech at the Elderslie Commemoration (Scottish Secretariat, Glasgow, 1943).

——. *A Clear Voice. Douglas Young Poet and Polymath. A Selection from his writings with a Memoir* (Loanhead, Macdonald Publishers, *c.* 1974).

Yule, Gen. Patrick, A Former Subscriber for a Wallace Monument, *Traditions, etc., respecting Sir William Wallace; Collected Chiefly from Publications of Recent Date* (Edinburgh, Oliver & Boyd, 1856).

SECONDARY SOURCES

Ainsworth, G. 'Repairing Wallace Monuments', One Day Wallace Conference, 17 May 1997, Stirling Smith Art Gallery and Museum.

Akroyd, R.J. *Lord Rosebery and Scottish Nationalism, 1868–1896*, unpublished PhD thesis, University of Edinburgh (1996).

Allanson, P. and Whitby, M. *The Rural Economy and the British Countryside* (London, Earthscan, 1996).

Anderson, B. *Imagined Communities: Reflections on the Origin and Spread of Nationalism*, revised edn (London, Verso, 1996).

Anderson, R.D. *Education and Opportunity in Victorian Scotland* (Oxford, Clarendon, 1983).

Anstruther, I. *The Knight and the Umbrella: An Account of the Eglinton Tournament 1839*, 2nd edn (Gloucester, Alan Sutton, 1986).

Appadurai, A. 'Disjuncture and Difference in the Global Cultural Economy', *Theory, Culture and Society*, Vol. 7, Nos 2–3, June (1990).

Armitage, D. 'Greater Britain: A Useful category of historical analysis?' *American Historical Review*, Vol. 104, No. 2 (1999).

Armstrong, J.A. *Nations before Nationalism* (Chapel Hill, University of North Carolina Press, 1982).

Ascherson, N. *Games With Shadows* (London, Radius, 1988).

Ash, M. *The Strange Death of Scottish History*, (Edinburgh, The Ramsay Head Press, 1980).

——. 'William Wallace and Robert the Bruce: the life and death of a national myth' in R. Samuel and P. Thompson (eds), *The Myths We Live By* (London, Routledge, 1990).

Bannerman, J. 'MacDuff of Fife', in A. Grant and K.J. Stringer (eds) *Medieval Scotland: Crown, Lordship and Community. Essays presented to G.W.S. Barrow* (Edinburgh, Edinburgh University Press, 1993).

Barrow, G. and Rogan, A. 'James Fifth Stewart of Scotland, 1260(?) – 1309', in K.J. Stringer, (ed.), *Essays on the Nobility of Medieval Scotland* (Edinburgh, John Donald, 1985).

Barrow, G.W.S. *Robert Bruce and the Community of the Realm of Scotland*, 4th edn (Edinburgh University Press, 1992).

Bellamy, J.G. *The Law of Treason in England in the Later Middle Ages* (Cambridge University Press, 1970).

Beveridge, C. and Turnbull, R. *The Eclipse of Scottish Culture* (Edinburgh, Polygon, 1989).

Bibliography

Bhabha, H.K. *Nation and Narration* (London, Routledge, 1990).

Billig, M. *Banal Nationalism* (London, Sage, 1995).

Boli, J. and Thomas, G.M. 'World Culture in the World Polity: A Century of International Non-Governmental Organization', in *American Sociological Review*, Vol. 62, April (1997).

Brown, S.J. '"Echoes of Midlothian" Scottish Liberalism and the South African War, 1899–1902', *Scottish Historical Review*, Vol. LXXI, 1, 2: No. 191/2 (1992).

Brown, F. and Hall, D. 'Introduction: the paradox of the peripherality', in F. Brown and D. Hall (eds), *Case Studies of Tourism in Peripheral Areas* (Bornholms Forskningscenter, 1999).

Brubaker, R. *Nationalism Reframed: Nationhood and the National Question in the New Europe* (Cambridge University Press, 1996).

Brunsden, G.M. 'Aspects of Scotland's Social, Political and Cultural Scene in the Late Seventeenth and Early Eighteenth Centuries, as Mirrored in the Wallace and Bruce Traditions', in E.J. Cowan and D. Gifford (eds), *The Polar Twins* (Edinburgh, John Donald Publishers, 1999).

Bryant, C.G.A. 'Social self-organisation, civility and sociology: a comment on Kumar's "Civil Society"', *British Journal of Sociology*, Vol. 44, No. 3 (1993).

Bryman, A. 'The Disneyization of Society', *Sociological Review*, Vol. 47, No. 1 (1999).

Calder, A. *Revolving Culture: notes from the Scottish Republic* (London, I.B. Tauris, 1994).

Campbell, I. *Kailyard*, (Edinburgh, 1981).

Cant, R.G. 'David Steuart Erskine, 11th Earl of Buchan: Founder of the Society of Antiquaries of Scotland', in A.S. Bell (ed.), *The Scottish Antiquarian Tradition: Essays to mark the bicentenary of the Society of Antiquaries of Scotland, 1780–1980* (Edinburgh, John Donald 1981).

Carnegie, A. *Autobiography of Andrew Carnegie* (Boston and New York, Riverside, 1920).

Carter, A. 'Kailyard: the literature of decline in nineteenth-century Scotland', *Scottish Journal of Sociology*, Vol. 1. (1976).

Child, F.C. *English and Scottish Ballads* (Boston, Little Brown, 1859).

Cohen, A.P. 'Culture as Identity: An Anthropologist's View', *New Literary History*, Vol. 24 (1993).

Conversi, D. 'Ernest Gellner as critic of social thought: nationalism, closed systems and the Central European tradition', *Nations and Nationalism*, Vol. 5, No. 4 (1999).

Cookson, J.E. 'The Napoleonic Wars, Military Scotland and Tory Highlandism in the Early Nineteenth Century', *The Scottish Historical Review*, Vol. LXXVIII, 1, No. 205 (1999).

Cornell, S. *Ethnicity and race: making identities in a changing world* (London, Pine Forge Press, 1998).

Cornell, S. 'That's the Story of our Life: Ethnicity and Narrative, Rupture and Power', in P.R. Spickard and W.J. Burroughs (eds), *We are a People: Narrative and Multiplicity in the Construction of Ethnic Identity* (Philadelphia, Temple University Press, 1999).

Corr, H. 'Where is the Lass o' Pairts: Gender, Identity and Education in Victorian Scotland', in D. Broun, R. Finlay and M. Lynch (eds), *Image and Identity: the making and remaking of Scotland through the ages* (Edinburgh, John Donald Publishers, 1998).

Coupland, A. 'Docklands: dream or disaster', in A. Thornley (ed.), *The Crisis of London* (London, Routledge, 1992).

Cowan, E.J. 'The political ideas of a covenanting leader: Archibald Campbell, marquis of Argyll 1607–1661' in R.A. Mason (ed.), *Scots and Britons: Scottish political thought and the union of 1603* (Cambridge University Press, 1994).

——. 'The Wallace Factor in Scottish History', in R. Jackson and S. Wood (eds), *Images of Scotland*, in *The Journal of Scottish Education*, Occasional Paper, No. 1 (Dundee, The Northern College, 1997).

——. 'Identity, Freedom and the Declaration of Arbroath', in Broun, Finlay, Lynch (eds), *Image and Identity*.

——. Finlay, R.J. and Paul, W. *Scotland Since 1688: struggle for a nation* (London, Cima Books, 2000).

Clements, A., Farquharson, K., Wark, K. *Restless Nation* (Mainstream, Edinburgh, 1996).

Craig, C. 'Myths against History, Tartanry and Kailyard in nineteenth-century Scottish literature', in C. McArthur (ed.), *Scotch Reels: Scotland in Cinema and Television* (London, BFI, 1982).

——. *Out of History: Narrative Paradigms in Scottish and English Culture* (Edinburgh, Polygon, 1996).

Craig, F.W.S. *British Parliamentary Elections 1885–1918*, 2nd edn (Aldershot, Parliamentary Research Services, 1989).

Craigie, W.A. 'Barbour and Harry as Literature', *The Scottish Review*, Vol. XXII (1893).

Craik, G.L. *A Compendious History of English Literature and the English Language from the Norman Conquest* (London, Griffen, Bohn & Co, 1861), Vol. 1.

Crang, M. 'On the heritage trail: maps of and journeys to olde Englande' *Environment and Planning D: Society and Space*, Vol. 13 (1994).

Davie, G.E. *The Democratic Intellect: Scotland and her Universities in the Nineteenth Century* (Edinburgh University Press, 1964).

——. *The Crisis of the Democratic Intellect: the problem of generalism and specialisation in twentieth-century Scotland* (Edinburgh, Polygon, 1986).

De Tocqueville, A. *Democracy in America*, G. Lawrence (trans.), J.P. Mayer (ed.) (London, Fontana, 1994).

Devine, T.M. *The Scottish Nation, 1700–2000* (Harmondsworth, Penguin, 1999).

Devine, T.M. and Mitchison, R. (eds), *People and Society in Scotland*, Vol. 1, 1760–1830 (Edinburgh, John Donald Publishers, 1988).

Dîaz-Andreu, M. 'The Past in the Present: the search for roots in cultural nationalism. The Spanish case', in J.G. Beramendi, R Máiz and X.M. Núñez (eds), *Nationalism in Europe: Past and Present*, Volume I (University Press of Santiago de Compostela, 1994).

Donaldson, G. *The Scots Overseas* (London, Robert Hale, 1966).

Donaldson, G. and Morpeth, R.S. *A Dictionary of Scottish History* (Edinburgh, John Donald, 1977).

Dunbar, A.H. *Scottish Kings: A Revised Chronology of Scottish History, 1000–1625* (Edinburgh, David Douglas, 1906).

Duncan, A.A.M. 'The Process of Norham, 1291', in P. Cross and S. Lloyd (eds), *Thirteenth Century England*, No. 5 (Woodbridge, Boydell, 1995).

Durie, A. 'Tourism in Victorian Scotland: the case of Abbotsford', *Scottish Economic and Social History*, xii (1992).

Edensor, T. 'National Identity and the politics of memory: remembering Bruce and Wallace in symbolic space', *Environment and Planning D: Space and Society*, Vol. 15, No. 2 (1997).

——. 'Reading Braveheart: Representing and Contesting Scottish Identity', *Scottish Affairs*, Vol. 21 (1997).

Edwards, O.D. *Macaulay* (London, Weidenfeld & Nicolson, 1988).

Eller, J.E. and Coughlan, R.M. 'The poverty of primordialism: the demystification of ethnic attachments', *Ethnic and Racial Studies*, Vol. 16, No. 2 (1993).

Ellis, P.B. and MacA'Ghobhainn, S. *The Scottish Insurrection of 1820* (London, Gollancz, 1970).

Eriksen, T.H. 'Formal and informal nationalism', *Ethnic and Racial Studies*, Vol. 16, No. 1 (1993).

Eskine-Hill, H. 'Literature and the Jacobite Cause: was there a rhetoric of Jacobitism?' in E. Cruikshanks (ed.), *Ideology and Conspiracy: Aspects of Jacobitism, 1689–1759* (Edinburgh, John Donald, 1982).

Evans, N. 'Introduction: Identity and Integration in the British Isles' in N. Evans (ed.), *National Identity in the British Isles* (Gwynedd, Coleg Harlech Occasional Papers in Welsh Studies, No. 3, 1989).

Fetherstone, M. 'Global Culture: an introduction', *Theory, Culture and Society*, Vol. 7, Nos 2–3, June (1990).

Finlay, R.J. 'Controlling the Past: Scottish Historiography and Scottish Identity in the nineteenth and twentieth centuries', *Scottish Affairs*, No. 9, Autumn (1994).

——. *Independent and Free: Scottish Politics and the Origins of the Scottish National Party, 1918–1945* (Edinburgh, John Donald, 1994).

——. 'Continuity and Change: Scottish Politics, 1900–45', in T.M. Devine and R.J. Finlay (eds), *Scotland in the Twentieth Century* (Edinburgh University Press, 1996).

Finlay, R.J. *A Partnership for Good? Scottish Politics and the Union since 1880* (Edinburgh, John Donald, 1997).

Fisher, A. *William Wallace* (Edinburgh, John Donald, 1986).

Forrest, M. 'The Wallace Monument and the Scottish National Identity', unpublished BA (Hons) dissertation, University of Stirling, 1993.

Foster, R. 'Storylines: narratives and nationality in nineteenth-century Ireland' in G. Cubitt (ed.), *Imagining Nations* (Manchester University Press, 1998).

Fraser, W.H. 'The Scottish Context of Chartism', in T. Brotherstone (ed.), *Covenant, Charter and Party: traditions of revolt and protest in modern Scottish History* (Aberdeen University Press, 1989).

——. *Scottish Popular Politics: From Radicalism to Labour* (Edinburgh, Polygon, 2000).

Fry, M. *Patronage and Principle: A political history of modern Scotland* (Aberdeen University Press, 1987).

——. 'The Whig interpretation of Scottish History', in I. Donnachie and C. Whatley (eds), *The Manufacture of Scottish History* (Edinburgh, Polygon, 1992).

Fujita, K. 'A World City and Flexible Specialisation', *International Journal of Urban and Regional Research*, Vol. 15, No. 2, June (1991).

Geddie, W. (ed.), *A Bibliography of Middle Scots Poets: with an introduction on the history of their reputations*, Scottish Text Society Vol. 61 (Edinburgh, Blackwood & Sons, 1912).

Gellner, E. *Nations and Nationalism* (Oxford, Basil Blackwell, 1983).

——. 'Reply: Do nations have navels?', *Nations and Nationalism*, Vol. 2, No. 3 (1996).

——. *Nationalism* (London, Weidenfeld & Nicolson, 1997).

Giles, J. and Middleton, T. 'Introduction', in J. Giles and T. Middleton (eds), *Writing Englishness 1900–1950* (London and New York, Routledge, 1995).

Gladstone, J. and Morris, A. 'Farm accommodation and agricultural heritage in Orkney' in F. Brown and D. Hall (eds), *Case Studies of Tourism in Peripheral Areas* (Bornholms Forskningscenter, 1999).

Goldstein, R.J. *The Matter of Scotland: Historical Narrative in Medieval Scotland* (Lincoln and London, University of Nebraska Press, 1993).

Grant, A. *Independence and Nationhood, Scotland 1306–1469* (London, Edward Arnold, 1984).

Grant, A. and Stringer, K. 'Introduction: the enigma of British History', in A. Grant and K. Stringer (eds), *Uniting the Kingdom? The Making of British History* (London and New York, Routledge, 1995).

Greenfeld, L. *Nationalism: Five roads to modernity* (Massachusetts, Cambridge, 1992).

Grierson, H.J.C. (ed.), *The Letters of Sir Walter Scott*, (London, Constable, 1932–7).

Bibliography

Grosby, S. 'The chosen people of ancient Israel and the Occident: why does nationality exist and survive?', *Nations and Nationalism*, Vol. 5, No. 3 (1999).

Guibernau, M. *Nationalisms: The Nation-State and Nationalism in the Twentieth Century* (Cambridge, Polity Press, 1996).

Hall, J.A. 'After the fall: an analysis of post-communism', *British Journal of Sociology*, Vol. 45, No. 4, December (1994).

Hall, S. 'The question of cultural identity', in S. Hall, D. Held and A. McGrew (eds), *Modernity and its Futures* (Cambridge, Polity Press, 1992).

Harvey, D. *Money, Time, Space, and the City* (Cambridge, Granta, *c.* 1985).

Harvie, C. *Scotland and Nationalism: Scottish Society and Politics, 1707–1994* (London, Routledge, 1994).

Hastings, A. 'Special peoples', *Nations and Nationalism*, Vol. 5, No. 3 (1999).

Hearn, J. *Claiming Scotland: national identity and liberal culture* (Edinburgh, Polygon, 2000).

Henderson, T.F. *Scottish Vernacular Literature: a succinct history* (London, David Nutt, 1898).

Hendrick, B.J. *The Life of Andrew Carnegie*, 2 vols (New York, Doubleday, Doran & Co., 1932).

Hewison, R. *The Heritage Industry: Britain in a Climate of Decline* (London, Methuen, 1987).

Hill Burton, J. *The History of Scotland* (Edinburgh, William Blackwood, new edn, 1897), Vol. II.

Hirst, P. and Thompson, G. *Globalization in Question* (Cambridge, Polity Press, 1996).

Hobsbawm, E.J. and Ranger, T. (eds), *The Invention of Tradition* (Cambridge, Canto, 1983).

Holt, J.C. *Robin Hood* (London, Thames and Hudson, 1983).

Hume Brown, P. *History of Scotland to the Present Time*, Vol. I (Cambridge University Press, 1911).

Hutchison, I.G.C. *A Political History of Scotland 1832–1924. Parties, Elections and Issues* (Edinburgh, John Donald, 1986).

Iwazumi, K. 'The Union of 1707 in Scottish Historiography, *c.* 1800–1914', unpublished MPhil thesis, University of St Andrews, 1996.

Johnson, N.C. 'Framing the past: time, space and the politics of heritage tourism in Ireland', *Political Geography*, Vol. 18, No. 2, Feb. (1999).

Johnston, T. *The History of the Working Classes in Scotland* (Glasgow, Forward Publishing, 1920, 1929).

Keane, J. (ed.), *Civil Society and the State: New European Perspectives* (London, Verso, 1988).

Kearney, H. *The British Isles: A History of Four Nations* (Cambridge University Press, 1995).

Bibliography

Keating, M. 'Response to Ethno-nationalist movements in Europe: a debate', *Nations and Nationalism*, Vol. 4, No. 4 (1998).

Keen, M. *The Outlaws of Medieval Legend* (London, Routledge & Kegan Paul, 1961).

Kidd, C. 'The Strange Death of Scottish History revisited: Constructions of the Past in Scotland, *c.* 1790–1914', *The Scottish Historical Review*, LXXVI, 201, April (1997).

——. 'Sentiment, race and revival: Scottish identities in the aftermath of Enlightenment', in L. Brockliss and D. Eastwood (eds), *A Union of Multiple Identities. The British Isles, c. 1750–c. 1850* (Manchester University Press, 1997).

King, A. 'Englishmen, Scots and Marchers: National and Local Identities in Thomas Gray's *Scalacronica*', *Northern History*, Vol. XXXVI, No. 2 (2000).

King, B. *The New English Literatures: cultural nationalism in a changing world* (London, Macmillan, 1980).

Knightley, C. *Folk Heroes of Britain* (London, Thames & Hudson, 1982).

Knox, W. 'The Red Clydesiders and the Scottish Political Tradition', in T. Brotherstone (ed.), *Covenant, Charter and Party: traditions of revolt and protest in modern Scottish History* (Aberdeen University Press, 1989).

Kumar, K. 'Civil Society: an inquiry into the usefulness of an historical term', *British Journal of Sociology*, Vol. 44, No. 3, September (1993).

Lacroix, J.G. and Tremblay, G. 'The Emergence of Cultural Industries into the Foreground of Industrialization and Commodification: Elements of Context', trans. R. Ashby, in *Current Sociology*, Vol. 45, No. 4, October (1997).

Laing, D. (ed.) *Early Popular Poetry in Scotland and the Northern Border*, in 1822/26. Rearranged and revised with additions and glossary by W. Carrew-Hazlitt, 2 vols (London, Reeves & Turner, 1895), Vol. II.

Landsman, N.C. 'Nation, Migration, and the Province in the First British Empire: Scotland and the Americas, 1600–1800', *American Historical Review*, Vol. 104, No. 2 (1999).

Langlands, R. 'Britishness or Englishness: The historical problem of national identity in Britain', *Nations and Nationalism*, Vol. 5, No. 1 (1999).

Leneman, L. *A Guid Cause: The Women's Suffrage Movement in Scotland* (Edinburgh, Mercat Press, 1991, 1995).

——. *Martyrs in our Midst: Dundee, Perth and the Forcible Feeding of Suffragettes* (Dundee, Abertay Historical Society, Publication No. 33, 1993).

Levitt, I. 'Scottish Sentiment, Administrative Devolution and Westminster, 1885–1964', in M. Lynch (ed.), *Scotland, 1850–1979*.

Lindsay, M. *History of Scottish Literature* (London, Robert Hale, 1977).

Llobera, J. *The God of Modernity: the Development of Nationalism in Western Europe* (Oxford, Berg, 1994).

Lowenthal, D. *The Past is a Foreign Country* (Cambridge University Press, 1985).

Bibliography

Lynch, M. 'A Nation Born Again? Scottish Identity in the Sixteenth and Seventeenth Centuries', in Broun, Finlay and Lynch (eds), *Image and Identity: The Making and Remaking of Scotland Through the Ages* (Edinburgh, John Donald, 1998).

——. *Scotland: A New History* (London, Century, 1991).

McArthur, C. 'Culloden: A pre-emptive strike', *Scottish Affairs*, No. 9 (1994).

——. '*Braveheart* and the Scottish Aesthetic Dementia', in T. Barta (ed.), *Screening the Past: Film and the Representation of History* (Westport, Praeger, 1998).

——. 'Scotland and the *Braveheart* Effect', *Journal of the Study of British Cultures*, Vol. 5, No. 1 (1998).

——. 'The Exquisite Corpse of Rab(elias) C(opernicus) Nesbitt', in M. Wayne (ed.), *Dissident Voices: the Politics of Television and Cutlural Change* (London, Pluto Press, 1998).

McCrone, D. *Understanding Scotland: the sociology of a stateless nation* (London, Routledge, 1992).

——. 'The Unstable Union: Scotland since the 1920s', in M. Lynch (ed.), *Scotland, 1850–1979: Society, Politics and the Union* (London, The Historical Association for Scotland, 1993).

——. 'Scotland – the Brand: Heritage, Identity and Ethnicity' in R. Jackson and S. Wood (eds), *Images of Scotland, The Journal of Scottish Education* Occasional Paper, No. 1 (Dundee, The Northern College, 1997).

——. *The Sociology of Nationalism: tomorrow's ancestors* (London, Routledge, 1998).

——, Morris, A. and Kiely, R. *Scotland – the Brand: The Making of Scottish Heritage*, (Edinburgh University Press, 1995, 1999).

Macdonagh, O. *States of Mind: A study of Anglo-Irish conflict, 1780–1980* (London, Allen & Unwin, 1983).

McDonald, T. 'Why has Scottish culture flourished in North America?' (unpublished MSc dissertation, University of Edinburgh, 2000).

Macdougall, N.A.T. 'The sources: a reappraisal of the legend', in J.M. Brown (ed.), *Scottish Society in the Fifteenth Century* (London, Edward Arnold, 1977).

McKay, K. *Mel Gibson* (Sidgwick & Jackson, London, 1988).

McKinlay, A. and Morris, R.J. (eds), *The ILP on Clydeside 1893–1932: from foundation to disintegration* (Manchester University Press, 1991).

MacNee, K. *Living in Rural Scotland: a study of life in four rural communities* (Edinburgh, The Scottish Office Central Research Unit, 1996).

McPherson, A. 'An Angle on the Geist: Persistence and Change in the Scottish Educational Tradition', in W. Humes and H. Paterson (eds), *Scottish Culture and Scottish Education, 1800–1980* (Edinburgh University Press, 1983).

MacPherson, J.A. 'Beyond the Memories: Drawing Strength from the Diaspora', in J.M. Fladmark (ed.), *Sharing the Earth* (London, Donhead, 1995).

MacQueen, J. 'The literature of fifteenth-century Scotland', in J.M. Brown (ed.), *Scottish Society in the Fifteenth Century* (London, Edward Arnold, 1977).

Magnusson, M. *Scotland: the Story of a Nation* (London, HarperCollins, 2000).

Mann, M. 'Nation-states in Europe and other countries: Diversifying, developing, not dying', in G. Balakrishnan (ed.), *Mapping the Nation* (London, Verso, 1996).

Maxwell, H.E. *The Early Chronicles Relating to Scotland* (Glasgow, Maclehose, 1912).

Mellor, R.E.H. *Nation, State and Territory: A Political Geography* (London and New York, Routledge, 1989).

Melucci, A. *Nomads of the Present: Social Movements and Individual Needs in Contemporary Society*, (London, Radius, 1989).

Mitchell, J. 'Conservatism in Twentieth Century Scotland: Society, Ideology and the Union' in M. Lynch (ed.), *Scotland, 1850–1979* (1993).

——. *Strategies for Self-Government* (Edinburgh, Polygon, 1996).

Mitchison, R. (ed.), *Why Scottish History Matters* (Edinburgh, Saltire Society, 1991).

Morris, A. and Morton, G. *Locality, Community and Nation* (London, Hodder & Stoughton, 1998).

Morris, L. 'Globalization, migration and the nation-state: the path to post-national Europe?', *British Journal of Sociology*, Vol. 48, No. 2, June (1997).

Morris, R.J. 'Scotland, 1830–1914: The making of a nation within a nation', in W.H. Fraser and R.J. Morris (eds), *People and Society in Scotland*, Vol. II, *1830–1914* (Edinburgh, John Donald Publishers, 1990).

——. 'Civil society and the nature of urbanism: Britain, 1750–1850', *Urban History*, Vol. 25, No. 3 (1998).

Morton, G. 'Review: Sir William Wallace and other tall stories (unlikely mostly)', *Scottish Affairs*, No. 14, Spring (1996).

——. 'Scottish Rights and "centralisation" in the mid-nineteenth century', *Nations and Nationalism*, Vol. 2, No. 2 (1996).

——. 'The Most Efficacious Patriot: the heritage of William Wallace in nineteenth-century Scotland', *Scottish Historical Review*, Vol. LXXVII, 2: No. 204 (1998).

——. 'What if? The significance of Scotland's missing nationalism in the nineteenth century', in D. Broun, R.J. Finlay and M. Lynch (eds), *Image and Identity: the making and remaking of Scotland through the ages* (Edinburgh, John Donald, 1998).

——. *Unionist-Nationalism: Governing Urban Scotland, 1830–1860* (East Linton, Tuckwell Press, 1999).

——. 'The First Home Rule Movement in Scotland, 1886 to 1918' in H. Dickinson and M. Lynch (eds), *Sovereignty and Devolution* (East Linton, Tuckwell Press, 2000).

Morton, G. and Morris, R.J. 'Civil Society, Governance and Nation: Scotland, 1832–1914', in W. Knox and R.A. Houston (eds), *New Penguin History of Scotland* (Harmondsworth, Penguin, 2001).

Moss, M. 'Telecommunications, world cities and urban policy', *Urban Studies*, Vol. 24 (1987).

Nairn, T. *The Break-up of Britain*, 2nd edn (London, Verso, 1981).

——. *The Enchanted Glass: Britain and its Monarchy* (London, Hutchinson, 1988).

——. 'Internationalism and the second coming', *Daedalus*, Vol. 122, No. 3 (1993).

——. *Faces of Nationalism: Janus revisited* (London, Verso, 1997).

Neilson, G. *John Barbour: Poet and Translator* (London, K. Paul, Trench, Trübner, 1900).

——. 'On Blind Harry's *Wallace*', *Essays and Studies* (by members of the English Association), Vol. I (Oxford, Clarendon Press, 1910).

Nenadic, S. 'Museums, Gender and Cultural Identity in Scotland', *Gender & History*, Vol. 6, No. 3 (1994).

——. 'Middle-Rank Consumers and Domestic Culture in Edinburgh and Glasgow, 1720–1840', *Past and Present*, No. 145 (1994).

Newby, H. *The Countryside in Question* (London, Hutchison, 1985).

Nicholson, R. *Scotland: The Later Middle Ages* (Edinburgh, Oliver & Boyd, 1974).

Norberg-Hodge, H. 'Break up the Monoculture', *The Nation*, 15–22 July (1996).

O'Halloran, C. 'Ownership of the past: antiquarian debate and ethnic identity in Scotland and Ireland' in S. J. Connolly, R.A. Houston and R.J. Morris (eds), *Conflict, Identity and Economic Development: Scotland and Ireland, 1600–1939* (Preston, Carnegie, 1995).

Page, R. 'The Archaeology of Stirling Bridge', One Day Wallace Conference, 17 May 1997, Stirling Smith Art Gallery and Museum.

Paterson, L. *The Autonomy of Modern Scotland* (Edinburgh University Press, 1994).

——. 'Civil Society and Democratic Renewal', in S. Baron, J. Field and T. Schüller (eds), *Social Capital: Social Theory and the Third Way* (Oxford University Press, 2001).

Pears, I. 'The Gentleman and the Hero: Wellington and Napoleon in the Nineteenth Century' in R. Porter (ed.), *Myths of the English* (Cambridge, Polity, 1993).

Pederson, R. 'Scots Gaelic as a tourism asset' in Fladmark (ed.), *Sharing the Earth*.

Pendreight, B. 'History in the faking', *The Scotsman*, 12 June 1995.

Petrie, D. *Screening Scotland* (London, BFI Publishing, 2000).

Pike, W.T. (ed.), 'Contemporary Biographies' in *Edinburgh and the Lothians at the Opening of the Twentieth Century*, A. Eddinton (Edinburgh, Pike & Co., 1904).

Pocock, J.G.A. 'The Limits and Divisions of British History: in search of an unknown subject', *American Historical Review*, Vol. 87, No. 2 (1982).

Pocock, J.G.A. 'Conclusion: Contingency, identity, sovereignty' in A. Grant and K. Stringer (eds), *Uniting the Kingdom? The Making of British History* (London, Routledge, 1995).

——. 'The New British History in Atlantic Perspective: An Antipodean Commentary', *American Historical Review*, Vol. 104, No. 2 (1999).

Prestwich, M. *War, Politics and Finance under Edward I* (London, Faber & Faber, 1972).

——. *The Three Edwards: War and State in England 1272–1377* (London, Weidenfeld & Nicolson, 1980).

Raeburn, A. *The Militant Suffragettes* (London, Michael Joseph, 1973).

Read, D. *The English Provinces,* c. *1760–1960: a study in influence* (London, Arnold, 1964).

Reid, N.H. 'Alexander III: The Historiography of a Myth' in N.H. Reid (ed.), *Scotland in the Reign of Alexander III 1249–1286* (Edinburgh, John Donald, 1990).

Renan, E. *Qu'est ce qu'une nation?*, trans. I. M. Snyder (Paris, 1882).

Rendall, J. 'Tacitus engendered: "Gothic feminism" and British histories, c. 1750–1800' in G. Cubitt (ed.), *Imagining Nations* (Manchester University Press, 1998).

Ritzer, G. *The McDonaldization of Society*, revised edn (California, Pine Forge Press, 1996).

Robertson, D., Wood, M. and Mearns, F.C. *Edinburgh 1329–1929* (Edinburgh, Oliver & Boyd, 1929).

Rogers, A. 'A Planned Countryside' in G. Mingay (ed.), *The Rural Idyll* (London, Routledge, 1989).

Rosie, G. 'Museumry and the Heritage Industry' in I. Donnachie and C. Whatley (eds), *The Manufacture of Scottish History* (Edinburgh, Polygon, 1992).

The Round Table: A Quarterly Review of the Politics of the British Empire, Vol. 11 (1920–1).

Samuel, R. *Theatres of Memory, Vol. 1: Past and Present in Contemporary Culture* (London, Verso, 1994).

Schama, S. *History of Britain*, BBC Television, Autumn 2000.

Schofield, W.H. *Mythical Bards and the Life of Sir William Wallace* (Cambridge, Mass., Harvard University Press, 1920).

Scholes, P.A. *God Save the Queen! The History and Romance of the World's First National Anthem* (Oxford University Press, 1954).

The Scottish Socialists: A Gallery of Contemporary Portraits (London, Faber & Faber, 1931).

Scott, P.H. 'The Distortions of Unionism', *Scotlands*, Vol. 5, No. 1 (1998).

Seal, G. *The Outlaw Legend: A cultural tradition in Britain, America and Australia* (Cambridge University Press, 1996).

Bibliography

Sellar, W.C. and Yeatman, R.J. *1066 and All That* (London, Methuen, 1930).

Sibbald, J. *Chronicle of Scottish Poetry from the thirteenth century to the Union of the Crowns, to which is added a glossary*, 4 vols (London, Longman & Rees, 1802).

Smith, A.D. *The Ethnic Origin of Nations* (Oxford, Basil Blackwell, 1986).

——. 'The myth of the "Modern Nation" and the myths of nation', *Ethnic and Racial Studies*, Vol. 11, No. 1 (1988).

——. *Nations and Nationalism in a Global Era* (Cambridge, Polity Press, 1995).

——. 'Memory and Modernity: reflections on Ernest Gellner's theory of nationalism', *Nations and Nationalism*, Vol. 2, No. 3 (1996).

Smout, T.C. *A Century of the Scottish People, 1830–1950* (London, Collins, 1986).

——. 'Perspectives on the Scottish identity', *Scottish Affairs*, No. 6, Winter (1994).

Stapleton, J. *Englishness and the Study of Politics: The Social and Political Thought of Ernest Barker* (Cambridge University Press, 1994).

Stones, E.L.G. 'The Submission of Robert Bruce to Edward I, *c.* 1301–2', *The Scottish Historical Review*, Vol. XXXIV, No. 118, October (1955).

Storry, M. and Childs, P. 'Introduction', in M. Storry and P. Childs (eds), *British Cultural Identities* (London, Routledge, 1997).

Sudjic, D. *The 100 Mile City* (London, André Deutsch, 1992).

Taylor, M. 'John Bull and the Iconography of public opinion in England, *c.* 1712–1929', *Past and Present*, Vol. 134 (1992).

Templin, J. Alton 'The ideology of a chosen people: Afrikaner nationalism and the Ossewa Trek, 1938', *Nations and Nationalism*, Vol. 5, No. 3 (1999).

Terry, C.S. *A Catalogue of the Publications of Scottish Historical and Kindred Clubs and Societies, 1780–1908* (Glasgow, MacLehose, 1909).

Thompson, E.P. 'Time, work-discipline, and industrial capitalism', *Past and Present*, No. 38 (1967).

Thompson, W. *The Good Old Cause: British Communism, 1920–1991* (London, Pluto Press, 1992).

Tilly, C., Tilly, L. and Tilly, R. *The Rebellious Century 1830–1930* (London, J.M. Dent & Sons, 1975).

Tramposh, W. 'Mickeying with the Muses: Disney World and Regional Identity', in Fladmark (ed.), *Sharing the Earth*.

Traquair, P. *Freedom's Sword* (London, HarperCollins, 1998).

Turnbull, M.T.R.B. *Monuments and Statues of Edinburgh* (Edinburgh, Chambers, 1989).

Urry, J. *The Tourist Gaze: Leisure and Travel in Contemporary Societies* (London, Sage, 1990).

Veitch, J. *The Feeling for Nature in Scottish Poetry*, Vol. I (Edinburgh, William Blackwood, 1887).

Wall, J.F. *Andrew Carnegie*, 2nd edn (Pittsburgh, University of Pittsburgh Press, 1989).

Wallerstein, I. *The Modern World System* (New York, Academic Press, 1989).

Watson, F. 'The Enigmatic Lion: Scotland, Kinship and National Identity in the Wars of Independence', in Broun, Finlay and Lynch (eds), *Image and Identity* (Edinburgh, John Donald, 1998).

——. *Under the Hammer: Edward I and Scotland, 1286–1306* (East Linton, Tuckwell Press, 1998).

Whatley, C.A. *Bought and Sold for English Gold? Explaining the Union of 1707* (Studies in Scottish Economic and Social History; no. 4: Glasgow, 1994).

——. *Scottish Society 1707–1830: Beyond Jacobitism, towards industrialisation* (Manchester University Press, 2000).

Williams, A.T.P. 'Religion' in E. Barker (ed.), *The Character of England* (Oxford, Clarendon Press, 1947).

Withers, C.W.J. 'The Historical Creation of the Scottish Highlands' in I. Donnachie and C. Whatley (eds), *The Manufacture of Scottish History* (Edinburgh, Polygon, 1992).

Wood, W. *Yours Sincerely for Scotland: The Autobiography of a Patriot* (London, Arthur Barker, 1970).

Wood, S. and Payne, F. *The Knowledge and Understanding of Scottish History of S4 Pupils in Scottish Schools* (Aberdeen, Northern College, 1997).

Woolf, S. (ed.), *Nationalism in Europe, 1815 to the Present* (London, Routledge, 1996).

Wright, P. *On Living in an Old Country: the National Past in Contemporary Britain* (London, Verso, 1985).

Young, A. *Robert the Bruce's Rivals: The Comyns, 1212–1314* (East Linton, Tuckwell Press, 1997).

Young, J.D. *The Very Bastards of Creation. Scottish-International Radicalism: A Biographical Study, 1707–1995* (Glasgow, Clydeside Press, *c.* 1996).

Index

Index